Company Law in Practice

Company Law in Practice

The City Law School
CITY UNIVERSITY LONDON

Authors
Professor Stuart Sime, Barrister, BPTC Course Director, The City Law School
Margot Taylor, Solicitor, formerly a Principal Lecturer at The City Law School

Editor
Professor Stuart Sime, Barrister, BPTC Course Director, The City Law School

Series Editor
Julie Browne, Barrister, Senior Lecturer, The City Law School

OXFORD
UNIVERSITY PRESS

OXFORD
UNIVERSITY PRESS

Great Clarendon Street, Oxford OX2 6DP
United Kingdom

Oxford University Press is a department of the University of Oxford.
It furthers the University's objective of excellence in research, scholarship,
and education by publishing worldwide. Oxford is a registered trade mark of
Oxford University Press in the UK and in certain other countries

Seventh edition 2008
Eighth edition 2010
Ninth edition 2012

Impression: 1

Published in the United States of America by Oxford University Press
198 Madison Avenue, New York, NY 10016, United States of America

British Library Cataloguing in Publication Data
Data available

ISBN 978-0-19-968690-2

Printed in Great Britain by
CPI Group (UK) Ltd, Croydon, CR0 4YY

FOREWORD

These manuals have been written by a combination of practitioners and members of staff of the City Law School (formerly the Inns of Court School of Law), and are designed primarily to support training on the Bar Professional Training Course (BPTC), wherever it is taught. They provide an extremely useful resource to assist in acquiring the skills and knowledge that practising Barristers need. They are updated regularly and are supported by an Online Resource Centre, which can be used by readers to keep up to date throughout the academic year.

This series of manuals exemplifies the practical and professional approach that is central to the BPTC. I congratulate the authors on the excellent standard of the manuals and I am grateful to Oxford University Press for their ongoing and enthusiastic support.

Peter Hungerford-Welch
Barrister
Assistant Dean (Professional Programmes)
The City Law School
City University London
2014

GUIDE TO USING THIS BOOK

The Bar Manuals series includes a range of tools and features to aid your learning. This guide will outline the approach to using this book, and help you to make the most out of each of the features within.

Practical-based approach

The authors have taken a practical-based approach to Company Law, focusing on the work typically encountered by practitioners specialising in this area of law.

Examples and exercises

This Manual includes sample exercises, and also a worked example of a Company Law Opinion and statement of case.

Court practice

This Manual has two chapters devoted to presenting company law cases in court.

Core texts and legislation

Company Law is a mix of statutory law and a large body of case law, together with the practice and procedures used by the Companies Court and Chancery Division. The main statute governing company law is the Companies Act 2006, which replaced earlier legislation. Insolvency is a substantial component of company law, with the main statute being the Insolvency Act 1986, which is supplemented by the Insolvency Rules 1986. Insolvency law is undergoing a thorough review, which has taken several years, and is not expected to be completed until at least 2014. There have been a number of substantial amendments to both the primary and secondary legislation in this area since 1986. The legislative material is gathered together in *Butterworths Company Law Handbook* (currently in its 27th edition, 2013), a book that is updated almost every year due to the rapid rate of change.

The leading practitioner texts are listed in Chapter 1 of this Manual, together with the two sets of law reports devoted to company law cases. Case law is a mix of well-established principles, often with leading cases from the nineteenth century, and the very modern, with important cases coming through all the time both in established and developing areas of company and insolvency law.

Practice and procedure is often to be found in the Civil Procedure Rules (CPR) and Practice Directions, as supplemented by the Insolvency Proceedings Practice Direction and the Chancery Guide, one of the official court guides. Insolvency procedure is based on the Insolvency Rules 1986, which adopt, with changes, many of the procedures laid down in the CPR.

ORC updates

For further material and updates to selected manuals in this series, please visit the Online Resource Centre at www.oxfordtextbooks.co.uk/orc/barmanuals/.

OUTLINE CONTENTS

DETAILED CONTENTS

TABLE OF CASES

TABLE OF LEGISLATION

UK Primary Legislation

UK Secondary Legislation

European Secondary Legislation

International Treaties and Conventions

1 Introduction

1.1 Company law practice

Much of the work in company law at the Bar is connected with corporate insolvency. Many junior practitioners, almost regardless of their chambers' specialisations, will find themselves being instructed to appear on winding-up petitions. Indeed for many practitioners, winding-up petitions are the full extent of their involvement with this area of law.

A small number of practitioners practise exclusively in company law. Many others combine a specialisation in company law with other areas of Chancery practice and commercial law. These practitioners may be instructed in a wide range of company matters, for example:

- Drafting a company's articles of association.
- Drafting applications and written evidence in miscellaneous matters where a company or its members can apply to the court under the Companies Acts.
- Advising in writing or in conference where shareholders claim they have been unfairly prejudiced and on innumerable other matters.
- Appearing in court on insolvency applications, applications to reduce share capital, in proceedings to disqualify directors from acting as such etc.

1.2 The course

The following chapters concentrate on a number of areas which are important and commonly met in day-to-day practice. An attempt has been made to preserve a balance between substantive company law and insolvency topics.

Company law is an area where you will need to develop the full range of barristers' skills, from organising the facts of your case, through researching the law and procedure, to drafting the necessary documents or advising the client or appearing in court.

1.3 Sources

You will find that company law is a broad subject, with many areas covered by detailed statutory provisions. Most barristers attend court with their papers, notebook and a copy of *Butterworths Company Law Handbook* (currently in its 27th edition, 2013).

The Handbook contains all the relevant legislation (including statutory instruments), and its usefulness cannot be overstated.

1.3.1 Law reports

Some areas of company law are based on case law, and many statutory provisions have been scrutinised many times by the courts. Cases are to be found in most of the main series of law reports, but, in addition, there are now two sets of reports dealing exclusively with company cases, namely:

- *British Company Cases (BCC),* published by Sweet & Maxwell (formerly CCH);
- *Butterworths Company Law Cases (BCLC).*

1.3.2 Practitioner texts

Atkin's Court Forms, vols 9 and 10.
British Company Law and Practice (Sweet & Maxwell).
Gore-Browne on Companies (Jordan Publishing).
Palmer's Company Law (Sweet & Maxwell).
Buckley on the Companies Acts (LexisNexis Butterworths).

1.3.3 Student texts

There are many excellent texts on company law. The following is only a selection:

Hannigan, Company Law, 3rd edn (OUP, 2012).
Mayson, French and Ryan on Company Law, 30th edn (OUP, 2013).

For reference:

Gower and Davies' Principles of Modern Company Law, 9th edn (Sweet & Maxwell).

1.4 Abbreviations

AGM	annual general meeting (of shareholders)
BCC	*British Company Cases*
BCLC	*Butterworths Company Law Cases*
BCP	*Blackstone's Civil Practice*
BIS	Department for Business Innovation and Skills. This is the government department responsible for company law. For many years it was called the Department of Trade and Industry, then the Department for Business, Enterprise and Regulatory Reform, before being renamed as the BIS. The Insolvency Service within the BIS is responsible for insolvency law
CA 1948	Companies Act 1948
CA 1980	Companies Act 1980
CA 1985	Companies Act 1985
CA 1989	Companies Act 1989

CA 2006	Companies Act 2006
CA	Court of Appeal
C(AICE)A 2004	Companies (Audit, Investigations and Community Enterprise) Act 2004
CDDA 1986	Company Directors Disqualification Act 1986
ChD	Chancery Division
CJA 1993	Criminal Justice Act 1993
CPR 1998	Civil Procedure Rules 1998
CVA	company voluntary arrangement (under IA 1986, ss 1–7)
EGM	extraordinary general meeting (of shareholders)
EUPLC Regs 2004	European Public Limited-Liability Company Regulations 2004, SI 2004/2326
HL	House of Lords. In October 2009 its judicial jurisdiction was transferred to the Supreme Court
IA 1986	Insolvency Act 1986
IPPD	Insolvency Proceedings Practice Direction pursuant to the Civil Procedure Rules 1998
IR 1986	Insolvency Rules 1986, SI 1986/1925. These rules are due to be replaced in 2014
Model articles	Default articles of association of companies registered under the CA 2006 in the Companies (Model Articles) Regulations 2008, SI 2008/3229
PD 49	Practice Direction 49 relating to the Civil Procedure Rules 1998
PD DDP	Practice Direction Directors Disqualification Proceedings
PF	prescribed form
reg	regulation
SC	Supreme Court. Successor to the House of Lords in its judicial capacity
SCA 1981	Senior Courts Act 1981. Until October 2009 this was known as the Supreme Court Act 1981
Table A	Default articles of association of companies for pre-CA 2006 companies under the Companies (Tables A to F) Regulations 1985, SI 1985/805

1.5 Reform of company law

Pressure for reform of company law comes from a number of sources. High-profile multinational company collapses, such as Enron, WorldCom and Parmalat, have led to calls to tighten regulation of the accounting and auditing professions. This was acted upon in the UK through the enactment of the C(AICE)A 2004, which sought to achieve a balance between strengthening auditing requirements and avoiding unnecessarily prescriptive and burdensome regulation. There are international pressures on questions such as international investment and allowing companies to prepare accounts in the same form no matter where they are incorporated. There are continuing pressures for the harmonisation of business law and practices across the EU, particularly in the area of employee and shareholder rights.

More substantial reform was made by the CA 2006, which came into force in stages between 2007 and 1 October 2009. It recognises the pivotal role played by companies in promoting enterprise, competitiveness and economic growth. It seeks to maintain and modernise the system, with the following objectives:

- facilitating enterprise by making it easy to set up and expand a business;
- encouraging the efficient allocation of capital by giving confidence to investors;
- promoting long-term company performance through shareholder engagement and effective dialogue between business and investors;
- maintaining the UK's position as one of the most attractive places in the world to set up and run a business.

Among the changes made by the CA 2006 are measures to provide better guidance to directors on their responsibilities (with statutory definitions of their fiduciary duties); more effective and efficient means of communication with shareholders; and better procedures for shareholders to exercise their rights of ownership. It recasts the most important regulatory provisions in plain English so that they are more accessible to the majority of business people who run smaller businesses (over 90 per cent of companies have no more than five shareholders). Previous legislation tended to be framed with large companies in mind, but with exceptions for smaller companies. It is recognised that this makes finding out the law more difficult than it needs to be for those running small businesses, and instead the CA 2006 adopts a 'think small first' approach.

There is an ongoing project to modernise the Insolvency Rules. It has proved more complicated than anticipated, and the implementation date has been postponed several times. It will involve the complete replacement of the IR 1986, which govern bankruptcy and company insolvency. The Insolvency Service has indicated that they are not likely to be brought into force before October 2014.

It is also recognised that excessive bureaucracy stifles business, and there is a project (the 'Red Tape Challenge') that is being implemented across a number of government departments which is designed to reduce the cost to business of complying with unnecessary regulations. This includes a consultation during 2013 on cutting the costs of insolvencies.

2

Companies proceedings

2.1 Jurisdiction

Many provisions in the CA 2006 provide for various applications to be made to 'the court'. This expression generally means the High Court or a county court (s 1156(1)). This is subject to any enactment or rule of law relating to the allocation of business between the courts (s 1156(2)), and a power to exclude particular county courts from having jurisdiction under the Companies Acts (s 1156(3)).

2.1.1 County courts

County court proceedings are issued out of the relevant county court office (PD 49A, para 5(2)(b)). Procedure in the county courts basically follows that in the High Court. The same forms of originating process are used, the only difference being the reference to the court in the title. When the Crime and Courts Act 2013, s 17, is brought into force there will be a single county court for England and Wales.

2.1.2 High Court

All applications under the CA 2006 and other legislation relating to companies are assigned to the Chancery Division (SCA 1981, Sch 1), and proceed in the Companies Court. The Chancery Division and Companies Court are located in the Rolls Building off Fetter Lane in London, as well as in ten Chancery district registries (Birmingham, Bristol, Caernarfon, Cardiff, Leeds, Liverpool, Manchester, Mold, Newcastle upon Tyne and Preston: see PD 49A, para 5(2)(a) and *Chancery Guide*, para 12.1).

2.1.3 Companies Court

The Companies Court is part of the Chancery Division. It is not a separate court, but a collection of judges and officials within the Chancery Division with relevant company law expertise, which allows for flexibility. It has a separate General Office for the issuing of originating process pursuant to the CA 2006 and IA 1986, filing witness statements etc. Judicial functions are performed by the Companies Court Registrar and by High Court judges.

2.2 Procedural provisions

A great deal of the litigation in the company law field is brought under Acts of Parliament. Different procedural codes apply depending on the statute governing the case. The general scheme is as follows:

- Proceedings under the CA 1985, CA 2006, the Financial Services and Markets Act 2000, Part VII, Council Regulation (EC) No 2157/2001 and the Companies (Cross-Border Merger) Regulations 2007 are governed by PD 49A.
- Insolvency proceedings are governed by IR 1986. The term 'insolvency proceedings' was said to be undefined in *Phillips v McGregor-Paterson* [2010] 1 BCLC 72 at [25], but is in fact defined in the IPPD, para 1.1(6), as covering any proceedings under the IA 1986, the IR 1986 and four sets of rules dealing with insolvent estates and insolvent partnerships.
- Proceedings under the CDDA 1986 are governed by the Directors Disqualification Proceedings Practice Direction pursuant to the CPR 1998.
- Unfair prejudice proceedings are governed by the Companies (Unfair Prejudice Applications) Proceedings Rules 2009, SI 2009/2469.

These rules often lay down detailed procedural provisions in addition to laying down the appropriate method of commencement. If no specific method of commencement is laid down, the application is commenced by issuing a claim form using the CPR, Part 8 procedure: PD 49A, para 5(1).

As mentioned previously, a great deal of company law litigation is brought under statute. In addition, company law often forms the basis of ordinary civil claims, for example proceedings commenced by claim form against directors for breach of their duties to their companies. Further, failure to comply with various provisions in the CA 2006 can result in criminal proceedings being brought against those in default.

We will now consider the various procedural rules in a little more detail, starting with applications under the CA 2006.

2.3 Proceedings under the Companies Acts

2.3.1 Part 8 procedure

2.3.1.1 Applications made by Part 8 claim form

Unless contrary provision is made (see **2.3.2** and **2.3.3**) all applications (other than interim applications) under the CA 2006 are begun by issuing a Part 8 claim form. Examples include applications under:

(a) CA 2006, s 229(5), for an order requiring a company to permit its shareholders to inspect its directors' service contracts or the written memoranda of its directors' terms of service.

(b) CA 2006, s 306, to summon meetings of a company and, if necessary, to declare such meetings quorate even if attended by fewer persons than the minimum number prescribed by the company's articles of association.

(c) CA 2006, s 358(7), to compel inspection or provision of copies of resolutions passed by the members and copies of the minutes of a company's general meetings.

(d) CA 2006, s 794, for an order imposing transfer and voting restrictions on shares in a company where a person interested in those shares has failed to give the information required by a s 793 notice served by the company.

(e) CA 2006, s 896(1), to order meetings of creditors or members where a compromise or arrangement is proposed. See PD 49A, para 15.

(f) CA 2006, s 1132, brought by the prosecuting authorities for an order for the production or inspection of a company's books in relation to investigations into offences connected with the management of the company's affairs. An order under this section is rather similar to a search warrant.

2.3.1.2 Title

In companies proceedings, the title of the claim form (and of any written evidence) must be entitled in the matter of the company in question and in the matter of the CA 2006 or other relevant statute (PD 49A, para 4(1), and *Chancery Guide*, para 20.5). The general form of title to proceedings is as follows:

IN THE HIGH COURT OF JUSTICE No of 2014

CHANCERY DIVISION

COMPANIES COURT

IN THE MATTER OF THE [NAME OF COMPANY]

AND IN THE MATTER OF THE COMPANIES ACT 2006

2.3.1.3 Parties

Where the application is adversarial in nature, such as applications under CA 2006, s 794 (see **2.3.1.1(d)**), the practice is to name the respective parties as claimants and defendants. The company involved is often, but not always, named as one of the parties. Any persons responsible for the default, such as directors and other officers of the company, may be joined as defendants. This is particularly so if the claimants intend to apply for an order for costs against such persons.

Unless an enactment makes a different provision, or the court orders otherwise, in Part 8 claims under the CA 2006 the company must be made a defendant (PD 49A, para 7(1)), except where the company is the claimant. PD 49A also contains specific provisions for applications under 11 sets of sections within the CA 2006. These specific provisions sometimes provide that stated affected persons (such as directors, members or auditors) must be notified of the application, and sometimes provide that the proceedings must be commenced by a Part 7 claim form (see **2.3.2**).

2.3.1.4 Evidence in support

The Part 8 claim form will invariably be supported by a witness statement setting out the relevant facts. It will be entitled in the same way as the Part 8 claim form, and is otherwise drafted and endorsed in the same way as other witness statements (see BCP, chapters 51 and 52, and *Atkin's Court Forms*, vol 9).

In the body of the evidence in support the witness will explain the nature of the application and give full particulars of the dispute. Relevant documents will be exhibited in the usual way. In addition, it is usual for evidence in support of applications under the CA 2006 to give some or all of the following details of the company in question:

- Its date of incorporation, its registered number and the nature of any limitation of liability.

- If it is a company limited by shares, its nominal, issued and paid-up share capital.
- The present ownership of its shares.
- The present directors.
- The address of its registered office.
- As an exhibit, a print of its memorandum and articles of association, together with any special resolutions.
- The nature of its objects, if any.

2.3.1.5 Subsequent steps

After the Part 8 claim form is issued by the court, it must be served on the company together with the evidence in support and a response pack for acknowledging service. Service must be effected by the claimant (PD 49A, para 28). A defendant who wishes to rely on written evidence must file it when acknowledging service (CPR, r 8.5(3)). The claimant then has 14 days to serve further evidence in reply (r 8.5(5)). A defendant who does not acknowledge service may attend the hearing, but may not take part unless the court grants permission (r 8.4(2)). Part 8 claims are treated as allocated to the multi-track (r 8.9(c)). The provisions in the CPR dealing with directions questionnaires and track allocation therefore do not apply (r 8.9(c)). However, CPR, Part 29, does apply, and this means that a case management conference may be held (r 29.3(1)).

The court may give directions immediately a Part 8 claim form is issued, either on the application of a party or of its own initiative (PD 8A, para 6.1). Directions may include a date for a case management conference or a date for the final hearing if the court considers this to be convenient. If the court does fix a hearing date on issue, obviously details of this have to be served with the claim form. At the hearing, depending on the nature of the claim, the registrar will either determine the application or give directions for the future conduct of the matter. In cases where the court does not fix a hearing date when the claim is issued, it will give directions (either with or without convening a case management conference) as soon as practicable after the defendants have acknowledged service, or after the period for acknowledging service has expired (PD 8A, para 6.2).

2.3.2 Part 7 claims under the Companies Act 2006

A small number of claims under the CA 2006 have to be commenced using the Part 7 procedure (the usual way of bringing adversarial claims in the civil courts). These are:

(a) proceedings to enforce a director's liability under CA 2006, s 370, in respect of political donations and political expenditure (PD 49A, para 11);

(b) proceedings under CA 2006, s 955, to enforce compliance with the Panel on Takeovers and Mergers rules on takeovers made under CA 2006, s 943;

(c) proceedings to recover compensation in relation to takeover bids of opted-in companies under CA 2006, s 968(6) (PD 49A, para 17); and

(d) derivative claims against directors for breach of duty.

There are detailed provisions dealing with derivative claims, which are discussed at **11.5.2.3**, and see CA 2006, ss 260–264 and CPR, rr 19.9–19.9F. Proceedings under CA 2006, ss 370, 955 and 968(6) are governed by PD 49A, which means that the rules relating to the title to the proceedings, service and allocation to the multi-track, as discussed previously, apply to these two types of claim. However, as they are Part 7 claims, the parties must file and serve statements of case, and directions will deal with matters such as disclosure by lists of documents, exchange of witness statements, experts and trial.

2.3.3 Petitions

Under the CA 1985, the former PD 49B, para 4(1), set out a list of 12 types of proceedings under the CA 1985 that had to be brought by petition. This was inconsistent with the policy of the CPR, part of which was to simplify the methods of commencing proceedings. Accordingly, under the CA 2006 and the current PD 49A the approach is that all applications under the CA 2006 must be brought by the Part 8 procedure, unless there is legislation or some other good reason for adopting a different method of starting proceedings. It is for this reason that there are only four types of claim which are commenced by Part 7 claim (see **2.3.2**, all of which are by their nature fundamentally adversarial, which is why the Part 7 procedure is appropriate). Applying the same policy, the only proceedings under CA 2006 which must be brought by petition are claims for unfair prejudice under CA 2006, ss 994 or 995. Unfair prejudice proceedings are governed by the Companies (Unfair Prejudice Applications) Proceedings Rules 2009, SI 2009/2469, which are discussed at **13.3**.

Petitions are also encountered in a variety of common situations under the IA 1986, see **2.4**.

2.4 Proceedings under the Insolvency Act 1986

Detailed procedural rules for applications under the IA 1986 are laid down in the IR 1986 and IPPD. The essential contents of many forms are specified in the IR 1986, and prescribed forms can be found in IR 1986, Sch 4 as amended by the Insolvency (Amendment) Rules 2010, SI 2010/686. Specific provision is made in the IR 1986 for the following types of applications:

(a) Administration orders. Application is by petition supported by a written statement in Form 2.2B (IR 1986, Part 2, ch 1).

(b) Winding-up orders. Application is by petition (IR 1986, Part 4, chs 3 and 4). For further details, see **Chapters 9** and **10**. Unopposed winding-up petitions in the High Court are heard by the Companies Court Registrar on Wednesdays.

Other types of applications are divided into:

(c) originating applications (to commence insolvency proceedings); and

(d) ordinary applications (made in pending proceedings).

2.4.1 Form of general applications

By the IR 1986, r 7.3(1), every application, whether originating or ordinary, must state:

- that the application is made under the Insolvency Act 1986;
- the parties' names;
- the name of the company;
- the name of the court;

- the insolvency proceedings number (if previously allocated);
- the nature of the remedy or order applied for or the directions sought from the court;
- the names and addresses of the persons intended to be served;
- the names and addresses of any persons who are required to be notified of the application by any statute or any rules; and
- the applicant's address for service.

The application must be authenticated by or on behalf of the applicant (IR 1986, r 7.3(3)). This means that the heading will take the following form:

IN THE HIGH COURT OF JUSTICE No of 2014

CHANCERY DIVISION

IN THE MATTER OF (name of company)

AND IN THE MATTER OF THE INSOLVENCY ACT 1986

The other details required by IR 1986, r 7.3(1) are set out in the body of the application. Originating applications must in addition set out the grounds on which the applicant claims to be entitled to the remedy or order sought.

An application is issued by filing copies at court, and paying a fee. It will be sealed and endorsed with details of where and when it will be heard.

2.4.2 Service

Generally, service must be effected at least 14 days before the date fixed for the hearing (IR 1986, r 7.4(5)). It is a sealed copy, endorsed with details of the hearing, that must be served (r 7.4(3)), together with any witness statement in support (r 7.8(1)(a)). Service may be effected by any of the methods laid down in CPR, Part 6 (see IR 1986, rr 12A.16 and 12A.17, and BCP, chapter 15). Except where different provision is made by the IR 1986, the CPR, Part 6 applies to service of insolvency applications with such modifications as the court may direct (r 12A.17).

The provisions of CPR, Part 6, relating to service outside the jurisdiction also apply in insolvency proceedings with such modifications as the court may direct (IR 1986, r 12A.20). Rule 12A.20 therefore gives the court a discretion to direct the use of a method for service outside the jurisdiction going beyond the confines of CPR, Part 6.

2.4.3 General procedure

By IR 1986, r 7.51A(2), the provisions of the CPR and any related PD apply to insolvency proceedings with any necessary modifications, except to the extent that they are inconsistent with the IR 1986. In particular, Parts 6 (service), 18 (further information), 31 (disclosure of documents), 32 (false statements of truth), 37 (payments into court), 44 and 47 (costs) and 52 (appeals) apply to insolvency proceedings with any necessary modifications and except to the extent that they are inconsistent with the IR 1986 (r 7.51A(1), (4)). Accordingly, for example, the principles in CPR, r 3.9, on relief from sanctions (see *A Practical Approach to Civil Procedure*, 16th edn (OUP, 2013), para 37.26) apply on applications to extend time in winding-up petitions under IR 1986, r 4.3 (*Re Metrocab Ltd* [2010] 2 BCLC 603). All insolvency proceedings are allocated to the multi-track, so CPR provisions relating to directions questionnaires and track allocation do not apply (r 7.51A(3)).

2.4.4 Evidence

Evidence in insolvency proceedings may be given by witness statement unless any specific provision of the IR 1986 provides otherwise or the court otherwise directs (IR 1986, r 7.7A). Official receivers may file reports instead of witness statements (r 7.9). As mentioned at **2.4.2**, the evidence in support must be served at least 14 days before the hearing together with the application. Any witness statement in reply should be filed and served at least five business days before the hearing (r 7.8(1)(b)).

2.4.5 Hearings

Applications before the registrar are heard in chambers. Unless the court otherwise directs, applications are heard in open court (IR 1986, r 7.6A(1)). The general rule is that applications must be made to the registrar. Applications which must be made to a judge are listed in the IPPD, para 3.2 and include applications for committal for contempt, applications to restrain the presentation or advertisement of a winding-up petition (for which, see **9.6**), and interim applications after the matter has been referred to the judge (a typical example would be an urgent validation application under IA 1986, s 127 (for which, see **9.7**).

2.4.6 Orders

Generally, the court draws up any order made other than orders on the application of the official receiver or for which the Treasury Solicitor is responsible (IPPD, para 8.1).

2.4.7 Bringing the wrong form of proceedings

Proceedings brought by ordinary claim form seeking unfair prejudice relief under CA 2006, s 994(1), rather than by petition under the Companies (Unfair Prejudice Applications) Proceedings Rules 2009, SI 2009/2469, were held in *Re Osea Road Camp Sites Ltd* [2005] 1 WLR 760 to be irremediably flawed, and were struck out. This was because the requirement to bring unfair prejudice proceedings by petition is expressly stated in CA 2006, s 994(1) ('a member of a company may apply to the court by petition ...'), and the power to correct errors of procedure in CPR, r 3.10, the only provision available to correct this type of mistake, could only apply to correct errors in procedures established by the CPR itself.

In contrast, bringing an ordinary application under the IR 1986 rather than an originating application (being an error because there were no existing insolvency proceedings, see *Re Continental Assurance Co of London plc (No 2)* [1998] 1 BCLC 583), or bringing proceedings by a Part 7 claim form under the CPR rather than by an originating application (being an error because the claims were insolvency proceedings, see *Phillips v McGregor-Paterson* [2010] 1 BCLC 72) were corrected under IR 1986, r 7.55. This was because r 7.55, which is the IR 1986 equivalent to CPR, r 3.10, covers formal defects in what should be insolvency proceedings. Orders to correct such errors are made where the court considers that no substantial injustice has been caused by the defect or irregularity.

2.5 Proceedings under the Company Directors Disqualification Act 1986

Procedure under the CDDA 1986 is governed by the Insolvent Companies (Disqualification of Unfit Directors) Proceedings Rules 1987, SI 1987/2023, and the Directors Disqualification Proceedings PD. The law is considered at **7.8**.

An application for the making of a disqualification order is commenced by issuing a Part 8 claim form in the format set out in the Annex to the Directors Disqualification Proceedings PD. It must state the section of the Act pursuant to which the claim is made, and it must set out the period of disqualification the court has power to impose. The claim form must be supported by an affidavit stating the matters by virtue of which it is alleged that the respondent is unfit to be concerned in the management of a company. The claim form is served together with the evidence in support (para 9.3(3)) and an acknowledgment of service form (para 7.4), which the respondent should return to the court within 14 days of service (para 8.3(1)). Within 28 days of service, the respondent may serve on the applicant and file at court affidavit evidence in opposition to the application (para 9.4). If this is done, the applicant has 14 days to serve and file further affidavit evidence in reply (para 9.6). Disqualification claims are automatically allocated to the multi-track (para 2.1).

The initial hearing of the application is before a registrar in open court, and must be at least eight weeks after the claim form was issued (para 10.1). Hearings are in public, and advocates wear robes. The registrar may determine the application on the initial hearing (para 10.3), but is more likely to give directions, such as for the service and filing of further evidence, and to direct whether the case is to be determined by a registrar or judge. The official receiver is entitled to use the investigatory powers in IA 1986, ss 235 and 236, for the purpose of obtaining evidence for use in the disqualification proceedings (*Re Pantmaenog Timber Co Ltd* [2004] 1 AC 158). The registrar will also give directions for the hearing of the claim. Many claims are tried by the registrar, but the more important or serious cases are referred to the judge (*Lewis v Secretary of State for Trade and Industry* [2001] 2 BCLC 597).

There are also detailed rules dealing with the summary procedure adopted in *Re Carecraft Construction Co Ltd* [1994] 1 WLR 172 (PD DDP, para 13), and for disqualification undertakings (paras 28 to 34, see **7.8.5**).

2.6 Interim applications in the Companies Court

Interim applications within proceedings assigned to the Companies Court are governed by the CPR and follow the same procedure as general proceedings in the Chancery Division (*Chancery Guide*, para 20.2). The detailed rules governing applications can be found in CPR, Parts 23 and 25, PD 23, PD 25A, PD 25B and PD 25C, discussed in BCP, chapter 32. Further guidance specifically for Chancery Division applications is set out in the *Chancery Guide*, paras 5.1 to 5.58, and see **10.5** to **10.7** of this Manual.

Most interim applications are commenced by issuing an application form in Form N244 (which is the same form as used in general litigation in the High Court and county courts), supported by evidence either in the application notice, or contained in witness statements filed and served with the application. The main exception relates to interim applications within proceedings under the IA 1986 (see **2.4**). These interim applications are brought using a form called an 'ordinary application', the format of which can be found in IR 1986, Sch 4. Evidence in support of ordinary applications is also given in witness statements.

2.7 Precedents

2.7.1 Part 8 claim form seeking order convening an extraordinary general meeting

Meetings are discussed at **6.4** and **6.5**. Shareholders' meetings are normally convened by the directors, although there is an exceptional power for shareholders to requisition meetings, discussed at **6.5.5**. The application in this precedent is made under CA 2006, s 306, and is designed to cope with the situation where a company is deadlocked and unable to hold effective, quorate meetings (see **6.6**).

Royal Arms	Claim Form (CPR Part 8)	In the High Court of Justice Chancery Division Companies Court Claim No 007914 of 2014

Claimant

MISS CATHERINE ANNE BARTON
6 University Mews,
Cambridge CB4 8RT SEAL

Defendants

(1) AT YOUR SERVICE LIMITED
(2) MISS AMANDA LOUISE SIMPSON

IN THE MATTER OF AT YOUR SERVICE LIMITED
AND IN THE MATTER OF THE COMPANIES ACT 2006

Does your claim include any issues under the Human Rights Act 1998? ☐ Yes ☐ No
Details of Claim (see also overleaf)

The Claimant seeks an Order pursuant to the Companies Act 2006, section 306:

1. that an extraordinary general meeting of the Company may be convened by the Court for the purpose of considering and if thought fit passing as ordinary resolutions:
   (a) that the second respondent Amanda Louise Simpson be removed as a director of the Company;
   (b) that Deborah Welsh of 12 Parkside Road, Cambridge, CB4 3LR be appointed as a director of the Company;
2. that the Court may give directions as to the manner in which the meeting is to be called, held and conducted and all such ancillary and consequential directions as it may think expedient, and in particular, that the Court may direct that one member of the Company present at the meeting be deemed to constitute a quorum;

3. that the costs of this application may be provided for.

Defendants' names and addresses

(1) At Your Service Limited, registered office 53 College Road, Cambridge, CB1 4LN

(2) Amanda Louise Simpson, 4 Sherwood Road, Lincoln, LN5 2WF

Part 8 of the Civil Procedure Rules 1998 applies to this claim which is made pursuant to CPR Part 49 and PD 49A, paragraph 5(1).

£
Court fee
Solicitor's costs
Issue date

The court office at Rolls Building, 7 Rolls Building, off Fetter Lane, London EC4A 1NL is open between 10 am and 4 pm Monday to Friday. When corresponding with the court, please address forms and letters to the Court Manager and quote the claim number.

Statement of Truth

(I believe) (The Claimant believes) that the facts stated in these details of claim are true. I am duly authorised by the Claimant to sign this statement.

Full name

Name of claimant's solicitor's firm — Jackson and Hussain.
Signed — position or office held
(Claimant) (Litigation Friend) — (if signing on behalf of firm or company)
(Claimant's solicitor) delete as appropriate

49 College Road Cambridge CB1 4LN	Claimant's or claimant's solicitor's address to which documents should be sent if different from overleaf. If you are prepared to accept service by DX, fax or e-mail, please add details.

2.7.2 Witness statement in support of Part 8 claim for an order convening an extraordinary general meeting

Made on behalf of: Claimant
Witness: C.A. Barton
Statement No: 1st
Exhibits: CAB1-CAB3
Made: 21.10.2014

IN THE HIGH COURT OF JUSTICE — No 007914 of 2014

CHANCERY DIVISION

COMPANIES COURT

IN THE MATTER of AT YOUR SERVICE LIMITED

AND IN THE MATTER of the COMPANIES ACT 2006

WITNESS STATEMENT OF
CATHERINE ANNE BARTON

1. I am CATHERINE ANNE BARTON, of 6 University Mews, Cambridge, CB4 8RT. I am a recruitment consultant and company director. I am the claimant.
2. I am a member and director of the above-named At Your Service Limited ('the Company'). I make this statement in support of my application under the Companies Act 2006, section 306, for an order of the Court convening an extra-ordinary general meeting of the Company, or alternatively an order of the Court directing me to convene such a meeting, to consider and if thought fit pass as ordinary resolutions resolutions to remove the second respondent Amanda Louise Simpson as a director of the Company and to appoint Deborah Welsh of 12 Parkside Road, Cambridge CB4 3LR as a director of the Company.
3. The Company was incorporated on 14 September 1984 under the Companies Acts 1948 to 1981 with company number 1334455 as a company limited by shares.
4. The nominal capital of the Company is £100 divided into 100 ordinary shares of £1 each all of which shares have been issued and are fully paid up or are credited as fully paid up.
5. I am the holder of 60 of the issued shares and the second defendant, Amanda Louise Simpson, is the holder of the other 40 issued shares. Amanda Louise Simpson is also the other director and secretary of the Company.
6. The registered office of the Company is situated at 53 College Road, Cambridge, CB1 4LN.
7. I refer to the print of the Memorandum and Articles of Association of the Company and copies of all special resolutions of the Company which have been passed since the incorporation of the Company marked as exhibit 'CAB1'.
8. The Company carries on business as a recruitment agency from premises in Cambridge. The business was originally intended to be a joint venture between the second defendant and myself. Indeed, from incorporation of the Company until July 2013 the only people employed by the Company were the second defendant and myself.
9. In the Spring of 2013 differences of opinion on business matters arose between the second defendant and myself, and in July 2013 the second defendant left Cambridge and set up in business in Lincoln. Since that time the second defendant has not attended the Company's premises, or attended any meetings of the Company or board of directors, or undertaken any duties in respect of the Company.
10. The Articles of Association of the Company incorporate part I of Table A in the First Schedule to the Companies Act 1948. Regulation 53 of Table A provides that:

    'No business shall be transacted at any general meeting unless a quorum of members is present at the time when the meeting proceeds to business; save as herein otherwise provided two members present in person or by proxy shall be a quorum.'
11. Furthermore, regulation 99 of Table A provides as follows:

    'The quorum necessary for the transaction of the business of the directors may be fixed by the directors and unless so fixed shall be two.'

    The quorum for board meetings was never fixed by the second defendant and myself, and I am advised and believe that the necessary quorum is two.
12. On 13 August 2014 I requisitioned the Company in writing to convene a general meeting of the Company for the purpose of considering a resolution for the removal of the second defendant as a director of the Company and called a

meeting of the directors for 20 August 2014 to consider the requisition. I refer to the true copy of that requisition and a true copy of a letter to the second defendant dated 13 August 2014 enclosing a copy of the requisition and notice of the board meeting marked as exhibit 'CAB 2'.

13. The second defendant failed to attend the board meeting fixed for 20 August 2014 which was therefore inquorate.
14. On 3 September 2014 I convened an extraordinary general meeting of the Company under the provisions of the Companies Act 2006, section 305, for the purpose of considering a resolution for the removal of the second defendant as a director of the Company, such meeting to be held on 2 October 2014. I refer to the true copies of the notice of this meeting and of a letter enclosing the notice sent to the second defendant marked as exhibit 'CAB 3'.
15. The second defendant failed to attend the extraordinary general meeting fixed for 2 October 2014, which was therefore inquorate.
16. In the circumstances I am advised and believe that it is not legally possible to hold meetings of the directors or of the Company or indeed for the Company to function without the order and directions sought from this Honourable Court.
17. It is essential in order to enable the Company to function in the ordinary way that an extraordinary general meeting should be held and that the above-named Deborah Welsh (who is now employed by the Company in place of the second defendant) or some other fit and proper person should be appointed a director of the Company. There would then be two directors able and willing to attend board meetings, and who could register transfers of shares so that quorate general meetings would be possible. I accordingly respectfully request this Honourable Court to make the order sought under the Companies Act 2006, section 306.

Statement of Truth
I believe that the facts stated in this witness statement are true.
Signed:
Catherine Anne Barton
Dated: 21 October 2014

2.8 Exercise 1

RE: BRIGHTWELL HOTELS LIMITED

INSTRUCTIONS TO COUNSEL TO
SETTLE PROCEEDINGS

Counsel will find herewith:

(1) Extracts from the company's articles of association;
(2) Relevant correspondence.

Counsel is instructed on behalf of Mrs Eleanor Owen, a financial services adviser. Late last year our client bought a block of 4,000 25p shares in Brightwell Hotels Limited from the present registered holder, Mr Keith Alan Hensley, for £16,500. As may have been appreciated from its name, the Company runs a number of hotels in the West Country.

On 12 December 2013, Mrs Owen sent the share certificate in the name of Mr Hensley and a completed form of transfer in her favour duly stamped in the sum of £82.50 to the Company's registered office. A card acknowledging receipt of these documents by the Company is dated 19 December 2013. However, nothing further was heard from the company, and our client has not been issued with a new share certificate.

Those instructing were consulted in February. On advice our client attended at the registered office on 24 February 2014 in order to inquire about her certificate. She was told by the manager that none of the directors was present and that he knew nothing about the shares. Instructing Solicitors wrote to the company on 25 February saying Mrs Owen would be attending again on 12 March for the purpose of collecting her share certificate. When Mrs Owen attended on 12 March she spoke to a Ms Karen Ruth Allott, who said the directors did not want to have her as a shareholder, and would not register the transfer. Mrs Allott then retreated into the office and our client was shown out by a member of the hotel staff. Subsequent letters to the company have been ignored.

From the particulars registered at Companies House it appears that the Company was incorporated on 18 June 1981. Its present directors are Mr Richard Hall, of 12 Station Road, Exeter EX6, Ms Karen Ruth Allott of 22 Moor Green, Okehampton, Devon and Mr Gladstone Lincoln Dyer of 31 Hopewell Road, Bristol BS9. Its present share capital is £12,000 divided into 48,000 25p shares. A total of 36,000 shares have been issued, and all appear to be fully paid-up.

Counsel is asked to settle proceedings and the evidence in support, which will be signed by Mrs Owen, for the purpose of compelling the Company to register this share transfer.

Counsel is instructed
to settle proceedings

Extracts from articles of association, Brightwell Hotels Limited.

Transfer of shares

22. The instrument of transfer of any share shall be executed by or on behalf of the transferor and transferee, and the transferor shall be deemed to remain a holder of the share until the name of the transferee is entered in the register of members in respect thereof.
23. Subject to such of the restrictions of these regulations as may be applicable, any member may transfer all or any of his shares by instrument in writing in any usual or common form or any other form which the directors may approve.
24. The directors may decline to register the transfer of a share (not being a fully paid share) to a person of whom they shall not approve, and they may also decline to register the transfer of a share on which the Company has a lien.
25. The directors may also decline to recognise any instrument of a transfer unless:—
    - (a) a fee of £0.13 or such lesser sum as the directors may from time to time require is paid to the company in respect thereof;
    - (b) the instrument of transfer is accompanied by the certificate of shares to which it relates, and such other evidence as the directors may reasonably require to show the right of the transferor to make the transfer.

42 Market Street,
Exeter,
Devon,
EX4 2TD

12 December 2013

The Directors,
Brightwell Hotels Limited,
Brightwell Hotel,
Bodmin Road,
Okehampton,
Devon

Dear Sirs,

I enclose a stock transfer form in my favour in respect of 4,000 shares recently purchased by me from Mr Keith Hensley. I also enclose Mr Hensley's share certificate and a cheque for £0.13 to cover transfer fees. Please register me as the new owner of these shares, and provide me with a new share certificate in my name.

Yours faithfully,

Eleanor Owen

Brightwell Hotels Limited
Regd. Office: Brightwell Hotel, Bodmin Road, Okehampton, Devon

Your ref:

Our ref: KRA 19 December 2013

We acknowledge receipt of your communication (and enclosures) dated 12 December 2013. A full reply will be sent in due course.

Beddoe and MacKenzie
SOLICITORS

25 Haymarket
Exeter
EX1 8BR

Tel: 01392 639051
Fax: 01392 639555

Our ref: CB/Owen
Your ref: KRA

25 February 2014

The Directors,
Brightwell Hotels Limited,
Brightwell Hotel,
Bodmin Road,
Okehampton,
Devon

Dear Sirs,

OUR CLIENT: Mrs ELEANOR OWEN

We are instructed on behalf of Mrs Eleanor Owen. On 12 December 2013 our client sent to you a stamped share transfer form, share certificate and transfer fee and requested that you register her as a shareholder and issue her with a share certificate. Yesterday, she attended at your registered office and orally requested her share certificate. To date none has been forthcoming. We have advised our client that she is legally entitled to be issued with a share certificate, and we are sure that you will agree. To this end our client will be attending again at your registered office at the Brightwell Hotel, Okehampton on 12 March 2014 at 2.30 pm to collect her share certificate. We should be grateful if you could make arrangements to ensure that it is available for collection at that time.

Yours faithfully,

Beddoe and MacKenzie

Beddoe and MacKenzie
SOLICITORS

25 Haymarket
Exeter
EX1 8BR

Tel: 01392 639051
Fax: 01392 639555

Our ref: CB/Owen
Your ref: KRA

13 March 2014

The Directors,
Brightwell Hotels Limited,
Brightwell Hotel,
Bodmin Road,
Okehampton,
Devon

Dear Sirs,

OUR CLIENT: Mrs ELEANOR OWEN

We refer to our letter to you of 25 February 2014.
Our client has still not been issued with a share certificate. Unless she is provided with one in the next 7 days, proceedings will be commenced to enforce the same. Legal costs will thereby be incurred which may be ordered against the company or its directors.

Yours faithfully,

Beddoe and MacKenzie

Beddoe and MacKenzie

SOLICITORS

25 Haymarket
Exeter
EX1 8BR

Tel: 01392 639051
Fax: 01392 639555

Our ref: CB/Owen
Your ref: KRA

27 March 2014

The Directors,
Brightwell Hotels Limited,
Brightwell Hotel,
Bodmin Road,
Okehampton,
Devon

Dear Sirs,

OUR CLIENT: Mrs ELEANOR OWEN

Take notice pursuant to the Companies Act 2006, s 782(1), that unless you make good the default in delivering the certificate for the 4,000 shares the subject of the transfer sent to you on the 12 December 2013 within 10 days after service of this notice on you an application will be made to the High Court for delivery of such certificate together with legal costs.

Yours faithfully,

Beddoe and MacKenzie

3

Constitution of companies

3.1 Formation of a company

3.1.1 Formalities required

A company is formed by one or more persons subscribing their names to a memorandum of association and complying with the requirements as to registration (CA 2006, s 7). Thus, under the CA 2006, any type of company (private, public or unlimited companies) may be formed with only one member (s 7). Under the CA 1985, a private company limited by shares or guarantee could be formed by a single person, but a public company and an unlimited company had to have at least two members.

The formalities required for registration, and the documents to be filed are set out in CA 2006, Part 2 (ss 7–16). Section 9 sets out the documents which need to be filed for a company to be registered.

3.1.1.1 Memorandum of association

This must be in a prescribed form and contain a statement that the subscribers wish to form a company and become members of that company when it is incorporated. If the company has share capital it must also state that the subscribers agree to take at least one share each. It must also be authenticated by each subscriber (CA 2006, s 8). Although this is the document which formally seeks to form the company, it is no longer a constitutional document unlike the position under the CA 1985. Under CA 1985 the memorandum also contained much of the information which is now in the application or other documents (see **3.10** for a brief explanation of the importance of the memorandum under CA 1985).

3.1.1.2 The application

The application sets out the company's proposed name, country of registration (in England and Wales (or in Wales), in Scotland or in Northern Ireland), liability of members (under the CA 2006, companies may be limited by shares or by guarantee or can be unlimited), and whether the company is to be private or public (CA 2006, s 9(2)). The application must also contain a statement of the intended address of the company's registered office (CA 2006, s 9(5)(a)). Thus it sets out the fundamental characteristics of the company to be formed which cannot be changed except as provided by CA 2006.

3.1.1.3 Articles of association

This sets out the internal regulations of the company, covering matters such as calling of company meetings; appointment, removal and powers of directors; keeping of accounts; payment of dividends; and issuing new shares and pre-emption rights. For more detail on the contents, alteration and effect of the articles, see **3.5**.

The contents are much the same as under the CA 1985 although they may also contain provisions which under the CA 1985 would have been contained in the memorandum (eg an objects clause, see **3.10**).

3.1.1.4 Statement of capital and initial shareholding/statement of guarantee

Companies which are to be registered under CA 2006 with a share capital need to deliver a statement of capital and initial shareholding. Companies limited by guarantee are required to deliver a statement of guarantee. Under CA 1985 some of the information provided in these documents was set out in the capital clause of the memorandum.

a) Statement of capital

If the company is to have a share capital, a statement of its share capital and initial shareholdings must be filed for registration to take place. This document does not form part of the company's constitution. It is merely 'a snapshot' of the company's share capital at the point of registration (CA 2006, s 10). It basically contains the total number of shares to be taken by the subscribers on incorporation, together with the total nominal value of those shares, the rights attaching to the shares and the amount paid up and unpaid in relation to each share.

Under the CA 1985 the amount of its share capital set out in the share capital clause in the memorandum under s 2(5)(a) determined the company's authorised share capital. The company could increase its authorised share capital at any time by ordinary resolution. Under the CA 2006, companies are no longer required to have an authorised share capital. A company may therefore issue as many shares as it likes, although members can insert provisions in the articles restricting the number of shares to be issued.

In relation to existing companies, the authorised share capital will continue to operate as a restriction in the company's articles. Transitional arrangements enable shareholders wishing to remove the deemed restriction from the articles to do so by ordinary resolution, rather than by special resolution (Companies Act 2006 (Commencement Order No 8, Transitional Provisions and Savings) Order 2008, SI 2008/2860, Sch 2, para 42).

b) Statement of guarantee

If the company is to be limited by guarantee, a statement of guarantee must be filed setting out the undertaking as to contribution required on winding up of the company (CA 2006, s 11).

3.1.1.5 Statement of proposed officers

Every private company must have at least one director and every public company at least two (CA 2006, s 154). Public companies must also have a company secretary (CA 2006, s 271). Private companies no longer need to have a company secretary although they may still do so if they wish (CA 2006, s 270). All existing companies formed under the CA 1948 or CA 1985 (or even earlier Acts) will have a company secretary. Transitional arrangements provide that they continue to do so unless they amend their articles to remove the requirement (Companies Act 2006 (Commencement Order No 5, Transitional Provisions and Savings) Order 2007, SI 2007/3495, Sch 4, para 4).

The statement of proposed officers gives details of the persons who are to be the first directors. It also states in respect of a public company the person who is to be the first secretary. If a private company has a secretary, it must also state who that is to be (CA 2006, s 12). The statement must also contain a consent to act by each person named.

3.1.1.6 Statement of compliance

This form, which is required by CA 2006, s 13, is the statement of compliance with the registration requirements of the Act. It is usually completed by the proposed company secretary.

3.1.2 Companies House file

On registration, a company will receive a certificate of incorporation and a number (which must be quoted on all company correspondence and is useful for tracing company records). On receipt of this certificate a private company may commence trading. A public company requires, in addition, the issue of a Trading Certificate in order to commence business (CA 2006, s 761). This will only be issued if the registrar is satisfied the proposed plc satisfies the capital requirements.

Once registered, various documents relating to the company will be available to the public at Companies House. These provide information as to the date of incorporation, any changes to the company's name, the nature of any limited liability of its members, details of its directors, secretary and shareholders, its constitution, any registered charges and, in due course, annual returns and statutory accounts. Registration and filing have traditionally been by posting hard copies of the relevant forms to Companies House, but electronic filing became permissible several years ago and is now positively encouraged by the CA 2006 (see ss 1068 and 1069). Information about companies, such as date of incorporation, current status and the date of last filed accounts, can be obtained by visiting www.companies-house.gov.uk.

3.1.3 Changing the status of a registered company

Once a company is registered there is limited provision for altering the country of registration, in that it can cease to be Welsh or become Welsh (CA 2006, s 88). Liability of members can be altered from limited to unlimited by assent of all the members (CA 2006, s 102) and from unlimited to limited by special resolution (CA 2006, s 105). Changing from being a private company to a public company requires a special resolution and fulfilment of conditions regarding share capital, net assets, company secretary etc (CA 2006, ss 90–96). Changing from public to private requires a special resolution (CA 2006, s 97). A company's registered office may be changed merely by giving notice to the registrar (CA 2006, s 87).

3.2 Restrictions on name

3.2.1 Choosing a name

There are the following restrictions on the choice of a corporate name:

(a) The name of a public company must end with the words public limited company (or plc), and of a private company with limited (or Ltd): CA 2006, ss 58 and 59. Certain private companies are exempt from this requirement (CA 2006, ss 60–62).

(b) A company shall not be registered with a name:
   (i) which is the same as a name appearing in the registrar's index of company names (CA 2006, s 66);
   (ii) the use of which would, in the opinion of the Secretary of State, constitute a criminal offence (CA 2006, s 53); or
   (iii) which, in the opinion of the Secretary of State, is offensive (CA 2006, s 53).

(c) Except with the approval of the Secretary of State, a company shall not be registered with a name which suggests a connection with government or a local authority, or which is specified in regulations by the Secretary of State (CA 2006, ss 54 and 55). CA 2006, ss 1192–1199 contain similar requirements concerning a company's business name if it is not its corporate name.

3.2.2 Disclosure of name

The Companies (Trading Disclosure) Regulations 2008, SI 2008/495, made under CA 2006, ss 82 and 84, require disclosure of the corporate name outside every office or place of business of the company (regs 3 and 4), on all letters, notices, invoices etc (reg 6) and of the registered number and address of the registered office on all letters and order forms (reg 7).

3.2.3 Changing the name

The company name can be changed by special resolution or other means provided for by the company's articles (CA 2006, s 77). Notice must be given to the registrar who, provided the name complies with these requirements, will enter the new name on the register in place of the former name and issue a new certificate of incorporation to reflect the change.

3.3 Legal personality

3.3.1 The general rule

On formation (ie from the date in the certificate of incorporation issued by the Registrar of Companies (see **3.1**)) a company becomes a legal person separate and distinct from its members (*Salomon v A Salomon and Co Ltd* [1897] AC 22). The principal effect of this is that, in the case of limited liability companies, the members are in general not liable for the company's debts. A company has separate legal capacity, and can therefore contract on its own behalf when conducting business. It therefore has title to the assets it owns, and is the proper party to be named in litigation when it asserts its rights, or when it is alleged to be in breach of its obligations. The separate personality of a registered company is part of the legal fabric of this country, and applies regardless of the legal basis of the relevant dispute. It applies, for example, even in matrimonial ancillary relief claims (*Prest v Petrodel Resources Ltd* [2013] 3 WLR 1).

A company has unlimited liability for its debts (which in practical terms is in fact limited to the amount of the company's assets). Unpaid creditors can petition for the winding up of the company if it fails to pay them what it owes. If creditors are not paid, the liability of its shareholders is limited to whatever sums remain unpaid on their shares. Once shares have been fully paid for, the shareholders have no further personal liability if the company becomes unable to pay its debts. Nowadays shares tend to be paid for in full either on issue or very soon after issue, so in practical terms shareholders are not required to contribute anything if their companies become insolvent. Limited liability companies therefore provide a convenient means through which business people can engage in risky business ventures, because if things go wrong they will not be putting their personal financial resources at risk.

It should be kept in mind, however, that financial institutions (principally the banks) can usually sidestep this result by requiring directors to enter into personal guarantees and contracts of suretyship as a condition of providing bank finance to limited liability companies. This does not infringe the limited liability principle, as the director's personal liability under a guarantee or surety arises under a separate contract. Likewise, although property owned beneficially by a company cannot be the subject of a property transfer order between a husband and wife in matrimonial ancillary relief proceedings, the separate corporate personality principle does not prevent such an order being made against the shares owned by a spouse in the company, nor does it prevent such an order being made in respect of property held by the company but which belongs beneficially to a spouse (*Prest v Petrodel Resources Ltd* [2013] 3 WLR 1).

3.3.2 The veil of incorporation and lifting the veil

The concept that a company is a legal person separate from its members and that the identity and motives of those who form and control the company are irrelevant as the outsider deals with the company and not its members, is often referred to as the veil of incorporation. The concept is that the outsiders deal with the company and are not allowed to go behind the company and get at those who formed or control it. Many of the consequences of formation set out previously are often quoted as examples of this veil of incorporation. There are problems with this concept, and exceptions to it, which are referred to as situations where the veil is pierced/lifted, have developed. Such situations include:

(a) *Enforcement of statutory rules*

(i) By IA 1986, s 213, where persons carry on the company with intent to defraud creditors they may be ordered to contribute to the company's assets.

(ii) By IA 1986, s 214, where a company goes into insolvent liquidation, and a director knew or ought to have known there was no reasonable prospect that insolvent liquidation could be avoided, and did not take every step to minimise loss to creditors, that director may be ordered to contribute to the company's assets.

(b) *Crimes committed* Where an offence requires mens rea, it is necessary to look behind the veil to see whether it was the company which had the necessary guilty mind (ie was the decision one of the members, board or senior officer to whom decision-making power has been properly delegated?). See *Tesco Supermarkets Ltd v Nattrass* [1972] AC 153.

(c) *Abuse of the company principle* For example, where an individual uses a company to evade legal obligations, the court may pierce the veil (see *Gilford Motor Co Ltd v Horne* [1933] Ch 935, where Horne set up a sham company to evade a restraint of trade clause he had entered into in his personal capacity). Piercing the corporate veil on this ground is appropriate where the company is used as a device or facade to conceal the true facts. The fact that a company has been involved in some impropriety which is not linked to the use of the company structure to avoid or conceal some liability is insufficient to justify piercing the corporate veil (*Trustor AB v Smallbone (No 2)* [2001] 1 WLR 1177). Cases where it will be appropriate to pierce the corporate veil on the basis that incorporation is being abused are comparatively rare (*VTB Capital plc v Nutritek International Corpn* [2013] 2 WLR 398; *Prest v Petrodel Resources Ltd* [2013] 3 WLR 1).

3.4 Consequences of incorporation

3.4.1 Main consequences

There are a number of further matters that arise once a company is incorporated:

(a) *Maintenance of capital rules* As a result of the fact that the company alone is liable for its debts and members usually have limited liability to contribute to the company to enable it to do this, the capital which has been or is promised to be contributed by the members must be maintained. The rules are aimed at issued share capital and include prohibitions against purchasing shares, giving financial assistance to purchase shares, payment of dividend out of capital etc (see **Chapter 4**).

(b) *Disclosure rules* A company is subject to fairly extensive disclosure duties which fall into three categories:

   (i) Documents delivered to the Registrar of Companies. On incorporation various documents must be delivered to the registrar. A file is opened on registration and a number given to the company to identify its file. The registration documents and any other documents filed during the life of the company are kept on this file which is open to public inspection. These may be inspected, for a fee, at Companies House (in Cardiff, with an office in London) or via the website www.companies-house.gov.uk. In addition there are specialist firms which will, at a cost, do the search and provide results within 24 hours including photocopies of all relevant documents.

   A company must annually file its accounts and an annual return which will give latest details on members, directors etc. In addition the company must file any changes in directors, capital, registered office, alteration of articles, change of objects etc with the registrar.

   (ii) Maintenance of registers and information at the company's registered office. There are statutory registers which the company must maintain and which are, by and large, open to public inspection, for example register of members, interests of directors in a company.

   (iii) Accounts must be prepared in a set format and audited. The CA 2006, Parts 15 and 16 set out detailed rules for the keeping, auditing and disclosure of company accounts both to members and the public by filing with the Registrar of Companies. Most small private companies with a turnover of £6.5 million or less are exempt from the auditing requirements (s 477).

(c) *Transferability of shares* The general rule is that a shareholder has a right to transfer shares whenever and to whomever she or he wishes, unless this right is restricted by the articles. The transferee takes over all the rights of the transferor.

(d) *Perpetual succession* A company comes into existence on the date stated in its certificate of incorporation and ceases to exist when it is dissolved and the name is removed from the register of companies. Any alteration in the membership between those dates does not alter the character of the company (even if all the members die: *Re Noel Tedman Holdings Pty Ltd* [1967] QdR 561).

(e) *Management* A company as a legal person must make decisions, but this must be done by the individuals controlling it. It is necessary to determine what decisions are decisions of the company and not just of the individuals. The members, as owners, make decisions collectively by voting in general meeting and such decisions will be decisions of the company. (CA 2006 requires certain formalities for such meetings with relaxation of the rules for private companies, see **Chapter 6**.) In theory decisions made without following the proper procedures are not valid. As it is impractical for the members to have general meetings to make all the decisions necessary to run the business, much of the decision-making power is delegated to the directors who must also act collectively through decisions at board meetings unless a power to sub-delegate has been given. There are thus two decision-making organs of the company, the general meeting and the board. As a general rule, once members have delegated their decision-making powers to the board, they cannot simultaneously exercise the delegated powers. This can cause problems where there is disagreement over the manner in which the business should be conducted.

(f) *Execution of documents* Under CA 2006, s 44, a document is executed by a company by affixing its common seal, or by two authorised signatories, or by a director in the presence of a witness who attests the signature. For problems that may arise with this, see *Williams v Redcard Ltd* [2011] 2 BCLC 350.

(g) *Contractual capacity* The company as a legal entity can contract in its own name, although there are limits on its capacity. It has no capacity before incorporation and any person who purports to contract on its behalf before this date will be personally liable on the contract (CA 2006, s 51).

(h) *Ownership of property* A company owns its own property and not the members. This can create problems in small private companies where the owners often treat company property as their own. See *Macaura v Northern Assurance Co Ltd* [1925] AC 619 and *Tunstall v Steigmann* [1962] 2 QB 593.

(i) *Company sues for wrongs done to it* This is known as the rule in *Foss v Harbottle* (1843) 2 Hare 461, and means that any decision to sue must be made by the members in general meeting, or the directors, and an individual member may not sue on behalf of the company. This can cause problems where errant directors are also majority shareholders and exceptions have developed to the rule. However, it is a difficult area of law and one where the concept of separate legal personality does not quite work (see **11.5**).

(j) *Company can create floating charges* A company can create floating charges, which are charges over a class of assets which change from time to time, and which the company can use and sell in the ordinary course of business, and on such sale the charge ceases to attach to the goods sold. One theory is that the charge 'floats above' all those goods in the class owned by the company at any one time and only attaches to the goods, preventing the company from using them, on crystallisation (see **5.4** and **5.5**).

3.4.2 Who is or may be a member?

The subscribers of a company's memorandum will be the first members of the company when it is registered (CA 2006, s 16(2)). They must be registered in the company's register of members (CA 2006, s 112(1)).

The members of a company are the registered holders of the shares (ie those persons whose names are on the register of members kept by the company either because they were subscribers to the memorandum or have agreed to be a member and had their name entered on the register (CA 2006, s 112(2)). The company will deal with the named person and, by CA 2006, s 126, no notice of any trust may be entered on the register. Thus, where there are nominee shareholders (X, the named shareholder, holds for Y on whose instructions X acts) the company must deal with X and not Y, even if X is not acting according to Y's instructions. Part 9 of the CA 2006 contains provisions which are designed to enable registered members to nominate persons who are entitled to receive information from the company, and they can also exercise voting and requisition rights (see **4.7**).

As nominee shareholdings have been used to build up voting control in companies, CA 2006, ss 791–828 gives public companies the power to obtain information about the interests in shares so as to enable the true ownership of its shares to be ascertained. There are also requirements to disclose substantial interests in shares in public companies traded on a regulated or prescribed market (eg the London Stock Exchange) under the Financial Services Authority Handbook Disclosure and Transparency Rules. Substantial interest is defined as 3 per cent or more of the issuer's voting rights.

Anyone may be a member of a company, including another company, although a company may not be a member of itself or its holding company (CA 2006, s 136). Capacity to be a shareholder is dictated by the ordinary law of contract and the articles, which may restrict membership to particular persons.

3.4.3 Divergence of private and public companies

In practice there is a great deal of difference between small private companies and large public companies. The CA 1985 largely treated them in the same way, although there were differences, such as the accounting rules which required the accounts to be drawn up in a particular format, audited, laid before members in general meeting (at the AGM) and filed with the Registrar of Companies every year. Some of the rules were relaxed for small and medium-sized private companies (which were defined on the basis of turnover, balance sheet totals and average number of employees).

One of the aims of the CA 2006 is to relax the formalities required by private companies. In particular, in recognition that most small private companies involve very few members and operate on an informal basis, private companies are no longer required to have general meetings (see **Chapter 6**).

3.4.4 Limited liability partnerships

In addition to limited liability companies registered under the CA 2006, it is possible to form limited liability partnerships ('LLPs') under the Limited Liability Partnerships Act 2000. Like a company, an LLP is a body corporate with a legal personality separate from that of its members (Limited Liability Partnerships Act 2000, s 1(2)). An LLP is formed by delivering an incorporation document to the registrar, and a statement from a solicitor or subscriber to the incorporation document that two or more persons are associated for carrying out a lawful business with a view to profit (s 2). Once incorporated an

LLP has unlimited capacity (s 1(3)). Like companies, they trade and conduct litigation in their own names rather than in the names of the individuals who manage or own them.

3.5 Articles of association

3.5.1 Constitutional documents

Part 3 of the CA 2006 deals with a company's constitution. Under these provisions, a company's constitution is defined (non-exhaustively) as the articles of association, and any resolutions or agreements that affect a company's constitution as listed in s 29 (see s 17). The memorandum of association, which under CA 1985 was also a constitutional document, no longer has this status.

3.5.2 Internal regulations/Model Articles

The articles are the internal regulations of the company which set out the basic administrative structure of the company and the division of powers between the members and the directors. On incorporation, the subscribers to the memorandum can adopt whatever articles they choose, and are free (subject to some limitations) to draft each regulation in whatever way they like. For limited companies registered on or after 1 October 2009, CA 2006, s 20, provides that if articles are not registered, or, if articles are registered, insofar as they do not exclude or modify them, the relevant model articles (so far as applicable) form part of the company's articles. By this means some degree of uniformity is found between different companies' articles. However, the Companies (Model Articles) Regulations 2008, SI 2008/3229, (made under CA 2006, s 19) contain different model articles for different descriptions of companies. The Model Articles for Private Companies Limited by Shares ('Model Articles Private Companies') contain 53 regulations. The Model Articles for Public Companies ('Model Articles Public Companies') are not surprisingly longer and more complex, containing 86 regulations. The areas covered by both sets, however, is much the same: interpretation, directors, general meetings, shares and distributions and various administrative matters.

Companies incorporated before CA 2006, s 20, came into force will be bound by their existing articles, although they are able to adopt the model articles under the CA 2006 if they wish. Default articles for companies registered between 1 July 1985 and 30 September 2009 are found in the Companies (Tables A to F) Regulations 1985, SI 1985/805. Table A is the set of articles applying to all companies limited by shares registered under the CA 1985. It contains 118 regulations dealing with numerous matters from accounts to winding up. It was subject to periodic minor amendment. Like provision is made for companies registered before 1 July 1985, the appropriate Table A being found in the legislation then in force, for example CA 1948, Sch 1.

These articles, Table A or the Model Articles Private Companies and Model Articles Public Companies, are frequently met in practice and repeated reference will be made to them on this course.

3.5.3 Altering the articles

3.5.3.1 Alterable by special resolution

With the passage of time, changes in a company's business and personnel may make it desirable to alter its original constitution. As with past Companies Acts, the general scheme of the CA 2006 is to permit any changes duly voted on by the shareholders, except where the change is in some way inequitable. Thus a company may by special resolution alter its articles under CA 2006, s 21(1).

Under the CA 1985, regulations in the articles could not be made unalterable (*Allen v Gold Reefs of West Africa Ltd* [1900] 1 Ch 656, CA). The former practice of permitting companies to entrench provisions relating to the constitution by putting them in the memorandum and providing that they could not be altered no longer exists with the new short form prescribed memorandum (see **3.1.1.1** and **3.10**). For companies incorporated under the CA 2006, provisions can be entrenched in the articles by providing that they can only be altered if specific conditions are met (s 22). The power to alter the articles by special resolution must not be abused by the majority shareholders, and any alteration may be set aside by the court if it is a fraud on the minority.

3.5.3.2 The principle

An alteration to the articles will be set aside if it was not made 'bona fide for the benefit of the company as a whole' (per Lindley MR in *Allen v Gold Reefs of West Africa Ltd* [1900] 1 Ch 656, CA). There is a fair amount of case law in this area, and it is not particularly easy to reconcile all the judgments that have been pronounced.

3.5.3.3 The hypothetical member

One of the leading cases in this area is *Greenhalgh v Arderne Cinemas Ltd* [1951] Ch 286, CA, in which Evershed MR said:

> Certain principles, I think, can be safely stated as emerging from those authorities. In the first place, I think it is now plain that 'bona fide for the benefit of the company as a whole' means not two things but one thing. It means that the shareholder must proceed upon what, in his honest opinion, is for the benefit of the company as a whole. The second thing is that the phrase, 'the company as a whole', does not (at any rate in such a case as the present) mean the company as a commercial entity, distinct from the corporators: it means the corporators as a general body. That is to say, the case may be taken of an individual hypothetical member and it may be asked whether what is proposed is, in the honest opinion of those who voted in its favour, for that person's benefit.

The hypothetical member contemplated is a member of the company in question. The court therefore considers the effect of the existing articles, how the company's powers are distributed between the directors and members, the rights attaching to different classes of shares etc. Conversely, the hypothetical member does not have any particular number of shares, so the court does not look exclusively at the effect of the alteration on the dissenting minority members.

3.5.3.4 Discrimination between members

Immediately after the passage from *Greenhalgh v Arderne Cinemas Ltd* [1951] Ch 286 quoted in the previous paragraph, Evershed MR said that, in practice, an alteration 'would be liable to be impeached if the effect of it were to discriminate between the majority shareholders and the minority shareholders, so as to give to the former an advantage of which the latter were deprived'. A similar approach was adopted by Lord Sterndale MR in *Sidebottom v Kershaw, Leese and Co Ltd* [1920] 1 Ch 154, CA, where he quoted from Buckley on the Companies Acts, saying that the majority shareholders cannot 'sacrifice the interests of the minority ... without any reasonable prospect of advantage to the company as a whole'. The effect is that an alteration may be valid despite adversely affecting minority interests, provided the overall (and, perhaps, long-term) effect is beneficial to the company as a whole.

3.5.3.5 Conflict between the approaches

Dr Sealy in his *Cases and Materials in Company Law* suggests, along with other commentators, that Evershed MR in *Greenhalgh v Arderne Cinemas Ltd* [1951] Ch 286 was trying to have the best of both worlds in that, on the one hand, it is the honest opinion of the majority shareholders that determines whether the alteration is valid, and, on the other, it is whether the alteration objectively discriminates between different shareholders.

3.5.3.6 Business policy

In this area, like many others in company law, there are occasions when the court considers that what has been done by the company is most properly characterised as a matter of business policy, and the court will not lightly interfere with the business judgement of the people involved. An example of a case where this factor weighed heavily in the court's decision is *Rights and Issues Investment Trust Ltd v Stylo Shoes Ltd* [1965] Ch 250.

3.5.3.7 Some examples

In *Greenhalgh v Arderne Cinemas Ltd* [1951] Ch 286 the original articles gave existing members pre-emption rights if any of them wished to sell their shares to outsiders. The majority wished to sell their shares to an outsider, but a minority shareholder was not prepared to forego his right of pre-emption. The majority therefore passed a special resolution to alter the articles so that the company could by ordinary resolution override the pre-emption provision. The court refused to make a declaration that the alteration was invalid, because any shareholder could in theory take advantage of the altered articles, even though, in practical terms, only the majority could pass the requisite ordinary resolution.

In *Rights and Issues Investment Trust Ltd v Stylo Shoes Ltd* [1965] Ch 250 the company's issued capital consisted of 4,000,000 shares, 90 per cent of which were ordinary shares carrying one vote per share, and 10 per cent were management shares carrying eight votes each. In practice, the holders of the management shares controlled shareholders' meetings. After taking over another company, a further 8,400,000 ordinary shares were issued. Resolutions were then passed at class and general meetings doubling the voting rights of the management shares. Again a declaration that the alteration was invalid was refused. The management shares' votes were not used at the meetings, the issue was regarded as one of business policy, the judge was satisfied that the resolutions were passed in good faith, and benefited the company as a whole.

Conversely, alterations compelling the minority to sell their shares have on occasion been held to be invalid. For example, in *Dafen Tinplate Co Ltd v Llanelly Steel Co (1907) Ltd* [1920] 2 Ch 124 the articles were altered to allow the company by ordinary resolution to require any member to sell its shares to the other members at a fair price, but exempted one named member from the provision. Peterson J held that the alteration was not in the interests of the company as a whole as it allowed the expropriation of a member's shares for no reason save the will of the majority. Further, the alteration was bad because it created a privilege for the one named member when the shares had originally been issued on an equal footing. Contrast *Sidebottom v Kershaw, Leese and Co Ltd* [1920] 1 Ch 154, CA, where an alteration to allow the expropriation of shares of any member carrying on a business in competition with the company was held to be valid.

3.6 Contractual effect of the articles

3.6.1 The statutory contract

Section 33 of the CA 2006, provides:

> *The provisions of a company's constitution bind the company and its members to the same extent as if there were covenants on the part of the company and of each member to observe those provisions.*

The section creates a statutory contract derived from the company's constitution between the company and its members, as did the similar provision in CA 1985.

This contract is a rather unusual contract in that:

(a) The remedies for breach are, generally, restricted to declarations and injunctions. Damages may be awarded in situations such as where there are arrears of dividends, but this is exceptional.

(b) There is no jurisdiction to rectify a company's articles of association: *Scott v Frank F Scott (London) Ltd* [1940] Ch 794, CA.

(c) There are only limited grounds for implying terms into the contract constituted by a company's articles of association: *AG of Belize v Belize Telecom Ltd* [2009] 1 WLR 1988.

(d) This contract can only be enforced by shareholders insofar as they are affected in their capacity as shareholders.

3.6.2 As shareholders

Buckley LJ in *Bisgood v Henderson's Transvaal Estates Ltd* [1908] 1 Ch 743, CA, said, 'The purpose of the memorandum and articles is to define the position of the shareholder as shareholder, not to bind him in his capacity as an individual'. So, in the leading case of *Hickman v Kent or Romney Marsh Sheep-Breeders' Association* [1915] 1 Ch 881 Astbury J reviewed earlier authorities on the section and said:

> I think this much is clear, first, that no article can constitute a contract between the company and a third person; secondly, that no right merely purporting to be given by an article to a person, whether a member or not, in a capacity other than that of a member, as, for instance, as solicitor, promoter, director, can be enforced against the company; and, thirdly, that articles regulating the rights and obligations of the members generally as such do create rights and obligations between them and the company respectively.

In this case one of the company's articles provided for disputes to be referred to arbitration. Hickman brought an action complaining of various irregularities, and the company applied for a stay (see BCP, chapter 56) relying on the article. Astbury J granted the stay because the article operated between Hickman and the company in Hickman's capacity as a member, was a general article applying to all members and so should have been complied with by him.

3.6.3 Who can enforce the statutory contract?

Case law has established that the statutory contract binds:

(a) Members in their dealings with the company (*Hickman v Kent or Romney Marsh Sheep-Breeders' Association* [1915] 1 Ch 881).

(b) The company in its dealings with its members as members (*Oakbank Oil Co v Crum* (1882) 8 App Cas 65, HL).

(c) Members in their dealings with each other as members, without the need to join the company in any action to enforce the contract (*Rayfield v Hands* [1960] Ch 1). This latter situation is the most controversial, and it may be that there are further limits on direct enforceability between members.

3.6.4 Authority of *Hickman's* case

Doubts have been raised against the decision in *Hickman v Kent or Romney Marsh Sheep-Breeders' Association* [1915] 1 Ch 881 on a number of grounds:

(a) The actual decisions in some of the earlier cases are not strictly consistent with the principles extracted from them by Astbury J.

(b) There are cases where the courts have enforced individual rights contained in the company's articles. An example is *Pulbrook v Richmond Consolidated Mining Co* (1878) 9 ChD 610, where a director obtained an injunction restraining the other directors from excluding him from the board.

Despite the above, *Hickman's* case undoubtedly states the law at the present time, and was accepted by the Court of Appeal in *Beattie v E and F Beattie Ltd* [1938] Ch 708.

3.6.5 Determining the meaning of the articles

The usual rules of construction as set out in *Investors Compensation Scheme Ltd v West Bromwich Building Society* [1998] 1 WLR 896 apply when construing the statutory contract in the articles of association. These are summarised at BCP, para 89.22. Generally the court will give the words used in the articles their plain and ordinary meaning. This can be departed from in various defined situations, such as when the ordinary meaning of the words leads to a commercial absurdity (*Thompson v Goblin Hill Hotels Ltd* [2011] 1 BCLC 587).

3.6.6 Limits on the statutory contract

There are two main limits on the enforcement of the statutory contract. First, the courts will not allow shareholders to use it to avoid the rule in *Foss v Harbottle* (see **11.5**), particularly where the shareholders are complaining of directors' breaches of fiduciary duty to the company (see *Prudential Assurance Co Ltd v Newman Industries Ltd (No 2)* [1982] Ch 204). Secondly, many breaches of a company's articles can be ratified by the company in general meeting, and if this has happened, members will be unable to complain.

3.7 Contracts incorporating provisions from the articles

As we have seen previously, the statutory contract can only be used to enforce 'insider rights' contained in a company's articles. A person undertaking to act as a company's director, solicitor etc is therefore best advised to enter into a separate contract with the company, rather than relying on provisions in the articles dealing with the terms of service of such post holders. Here we deal with the situation where such a separate contract incorporates terms from the articles. If provisions are incorporated expressly into the contract there should be no undue problem and any breach of the terms contained in the articles can be enforced under the external contract.

In the absence of express provision, the court may be prepared to infer that provisions from the articles have been incorporated into the contract. In *Re New British Iron Co, ex p Beckwith* [1898] 1 Ch 324 the court implied a term fixing the directors' remuneration from the articles on the footing that the directors had been employed by the company and had accepted office. Provisions will not be implied from the articles if the contract deals expressly with the same matters (*Nelson v James Nelson and Sons Ltd* [1914] 2 KB 770, CA), but the articles can be used to infer terms on matters where the express terms of the contract are silent (*Read v Astoria Garage (Streatham) Ltd* [1952] Ch 637, CA).

However, the courts have on occasion been reluctant to imply contracts incorporating articles solely on the basis of the parties having acted on the provisions of the articles, see *Browne v La Trinidad* (1887) 37 ChD 1 and *Newtherapeutics Ltd v Katz* [1991] Ch 226.

3.8 Contracts and alterations to the articles

3.8.1 Alteration constituting a breach of contract

An alteration to a company's articles, or acting on such an alteration, may constitute a breach of contract by the company. Thus, in *Southern Foundries (1926) Ltd v Shirlaw* [1940] AC 701, HL, the claimant was appointed managing director for ten years. Later, an article was added allowing a director to be removed by two directors and a secretary, and the claimant was removed under this provision. Although the company was entitled to alter its articles in this way, by doing so it was in breach of its contract with the claimant and was liable in damages.

3.8.2 Alteration to justify a breach of contract

Where there is an ordinary contract between a person (outsider or member) and the company, the company cannot resile from the agreed terms and justify a breach of the contract by altering its articles (*Baily v British Equitable Assurance Co* [1904] 1 Ch 374, CA). This principle was approved on appeal [1906] AC 35 by Lord Macnaghten, though the House of Lords reversed the decision of the Court of Appeal. The House of Lords construed the contract as incorporating the articles of the company and as being alterable from time to time, so there was no breach of contract when the articles were altered.

3.9 Shareholders' agreements

Shareholders may, before incorporation of the company, enter into an agreement between themselves about participation in the management of the business, sharing profits and the arrangements for buying each other out. Such an agreement would almost certainly be considered by the court in the event of a 'just and equitable' winding-up petition or unfair prejudice petition being brought by one of the members (see **Chapters 12** and **13**).

Alternatively, the company may by contract confer rights on individual members on matters such as the composition of the board of directors and the payment of dividends.

Although such matters can be dealt with in the articles, there are two main differences in their legal effect:

(a) Provisions in the articles run with the shares, so as to bind successive share owners. A contractual obligation, on the other hand, is purely personal and binds only the contracting parties.

(b) Regulations in the articles can always be altered by the company in general meeting, despite the objections of the individual member. Contractual obligations can only be altered by mutual consent.

There may be arguments about the validity of terms in these extra-statutory documents. Possible grounds include being contrary to public policy or illegal, particularly if the agreement is construed as being a bribe. The agreement may be a fetter on the company's power to alter its articles (see **3.5.3**) or, if only some of the shareholders are party to the agreement, may give grounds to the others to apply for minority remedies (see **Chapters 12** and **13**).

In *Russell v Northern Bank Development Corporation Ltd* [1992] 1 WLR 588, HL, a shareholders' agreement was entered into by four of the company's shareholders including the claimant, who between them held 40 per cent of its shares, and the company. The agreement provided that its terms should take precedence over the articles of association and that no further share capital would be issued or created without the written consent of all the parties to the agreement. Some years later the board of directors convened an EGM to consider increasing the company's share capital, whereon the claimant applied for injunctions. It was held that the agreement was an unlawful fetter on the company's statutory powers to increase its capital insofar as it purported to bind the company, but was a valid, personal, agreement outside the articles insofar as it bound the individual shareholders. The invalid part of the agreement was severable from the valid part, and a declaration as to the validity of the agreement as between the shareholders was granted.

The interrelation between a shareholders' agreement and a director's service contract was considered by the Court of Appeal in *Morris Angel and Son Ltd v Hollande* [1993] 3 All ER 569. The defendant was a party to the shareholders' agreement, and was a director of the company employed on the terms of a service contract entered into on the same date as the shareholders' agreement. The company's business was sold to the claimant. There was a triable issue as to whether the other parties were in breach of a term of the shareholders' agreement not to sell the company's business without his consent. The claimant immediately sacked the defendant, and brought an application for an injunction to restrain an alleged breach of a covenant in his service contract. It was held that the alleged breach of the shareholders' agreement had no bearing on the discretion to grant the proposed interim injunction, which was granted.

3.10 Memorandum of association: CA 2006 and CA 1985 contrasted

3.10.1 Companies formed under Companies Act 2006

The memorandum for companies formed under the CA 2006 must be in a prescribed form and simply contain a statement that the subscribers wish to form a company and become members of that company when it is incorporated and, in the case of a company that is to have a share capital, to take at least one share each (CA 2006, s 8). It is not part of the company's constitution and contains no other clauses. The memorandum is simply a 'snapshot' of the company at that particular point in time. It cannot be amended or updated. It is therefore a very different document to the memorandum of companies formed before the implementation of CA 2006.

3.10.2 Companies formed before implementation of CA 2006

The memorandum of companies formed under previous Companies Acts was a constitutional document and contained a number of important clauses. It contained a clause similar to that required by CA 2006, s 8 (see previously) which was called the 'Association Clause' (ie a formal request that the company be formed by the subscribers). The other clauses, which are not contained in the memorandum of companies formed under CA 2006, are treated as if they formed part of the articles (CA 2006, s 28). These clauses included clauses covering information now contained in the application of companies registering under CA 2006 (see **3.1.1.2**):

(a) name clause: setting out the corporate name;

(b) public company clause: a public company had to have a clause stating it was a public company; this clause did not exist in the memorandum of a private company;

(c) office clause: setting out the country in which the registered office was located;

(d) liability clause: if the members' liability was limited, a clause stating this fact.

Another clause in the memorandum was the capital clause. A company with share capital had a clause stating the amount of authorised capital and the division of that capital into shares of fixed amounts (eg £50,000 being 50,000 £1 shares). A company limited by guarantee had a clause stating the amount each member guaranteed to contribute in the event of an insolvent liquidation. This has been replaced by the statement of capital and initial shareholding (companies limited by shares) and statement of guarantee (companies limited by guarantee) (see **3.1.1.4**).

The other clause in the memorandum was the objects clause, which was extremely important.

3.10.3 Importance of the objects clause in pre-CA 2006 companies

The objects clause defined the business that a company could carry out (eg to make and sell, or lend on hire, railway carriages and wagons and all kinds of railway plant, fittings, machinery and rolling stock). Historically the basis for the clause was to enable investors to see if a company was in a business which was likely to be profitable. The *ultra vires* rule, that contracts outside the objects were *ultra vires* and void, ensured that the company did not embark on speculative ventures outside those objects. Outsiders dealing with the company were unable to enforce *ultra vires* contracts as they had constructive notice of the contents of the memorandum which was a public document. Companies therefore developed very long, complicated objects clauses. However, over time it became accepted that the *ultra vires* rule was unfair to outsiders, putting the onus on them to read and understand the object clause.

The CA 1989 made amendments to the CA 1985 which enabled companies to incorporate with a very wide objects clause, ie '*to carry on business as a general commercial company*' (CA 1985, s 3A) and empowered a company to alter its objects clause by special resolution enabling companies to adopt this new clause (CA 1985, s 4).

Under CA 2006, any objects clause in the memorandum is treated as forming part of the articles of association (CA 2006, s 28). CA 2006, s 31, provides that unless a company's articles specifically restrict the objects of the company, the objects are unrestricted. A company may amend its articles by special resolution (CA 2006, s 21(1)). Where this amendment is to add, remove or alter a statement of the company's objects, it must give notice to the registrar (CA 2006, s 31). Thus companies with objects clauses can simply remove them.

3.10.4 Exceeding authority and acting outside capacity

Where companies have retained less broad objects clauses, the *ultra vires* rule is effectively nullified by what is now CA 2006, s 39(1). This provides that the validity of an act done by a company shall not be called into question on the ground of a lack of capacity by reason of anything in the company's constitution. However, the actual authority of directors is still limited by the provisions of any objects clause. Where directors exceed this authority, CA 2006, s 40(1), gives protection to outsiders dealing with the company in good faith, by providing that the power of the directors 'to bind the company ... is deemed to be free of any limitation under the company's constitution'. Members have the right to restrain a proposed *ultra vires* act by directors (CA 2006, s 40(4)), and directors are liable for *ultra vires* acts to which they committed the company (CA 2006, s 40(5)), although the members may ratify their actions and excuse them from liability (CA 2006, s 239).

4 Share capital

4.1 Introduction

The topic of share capital covers both the rules relating to individual shareholders' rights and duties and the rules requiring the company to maintain its share capital as a whole.

The CA 2006 provisions on share capital are largely contained in Parts 17, 18, 20 and 21. Parts 17 and 18 together deal with provisions about issue of shares and maintenance of capital. Part 20 deals with the difference between rules prohibiting private companies from making public offers of shares and minimum share capital requirements of public companies. Part 21 deals with certification and transfer of shares.

4.2 Issue and transfer of shares

The two methods by which a person can become a member of a company are the allotment of shares by the company to the original allottee and the subsequent transfer of shares to another person.

4.2.1 Issue

4.2.1.1 General

An original allotment of shares may be by a fresh issue of shares, a rights issue (fresh issue of shares to existing members who may or may not decide to purchase them) or a bonus issue (where profits are capitalised and shares are issued to members in lieu of dividend). Where shares are offered to existing members, they may be offered by way of a renounceable letter of allotment, which enables the existing shareholder to take up the issue or renounce it in favour of someone else either by sale or gift. Whoever wishes to take up the shares will return the relevant document to the company, which will enter the appropriate name in the register of members and issue a share certificate.

4.2.1.2 Rules on the issue of shares

The following is an outline of the rules on the issue of shares:

(a) *Power of directors to issue* The CA 2006, s 549, provides that directors cannot allot shares except in accordance with s 550 or 551.

(i) *Private companies with one class of shares* By s 550 directors can allot shares where the company is a private company with only one class of shares (see definition in s 629), unless they are prohibited from doing so by the articles. Therefore in the circumstances prescribed by s 550, directors are empowered by statute to allot shares and do not need to rely on authority under the constitution, or from the members. However, the members can, if they wish, restrict or limit the directors' power to do so by the articles.

(ii) *Public companies and private companies with more than one class of share* For these companies, s 551 provides that the directors may only allot shares if they have been given prior authorisation to do so by the members passing a resolution to that effect, or by the articles. Any such authorisation must state the maximum number of shares to be allotted under it and must specify the date on which it will expire, which must be for a period of no more than five years.

(iii) *Transitional arrangements* For companies registered before the CA 2006, transitional arrangements ensure that any existing authorities, whether in the articles or by resolution, will continue to have legal effect (Companies Act 2006 (Commencement Order No 8, Transitional Provisions and Savings) Order 2008, SI 2008/2860, Sch 2, para 45).

(b) *Statutory pre-emption rights must be observed* CA 2006, s 561, provides that subject to certain exceptions, a company shall not allot equity securities (see s 560 for the definition) without first offering them on a pro rata basis to existing shareholders at the same or more favourable terms as will be offered to outsiders. Shareholders have a stated period, which must not be less than 14 days, to accept, and the offer cannot be withdrawn by the company during that period (s 562). A private company may exclude s 561 in its articles (s 567), and a public company may exclude it by special resolution when delegating the power to issue to the directors (s 570). The statutory pre-emption rights will not apply if the company has written pre-emption provisions into its articles, except for the provisions in the CA 2006 which relate to the communication of the offer to shareholders (s 568). The directors have the right to disapply or modify the statutory pre-emption rights if they are authorised to do so by the articles or by special resolution (ss 569–573).

(c) *Shares may not be issued at a discount but may be issued at a premium* Every share must have a fixed nominal value (CA 2006, s 542). Shares may not be issued for consideration of less value than the nominal value of the shares. There are special rules for public companies to ensure that where shares are issued for a non-cash consideration, it is not less than the nominal value (CA 2006, ss 580–609). Shares may be issued at more than the nominal value, but the premium is treated as capital and is subject to the maintenance of capital rules (CA 2006, ss 610–616).

(d) *A return of allotment* This must be made to the Registrar of Companies showing the names and addresses of the allottees, the number and nominal value, etc of the shares (CA 2006, s 554) together with a statement of capital, which shows the amount of issued share capital at that point in time (CA 2006, s 555). This means that for both public and private companies, the Registrar of Companies will have up-to-date information about a company's share capital, which can be obtained by a company search.

(e) *Issues to the public* A private company is prohibited from issuing shares to the public (CA 2006, s 755), thus limiting the pool of potential investors. A court may order a company which is proposing to or has acted in contravention of s 755 to re-register as a public company unless it does not meet the requirements for public companies (see **4.10.2**), in which case the court may order it to be wound up compulsorily (ss 757–758). If a public company wishes to offer shares to the public, it must comply with provisions as to form, content, approval and publication of the prospectus or listing particulars in the Financial Services and Markets Act 2000.

4.2.1.3 Removal of concept of authorised share capital

Companies registered before the implementation of the CA 2006 filed a memorandum of association containing a capital clause which set out the amount of its authorised share capital. If shares had been issued up to that amount, the authorised capital had to be increased by ordinary resolution of the members before further shares were issued. The memorandum of companies registering under the CA 2006 does not contain a capital clause, and there is therefore no longer a requirement to increase this before issuing shares. CA 2006, s 28, provides that the clauses in the memoranda of companies registered before the implementation of CA 2006 which are not contained in the CA 2006-style memorandum are to be treated as provisions in the company's articles. Thus these companies which have issued shares to the amount stated in the capital clause and wish to issue further shares should vary the articles either to remove the clause or increase the amount.

4.2.2 Transfer

4.2.2.1 Shares are saleable investments

The general rule is that a shareholder has the right to transfer shares unless the articles restrict the right. Public companies generally do not restrict the right to transfer fully paid shares and cannot obtain official listing if they do. Before 1980, private companies were required to impose some restrictions and still often do in practice. The two most common restrictions are:

(a) Pre-emption rights of other members. The shareholder must first offer the shares to existing shareholders and may only transfer to others if the pre-emption right is not exercised.

(b) Power of directors to refuse to register transfers. This may be a general power giving the directors absolute discretion (eg Model Articles Private Companies, reg 26(5)), or a specific power enabling the directors to refuse to register a transfer only on specified grounds (eg 1985 Table A, reg 24, contains such a provision for partly paid shares whether of a public or private company). The power is given in small private companies usually to ensure that shares remain in a family or among a closed group of members.

Any ambiguity or uncertainty in the provisions is construed in favour of the shareholder wishing to transfer. The company must register the transfer or notify the transferee of any refusal to register the shares and give reasons for its refusal 'as soon as practicable, and in any event within two months of the transfer being lodged with' the company (CA 2006, s 771). Where the directors refuse to register the transfer, the transferee is entitled to receive such information as he may reasonably require regarding the reasons for the directors' refusal. However, the transferee is not entitled to obtain copies of the board minutes.

The transfer is completed by entering the name of the transferee in the register of members whereby the newly registered member has a fresh contract with the company (ie he is not an assignee).

In the event of refusal to register, the transferor's name will remain on the register of members as the legal owner of the shares. The transferee will be the equitable owner although his or her interest will not be on the register as CA 2006, s 126, will not permit any notice of a trust to be entered on the register. The transferor will remain liable for calls on the shares (where a company calls for money to be paid up on unpaid or partly paid shares). He or she will have to account to the transferee for any dividends received and will even have to attend and vote at company meetings at the behest of the transferee. A transferee who considers that the transfer has been wrongfully refused may apply for rectification of the register of members (CA 2006, s 125, see **4.8**).

Transmission of shares occurs when the shareholder dies or is adjudicated bankrupt and the shares fall under the control of his or her personal representatives or trustee in bankruptcy, who may, if they wish and the articles allow, be registered as shareholders or transfer them without being so registered (CA 2006, s 774).

4.2.2.2 Procedure for transferring shares

It is not lawful for a company to register a transfer of shares unless a proper instrument of transfer has been delivered to it or the transfer is an exempt transfer within the Stock Transfer Act 1982 or is made in accordance with the Uncertificated Securities Regulations 2001, SI 2001/3755 (CA 2006, s 770). Most transfers will come within the Stock Transfer Act 1963, which allows a single form of transfer for fully paid shares, or the Uncertificated Securities Regulations governing the CREST system. Although the method of transferring shares remains the same under the CA 2006 as it was under CA 1985, at some point in the future, the Government is likely to make regulations enabling all shares to be transferred electronically without the need for a written instrument. The existing method of transfer of shares depends on whether or not the shares are listed on the London Stock Exchange.

(a) *Shares not on the London Stock Exchange* Shares not listed on the London Stock Exchange are transferred directly from transferor to transferee. The transferor completes a transfer form in the name of the transferee. If the transferor is selling the whole of the shareholding, the transfer form and share certificate are given to the transferee who forwards the transfer form and share certificate to the company. The company enters the name of the transferee on the register of members and enters a note that the transferor is no longer a member. The old share certificate is cancelled and a new one is issued in the name of the transferee.

If the transferor is selling only part of the shareholding, the procedure is more complicated. The completed transfer form and share certificate are sent by the transferor to the company. The company endorses the transfer form 'certificate lodged' and returns the transfer form to the transferor who passes it to the transferee. The share certificate is retained by the company for cancellation. The transferee sends the transfer form to the company which alters the register of members accordingly and issues two new certificates, one in the name of the transferee for the shares transferred and one in the name of the transferor for the shares retained.

(b) *Shares on the London Stock Exchange* Almost all share trades on the Stock Exchange are conducted electronically using the CREST system. This is a large messaging system that conveys information about share trades, and usually results in share trades being settled within three working days. The London Stock Exchange has its own electronic system (SETS), which matches buyers and sellers constantly through the day. Further details can be found at www.londonstockexchange.com/traders-and-brokers/private-investors/private-investors/selecting-analysing-shares/buying-selling-shares/buying-selling-shares.htm.

4.3 Ceasing to be a member

A person ceases to be a member when his or her name is removed from the register or he or she dies. The name may be removed for a variety of reasons, for example transfer to another whose name is registered, purchase, redemption, forfeiture by the company or surrender to the company of shares which are then cancelled or reissued, or the company being dissolved. In addition, where a share warrant is issued, the company will strike the name of the member off the register and substitute a statement that a warrant has been issued, the shares included in the warrant and the date of issue of the warrant. CA 2006, s 122, makes it clear that a shareholder with a share warrant is not a member but may be deemed to be so if the articles so provide. Share warrants are negotiable instruments whereby the bearer is entitled to the shares represented by the warrant and legal title is transferred by delivery, so no entry is made in the register of members on transfer. Share warrants are not very common.

4.4 Register of members

The subscribers to the memorandum will automatically become members on incorporation and their names will be entered in the register of members (CA 2006, s 112(1)). All other shares will be allotted by the company on an application by a person to become a member of the company. CA 2006, s 112(2), provides that every other person who agrees to become a member of a company and whose name is entered in its register of members, is a member of the company. CA 2006, s 113, requires every company to keep a register of members containing the following information: the names and addresses of the members, the date on which each person was registered as a member and ceased to be a member, the shares held by each member, the class and number of those shares and the amount paid on each share. CA 2006, s 114, requires that the register be kept at the company's registered office or at the office of the place where it is made up, in which case notice of that address must be given to the registrar.

The register is open to inspection by any member free of charge and any other person who may be required to pay. In an attempt to curb abuse, CA 2006, s 116, requires the person making the request to specify the purpose for which the information will be used and to provide their name and address and the name and address of any other person to whom they intend to disclose the information. It is an offence knowingly or recklessly to give false information in relation to a request, and to disclose that information to any other person who they know or suspect may use it for an improper purpose (s 119). The company must comply with the request within five days or apply to the court for relief from the obligation if they suspect that the request has been made for an improper purpose (s 117). The register must be kept open for inspection at all times. Generally under the CA 1985 provisions, the court would make an order once a contravention of the section had been established, but the court retained a discretion to refuse to make an order if there were special circumstances. These could include cases where inspection had been given (albeit late), where the list of members had been lost or destroyed, or where an undertaking had been offered which met the justice of the case. In appropriate cases, an order could be made subject to conditions regarding the confidentiality and use of the information given (*Pelling v Families Need Fathers Ltd* [2002] 2 All ER 440). It remains to be seen how the court will deal with applications under the CA 2006.

4.5 Share certificates

Share certificates are not issued for uncertificated shares recorded in the CREST system under the Uncertificated Securities Regulations 2001, SI 2001/3755 (reg 38(2)). For all other shares, the company must within two months of allotment or transfer issue a share certificate (CA 2006, s 769). It will state that the named person is the registered holder of a specified number of shares of a particular class which are fully paid or paid up to a stated amount. The share certificate is not a document of title. CA 2006, s 768, provides that it is prima facie evidence of title to the shares of the person named in it. This presumption may be rebutted. The share certificate operates as a representation by the company that at the time it was issued the person named in it held the specified number of shares and that those shares were paid up to the extent specified (*Alipour v UOC Corp* [2002] 2 BCLC 770). The company may be estopped from denying statements in the certificate against persons who have relied on them. It may be estopped in respect of the statement of the amount paid up on the shares (*Bloomenthal v Ford* [1897] AC 156) or in respect of the statement as to title (*Re Bahia and San Francisco Railway Co Ltd* (1868) LR 3 QB 584).

4.6 Legal and equitable interests in shares

The legal owner of the shares is the person whose name is on the register of members. Equitable interests may arise in a variety of circumstances: a trustee holding shares for beneficiaries under an express trust; a nominee shareholder holding shares for the true controller of the shares; the seller of shares where an unconditional contract has been entered into holding as trustee for the purchaser until the purchaser is registered; on the mortgage of shares.

4.6.1 Notice of equitable interests

CA 2006, s 126, provides that:

No notice of any trust, expressed, implied, or constructive, shall be entered on the register of members of a company registered in England and Wales or Northern Ireland, or be receivable by the registrar.

This almost certainly extends to all equitable interests. Thus, although priority and protection of equitable interests are usually given by notice, this cannot be done in respect of such interests in shares in a company.

4.6.2 Stop notices

A person with a beneficial interest in shares can protect that interest by issuing a stop notice. The procedure for obtaining a stop notice and enforcing it is governed by the Charging Orders Act 1979 and CPR, rr 73.16–73.21. Stop notices are issued by the Chancery Division on the filing of a witness statement or affidavit and copies of the notice to be served on the company. The notice informs the company that the applicant has an interest in specified shares and that the notice is to prevent the registration of transfers of the shares and, possibly, the payment of dividends to the registered holder. As long as the stop notice remains in force the company must notify the applicant at least 14 days before any register of transfer or, where applicable, payment of dividend. This is to give the applicant time to apply to the court for an injunction to prevent the transfer being registered (or dividend being paid).

4.6.3 Disclosure of interests

The risks of hidden interests in shares through nominee shareholdings in public companies and the power of companies to obtain information and the requirement to disclose substantial interests in shares traded on regulated or prescribed markets has been briefly covered in **3.4.2**.

4.7 Exercise of members' rights

Section 145(1) of the CA 2006 applies where a company's articles enable members to nominate another person or persons to enjoy or exercise all or any specified rights of the member in relation to the company. Part 9 (ss 145–153) sets out the requirements to be fulfilled and the rights of the nominees, etc in some detail. These provisions were implemented to enable investors who increasingly hold shares through an intermediary to obtain information from the company and give instructions on how they wish the shares to be voted.

4.8 Rectification of the register

CA 2006, s 127, provides:

The register of members is prima facie evidence of any matters which are by this Act directed or authorised to be inserted in it.

It may, therefore, be challenged, and this is done by asking for the register to be rectified. It is unclear whether the company can rectify the register on a request without obtaining a court order first (see, eg *Reese River Silver Mining Co v Smith* (1869) LR 4 HL 64).

CA 2006, s 125(1), provides:

If—

(a) the name of any person is, without sufficient cause, entered in or omitted from a company's register of members, or

(b) default is made or unnecessary delay takes place in entering on the register the fact of any person having ceased to be a member,

the person aggrieved, or any member of the company, or the company may apply to the court for rectification of the register.

An application to rectify the register is usually made by a Part 8 claim form to the Companies Court unless the case is complicated or other relief is sought when it should be begun by ordinary claim form. The summary procedure may be used where the company wrongfully refuses to register a transferee, there is a dispute about title where the facts are agreed or easily ascertained, or where an allotment is void or voidable because of misrepresentation inducing the purchase. Written evidence must be filed setting out the facts supporting the application to rectify. Where there is a substantial dispute of fact the court may decide to strike out an application under the summary procedure in s 125(1), but by s 125(3), the court may decide any question relating to the title of any party to have his name entered in or omitted from the share register. Since the introduction of the CPR, and in keeping with the overriding objective in r 1.1 and the court's active case management function, the court may allow proceedings started under s 125 to continue with suitable directions for filing statements of case and for the future progress of the claim (*Re Hoicrest Ltd* [2000] 1 WLR 414).

4.9 Classes of shares and variation of class rights

4.9.1 Classes of shares

A company may have classes of shares, that is, where different shares have different rights, for example to vote or to receive dividends in return for their capital contributions. Shareholders receive their share of the profits by way of payment of a dividend. The right to a dividend only arises if there are distributable profits out of which a dividend has been declared. When and how this is done will depend on the articles. Shareholders may receive a return of their capital investment on liquidation of the company or a reduction of capital in accordance with the provisions in CA 2006, ss 641–653.

These rights to dividend and return of capital will be set out in the articles or terms of issue of the shares. If different shares have different rights there will be classes of shares. The two most common classes of shares are:

- Ordinary shares (equity shares) which are the vast majority of shares and will have the usual rights without any special definition.
- Preference shares which have preferential rights to dividend and/or return of capital.

There are two general presumptions on these rights:

- A presumption of equality, that is, all shares are presumed to rank equally in the absence of special provisions.
- A presumption of priority rights being exhaustive.

Preference shares usually have a preferential dividend measured as a percentage of the nominal value of the share (10 per cent preferential dividend on shares of £1 nominal value). Such dividend is presumed to be cumulative unless otherwise stated. Thus if no dividend is paid one year, a 20 per cent dividend will be paid the next year. The priority on the dividend means that although dividends will be paid more regularly, they will always be exactly the same and will not increase if, for example, substantial profits are made. Ordinary shares, on the other hand, have less of a guarantee of payment of dividend regularly but stand to benefit where a large profit has been made.

Preference shares will also usually be given priority in the return of capital in a liquidation although, given the presumption of equality, this is not necessarily so just because they have a preference to dividend. If given priority to return of capital, the preference shares again are a more secure investment than ordinary shares, as they are more likely to have capital returned even where there is insufficient to pay all shareholders. However, they are also potentially less profitable as they will not share in any surplus.

Note that there are also participating preference shares which combine the benefits of priority of preference shares and of sharing in the remaining profits or surplus of capital of ordinary shares.

4.9.2 What is a variation of class rights?

There will be a variation of class rights where the rights attached to the shares have been varied. This will not include actions which do not alter those rights but nevertheless affect the commercial value of the shares. Many of the cases on this point are concerned with the grant or increase of rights to other members which reduces the value of existing rights without actually altering them. Thus it has been held that a subdivision of ordinary shares which reduces the voting powers of preference shares was not a variation of the rights of the preference shareholders (*Greenhalgh v Arderne Cinemas Ltd* [1946] 1 All ER 512). Also, a reduction of capital by which the amount of dividend payable on preference shares was reduced was not a variation of class rights (*Re Mackenzie and Co Ltd* [1916] 2 Ch 450).

4.9.3 Procedure

Variation of class rights of shareholders is governed by CA 2006, s 630. In all cases, rights may be varied in accordance with the company's articles or where the articles make no provision for variation of class rights, by special resolution or written consent of the holders of at least three-quarters in nominal value of the issued shares of that class. Thus, if the articles require a simple majority, this will suffice. In addition, as s 630(3) provides that the provisions are without prejudice to other restrictions on variation, if the articles require a higher percentage, this must be fulfilled or if the class rights are entrenched in the articles, that protection must be respected. There are no provisions for variation of class rights in the Model Articles—Private Companies or Public Companies. Section 631 makes similar provision for variation of class rights in companies without share capital.

CA 2006, s 633, provides that the holders of at least 15 per cent of the class of affected shares who did not consent to the variation may within 21 days apply to the court to disallow the variation. The variation does not then take effect until the court confirms it. The most usual ground for complaint is that the majority who consented did not act in the interests of the class but to secure some other advantage, for example they held shares of another class which would benefit by the variation (*Re Holders Investment Trust Ltd* [1971] 1 WLR 583, and see **3.5.3**). Section 634 gives a similar right in respect of variation of class rights in companies without share capital.

4.10 Maintenance of share capital

It is important to differentiate between:

- Authorised share capital—a concept not carried forward in the CA 2006, but which may still be relevant to companies registered before the implementation of CA 2006—see **4.2.1.3**).
- Issued or allotted share capital—the total nominal amount actually issued to shareholders at any time.
- Paid-up share capital—the amount so far paid on shares which have been issued.
- Uncalled share capital—the amount which the company is entitled to call on shareholders to contribute.

Most shares are now issued as fully paid shares: it is rare to have partly paid shares with the resulting uncalled capital.

The members together provide the company with its share capital. The money or assets so contributed become the property of the company. If the company does well, it will have assets worth more than the nominal value of its issued share capital. If it does poorly the sum total of the assets may be less. Thus the capital may be dissipated through trading losses. However, there are stringent rules on not returning to the shareholders the share capital which they have contributed. These rules extend to ensuring that the consideration given by each shareholder in exchange for shares is at least equal in value to the nominal value of the shares. The rules have developed in recognition of the fact that the share capital is the 'creditors' buffer' in that it is the company which is their debtor and whose assets must be used to pay their debts.

Thus a company may not:

(a) Issue shares at a discount (see **4.10.4**).

(b) Provide financial assistance for the purchase of its shares except as provided in the Companies Acts (see **4.11**).

(c) Reduce its issued share capital without following the procedure set out in the Companies Acts (see **4.13**).

(d) Purchase its own shares except as provided in the Companies Acts.

(e) Pay a dividend except out of distributable profits (see **4.16**).

4.10.1 Nominal value and premium and no par shares

All shares issued in the UK have a nominal or par value. This is the face value which appears on the share certificate and in the statement of capital. It is not usually more than £1. No par shares are used in other countries, for example Canada and the USA, but not in this country. The principal reason for this is that the measure of a shareholder's liability to contribute to the company is the nominal value of the shares.

The nominal value of all the issued shares of the company is its share capital which must be maintained. However, companies frequently issue shares for more than their nominal value. Any amount over and above the nominal value is a premium. The premium obtained is treated as the equivalent of share capital. It must be credited to the share premium account which is subject to the rules on reduction of capital and can only be applied for certain purposes: to pay up bonus shares to be issued as fully paid to members; and in writing off the expenses of and commission paid on the issue of these particular shares (CA 2006, s 610).

4.10.2 Minimum capital requirements

There is no minimum share capital requirement for private companies. However, public companies must have a minimum of £50,000 issued share capital on which at least one quarter of the value and all the premium has been paid (CA 2006, ss 761–763). Where the issued share capital of a public company falls below that minimum it must re-register as a private company.

4.10.3 Partly paid shares

The issue of shares creates a debt due from the allottee to the company. It need not be paid at once. However, a public company must not allot shares unless at least one quarter of the nominal value and the whole of the premium has been paid (CA 2006, s 586). Shares may be issued as partly paid on the basis that the remainder will be paid by instalments on fixed dates or when demanded by the company. Most shares are now issued fully paid.

4.10.4 Issue at a discount

A company may not allot shares for a consideration which is less than the nominal value of the shares. Any allotment in contravention of this provision results in the allottee being liable to pay the discount (ie the shares are treated as partly paid) plus interest on that amount at 5 per cent a year (CA 2006, ss 580 and 592).

4.10.5 Payment in cash or kind

Shares allotted by a company and any premium on them may be paid up in money or money's worth (including goodwill and know-how) (CA 2006, s 582). Where the company receives non-cash consideration for shares it must be of a value at least equal to the nominal value of the shares. If it is of a value which is more than the nominal value of the shares there will be a premium which must be credited to the share premium account (*Henry Head and Co Ltd v Ropner Holdings Ltd* [1952] Ch 124).

The allotment of shares for a non-cash consideration may result in shares being issued at a discount where the value of the non-cash consideration is less than the nominal value of the shares. Private companies enjoy substantial freedom to determine the value of what is received. The court will only interfere with such valuation where it is patently inadequate, illusory or fraudulent (*Re Wragg Ltd* [1897] 1 Ch 796).

There are a number of statutory restrictions on public companies to ensure that shares are not in fact issued at a discount. Public companies may not:

- allot shares for a non-cash consideration unless the consideration has been independently valued in accordance with CA 2006, ss 593–609; or
- accept in payment for their shares an undertaking to perform services for the company (CA 2006, s 585); or
- allot shares for a consideration which includes an undertaking which may be performed more than five years after the allotment (CA 2006, s 587).

If a public company does issue shares in contravention of these rules, the allotment is valid but the allottee is liable to pay the nominal value and the whole of the premium (or so much of that aggregate as is treated as paid up by the consideration) with interest at 5 per cent a year (CA 2006, ss 604 and 609). Any person so liable may apply under CA 2006, s 589 or 606 for relief from liability.

4.11 Financial assistance by a company for purchase of its own shares

4.11.1 The prohibition

Subject to a number of exceptions, it is unlawful for a public company or any of its subsidiaries to give financial assistance for the acquisition of shares in the company (CA 2006, s 678). It is also unlawful for a public company which is a subsidiary to a private company to give financial assistance for purchase of shares in its private holding company (CA 2006, s 679). Contravention of either section is an offence (CA 2006, s 680). To be 'for the purpose' of the acquisition of shares, the benefit must be given with the objective of furthering the acquisition (*Chaston v SWP Group plc* [2003] 1 BCLC 675). Note that it is not unlawful for a holding company to give financial assistance for purchase of shares in a subsidiary.

4.11.2 Financial assistance

Financial assistance is widely defined in CA 2006, s 677, to include assistance by way of: gift; guarantee, security or indemnity; release or waiver of a right or obligation; loan or any other agreement under which the obligations of the person giving the assistance are to be fulfilled at a time when in accordance with the agreement any obligation of another party to the agreement remains unfulfilled; novation or assignment of the rights arising under a loan or such other agreement; any other financial assistance given by a company which reduces the net assets of the company to a material extent or by a company with no net assets. Thus it would cover, for example, the situation whereby a takeover bidder borrows money to buy shares in a company and having acquired the shares uses company money or assets to repay the loan. Payment of the purchaser's professional fees was held to be 'financial assistance' in *Chaston v SWP Group plc* [2003] 1 BCLC 675, and it was irrelevant that there was no detriment to the company. A rescheduling, which did not involve the company giving anything new to the purchaser, was not 'financial assistance' in *MT Realisations Ltd v Digital Equipment Co Ltd* [2003] 2 BCLC 117.

The definition has been widely drafted on purpose. However, the precise meaning, in particular of the last provision (assistance reducing the net assets) is not clear, see *Belmont Finance Corporation Ltd v Williams Furniture Ltd (No 2)* [1980] 1 All ER 393 and *Charterhouse Investment Trust Ltd v Tempest Diesels Ltd* [1986] BCLC 1 on the interpretation of CA 1948, s 54 (the predecessor to what is now s 677).

4.11.3 Exceptions

The provisions of CA 2006, s 678, are subject to a number of technical exceptions to be found in s 681, for example distributions by way of dividends lawfully made, in the course of a company's winding up, are not prohibited. Further exceptions are available under s 682 where a private company gives assistance or a public company gives assistance which does not reduce the net assets or is provided out of distributable profits. These exceptions include lending money in the ordinary course of business and assistance for an employee share scheme.

4.12 Alterations in capital

4.12.1 Consolidation and division

Consolidation is the combining of a number of shares into one new share of commensurate value, thus five 20p shares may be consolidated into one £1 share. Division is the opposite. CA 2006, s 618, enables consolidation and division by ordinary resolution provided there is no express prohibition in the articles.

4.12.2 Reduction of capital

This is the reducing of the company's issued capital and is subject to general maintenance of capital rules. Such reduction needs court approval. The formal procedure is covered at **4.13**.

The court also has power to reduce the company's share capital when ordering the company to purchase a member's shares on a petition under CA 2006, s 994 (unfair prejudice, see **13.6**).

In addition, the company may reduce its share capital without confirmation of the court where it redeems redeemable shares (see CA 2006, ss 684–689); purchases its own shares (see CA 2006, ss 690–692); or forfeits or accepts surrender in lieu of forfeiture of shares.

4.13 Reduction of share capital

The general maintenance of capital rule restricts the return of share capital to members or the reduction of liability on shares. However, a reduction of share capital is allowed by private companies without court approval and by any company with court approval.

4.13.1 Reduction by private company using solvency statement procedure

Provided there are no provisions in the company's articles restricting or prohibiting the reduction of the company's share capital, a private company may reduce its share capital without court approval by following the requirements in CA 2006, ss 642–644. These include:

(a) after the reduction there must be at least one member remaining and that member must hold shares other than redeemable shares. This is to prevent a reduction which would enable a company to reduce its share capital to zero;

(b) the directors must make a statement of the solvency of the company (ie that having taken into account the company's liabilities, they are satisfied that there is no reason the company will be unable to pay its debts);

(c) the statement of solvency must be made available to members who then pass a special resolution approving the reduction;

(d) copies of the statement of solvency and the resolution must be filed together with a statement of capital with the Registrar of Companies.

4.13.2 Reduction with court approval

Any company may reduce its capital by special resolution and court approval provided there is no provision in the company's articles restricting or prohibiting the reduction of the company's share capital and the procedures and precautions set out in CA 2006, ss 645–651, are fulfilled. Although CA 2006, s 641, provides a general power to sanction schemes of reduction, the three most common types of cases are discussed in the following section.

4.13.2.1 Extinguishing or reducing the liability on shares not fully paid

For example, a company with issued capital of 1,000 £1 shares partly paid (50p per share) cancels the unpaid sum on each share. This would reduce the nominal value of each share to 50p and the issued share capital of the company to £500. The capital available to pay the company's debts is therefore reduced. This type of reduction of capital is not now very common as most shares are issued fully paid.

4.13.2.2 Cancelling paid-up share capital which is lost or unrepresented by available assets

For example, a company with issued capital of 1,000 £1 shares fully paid has assets worth only £500 because of depreciation or trading losses. The company wishes to alter its share capital to reflect the true financial position of the company. It therefore cancels 50p per share leaving the shareholders with 50p shares. Its issued share capital is then £500.

This is the most frequent type of reduction. Depreciation and trading losses are facts of business life. In *Re Jupiter House Investments (Cambridge) Ltd* [1985] 1 WLR 975, it was held that 'loss' meant permanent loss, but where it could not be proved to be so the court would in exceptional circumstances confirm the reduction if the company gave an undertaking that if the loss was recovered it would not be distributed as dividends. In *Re Grosvenor Press plc* [1985] 1 WLR 980, it was held that there was no need for a reserve to be set aside indefinitely, as future creditors were protected by the various statutory provisions. An undertaking was given to treat any recovery of the loss as an undistributable reserve for as long as there remained outstanding any liabilities admissible to proof in a winding up commencing on the date the reduction of capital took effect.

4.13.2.3 Repaying paid-up capital which is in excess of the company's wants

For example, a company with issued capital of 1,000 £1 shares fully paid returns 50p per share to its shareholders. The shares now have a nominal value of 50p and the issued share capital of the company is £500. The capital available to pay the company's debts is therefore reduced. This method of reduction will usually arise where the company has reduced its business by selling off part of it or where it can obtain finance more cheaply from other sources. The repayment can be in cash or in kind, for example the company may offer the option of taking debentures or preference shares instead of cash.

4.13.2.4 Procedure

(a) If the articles contain a provision restricting or prohibiting a reduction, they will have to be altered by special resolution to remove it.

(b) The company must pass a special resolution setting out the terms of the reduction (CA 2006, s 641). Although there is a general rule that a resolution can be treated as validly passed if all the members entitled to attend the meeting agree to treat it as binding, it would appear that the court requires a special resolution to be passed at a general meeting for a reduction of capital and will not treat unanimous consent as an adequate substitute (*Re Barry Artist Ltd* [1985] 1 WLR 1305).

(c) Once the resolution has been passed the company applies to the Companies Court to confirm the reduction (CA 2006, s 645(1)). Written evidence must be filed, usually made by one of the directors, setting out the reasons and circumstances of the reduction and submitting a statement of assets and liabilities. If possible the position of creditors will be safeguarded in advance by obtaining bank guarantees that all creditors will be paid in full.

(d) An application for directions is taken out and at the hearing before the registrar directions for the publication of notices and steps to protect creditors are given. Where the reduction involves the reducing of liability on unpaid shares or the repayment of capital to shareholders, the creditors are entitled to object to the reduction (CA 2006, s 645(2)).

The court must, under CA 2006, s 646, settle a list of creditors entitled to object. In practice the list is dispensed with under CA 2006, s 645(3), as petitioners invariably obtain the agreement of creditors and provide bank guarantees. If a creditor does not consent to the reduction the court may dispense with that creditor's consent on the company securing the full amount or an amount fixed by the court where the company disputes the full amount (CA 2006, s 646(4)). Where the reduction does not reduce shareholders' liability or return capital to them, the creditors have no right to object unless the court so directs.

(e) At the full hearing the court, if satisfied that every creditor entitled to object under s 646 has either consented to the reduction or has been paid or secured, may make an order confirming the reduction on such terms and conditions as it thinks fit (CA 2006, s 648).

In addition to considering the position of creditors, the court will also ensure that the reduction is fair between classes of shareholders. Where there are ordinary and preference shares the right to return of capital on liquidation is considered in determining what is fair as a reduction of capital is really a 'mini-liquidation'. If the preference shares carry no priority for repayment of capital they are likely to suffer a reduction of capital rateably with ordinary shares. This may result in a reduction of dividend payable on the preference shares, as preference dividends are calculated as a fixed percentage of the paid-up or nominal value. Such a variation is not a variation of class rights and requires no separate class consent (*Re Mackenzie and Co Ltd* [1916] 2 Ch 450). If the preference shares do carry a right to repayment of capital in priority to ordinary shares and surplus cash is returned, it will normally be returned to the preference shareholders first. Although such a reduction may eliminate a class entirely, in the absence of a provision in the articles no class consent is required for the reduction as this again is not a variation of their rights but a satisfaction or fulfilment of rights which then cease to exist (*House of Fraser plc v ACGE Investments Ltd* [1987] AC 387). If preference shares do carry a right to repayment of capital in priority to ordinary shares, and capital is lost, the ordinary shares should bear the loss first. The court is reluctant to confirm a reduction which cancels the ordinary shareholding entirely.

Where the court confirms the reduction, it may direct the company to add to its name the words 'and reduced' and require the company to publish the reasons for the reduction (CA 2006, s 648(4)). Such directions are very unusual.

(f) A copy of the order and a statement of capital showing the altered share capital, in particular, the amount of the share capital, the number of shares and amount of each share and the amount deemed to be paid on each share, must be registered with the Registrar of Companies.

The resolution takes effect on registration (CA 2006, s 649(3)). Where a public company has reduced its capital below the required minimum, the registrar will not register the order until the company has re-registered as a private company (CA 2006, s 650). On registration the registrar issues a certificate, which is conclusive evidence that the requirements of the Act have been fulfilled and that the company's capital is as stated in the minute.

4.14 Serious loss of capital by public company

Where a public company suffers a serious loss of capital there is an obligation on the directors to call an extraordinary general meeting within 28 days from the earliest date on which any director knew of that fact (CA 2006, s 656). Such loss is defined as where the net assets of the company are half or less of its called-up share capital. The purpose of the meeting is to notify the shareholders of the situation and to discuss what measures should be taken. One obvious measure is a reduction of capital (see **4.13**).

4.15 Compromise or arrangement with creditors

The Companies Act 2006, ss 895–901, enable a company to enter into a compromise or arrangement with its creditors or any class of them, or its members or any class of them, which, if approved by the requisite majority of creditors and members and sanctioned by the court, becomes binding on the company, members and creditors. The provisions may be used for a wide variety of purposes from mergers of two or more companies to altering rights attached to debentures and/or shares.

The procedure is as follows:

(a) An application is made to the court under Part 8 setting out the proposed scheme. There is no need to name a defendant unless the court otherwise orders. Details to be included in the Part 8 claim form are set out in PD 49A, para 15(4).

(b) If the court is satisfied that the documents are in order and the scheme is not being used improperly it will order meetings to be held of each affected class of creditor or member. The notice of the meeting must include a statement explaining the effect of the proposed compromise or arrangement and any material interests of the directors in the proposal.

(c) If the scheme is approved at each of the meetings by a majority representing at least three-quarters in value of those who attend and vote, a further application is made to court. The court will ensure that the procedure has been properly followed, the requisite meetings and majority votes have been obtained, and that the proposal is such that an intelligent and honest person (being a member of the class concerned and acting in his own interests) might reasonably approve.

(d) If sanctioned by the court, the scheme becomes binding on the company, creditors and members.

(e) Where the compromise or arrangement is for the reconstruction of a company or the merger of two or more companies and involves the transfer of some or all of the property from one company to another the court has additional powers to make provision for, *inter alia*, the transfer of property or liabilities, the allotment of shares or the dissolution of the transferor company.

The court order is ineffective until a copy is received by the registrar.

4.16 Payment of dividends out of profits

A basic aspect of the maintenance of capital rule is that the company cannot make a distribution (eg pay dividends) out of capital. It can only pay a dividend if there are distributable profits out of which it may be declared (CA 2006, s 830).

4.16.1 Distributable profits

Distributable profits are defined as the accumulated, realised profits, so far as not previously utilised by distribution or capitalisation, less the accumulated, realised losses, so far as not previously written off in a reduction or reorganisation of capital duly made. (There are special rules for investment companies and insurance companies.)

The definition does not distinguish between capital and revenue profits. However, it does require the profits and losses to be accumulated. Thus the balance of profit or loss from previous years must be brought into account in the current period. In addition, it requires the profits and losses to be realised. The term 'realised' is not defined in the Act. However, various accounting guidelines have been issued setting out criteria and standards for determining what is and is not a realised profit or loss. The Act itself also makes some detailed provisions, for example on the treatment of development costs.

4.16.2 Accounts

The amount of the distribution which may be made is determined by reference to the last audited annual accounts or, where the figures derived from the latest annual accounts would preclude the payment of a dividend, interim accounts may be used but they must be such as are necessary to enable a reasonable judgement to be made. In addition, if the company has not yet produced its first annual accounts, 'initial' accounts may be prepared for the purpose of declaring a dividend, subject to the same qualification as applies to interim accounts.

4.16.3 Dividends by public companies

There are additional rules for public companies under CA 2006, s 831, which prohibits a public company making a distribution unless its net assets are at least equal to the aggregate amount of its called-up share capital and undistributable reserves and the distribution would not reduce the amount of those assets to less than that aggregate. Thus this takes into account unrealised losses. Undistributable reserves are defined in the section as the share premium account, the capital redemption reserve, unrealised profits less unrealised losses unless previously written off and any other reserve which the company is prohibited from distributing by any statute or by its memorandum or articles.

4.16.4 Unlawful distributions

A member who receives a dividend which is wholly or partly in breach of the rules, knowing, or having reason to believe, that it is paid in breach of the rules, is liable to repay to the company all or so much of it as is paid in breach of the rules (CA 2006, s 847). In addition, directors who authorise or recommend a dividend in breach of the rules are in breach of their duty to the company and can be required to make good the breach (*Re Exchange Banking Co, Flitcroft's Case* (1882) 21 ChD 519). Directors are liable to repay unlawful dividends even if the company is solvent, and can be ordered to repay the whole of the dividends. Further, their liability is not limited to the difference between what they could have lawfully declared and what they in fact declared (*Bairstow v Queens Moat Houses plc* [2001] 2 BCLC 531), although their liability may be reduced or extinguished by an application for relief under CA 2006, s 1157.

4.16.5 Payment of dividends

Dividends are only due when they have been declared. Under Model Articles Public Companies, reg 70, and Private Companies, reg 30, and 1985 Table A, reg 102, the general meeting declares the final dividend although the directors have the power to declare interim dividends and the final dividend cannot be higher than that recommended by the directors. Payment of a dividend must be in cash unless the articles allow payment in some other form such as bonus shares. Bonus shares may be issued where the company has the power to capitalise its profits and apply the amount so capitalised in the issue of bonus shares issued to members in the same proportion as a cash dividend would have been distributed: see 1985 Table A, reg 110.

5 Debentures

5.1 Introduction

5.1.1 General

Most companies are unable to finance their activities solely from their paid-up share capital. Companies with share capital under £100 and £1,000 are very common, and few businesses can be run without considerably more funds. Most companies raise further finance by borrowing. In the past it was quite common for companies to raise finance by borrowing small amounts, often about £100 each, from a large number of private investors. This is now extremely unusual. It is far more common today for companies to borrow, either long or medium term, or on overdraft, from a bank, or for money to be lent by persons or companies connected with the borrowing company (such as shareholders or directors).

5.1.2 Power to borrow and give security

Under the pre-CA 2006 system, companies had to state their objects in their memorandum of association. These would often give the company express power to borrow for the purposes of its undertaking and to give security to the lender. Even if such powers were not given expressly, they would be implied at common law if the company was a trading or commercial one. Under the CA 2006, s 31(1), unless a company's articles specifically restrict the objects of the company, its objects are unrestricted. This allows such companies to enter into all types of borrowing and security transactions. For companies registered under the pre-CA 2006 system, their old-style objects clauses are treated by CA 2006, s 28(1), as provisions of their articles. If these restrict the company's borrowing and security powers they will continue to have that effect unless they are deleted by special resolution under CA 2006, s 21.

5.1.3 Debentureholders and shareholders compared

A long-term loan to a company is a form of investment whereby the creditor's return is the interest on the amount lent (as opposed to the dividend paid to shareholders). The loan contract is called a debenture and the lender/creditor, a debentureholder. Although debentures and shares are both forms of investment in a company, there are substantial differences.

(a) *Position of shareholder/debentureholder* A shareholder is a part owner of the company, whose rights will be set out in the articles or terms of issue. Shareholders may only be paid dividends if there are distributable profits, and dividends only become due if and when declared. A debentureholder is a creditor whose rights are set out in the debenture and whose interest in the company is a debt due from the company, payable even if there are no profits.

(b) *Treatment of share/loan capital* The maintenance of capital rules apply only to share capital and thus debentures may be issued at a discount, purchased freely by the company, and interest may be paid out of capital as an expense of the business which will reduce profits.

There are, however, also similarities in that CA 2006, ss 549, 551 (directors' authority to issue) and 561 (pre-emption rights) apply to shares and debentures convertible into shares, and the rules on issue to the public in the Financial Services and Markets Act 2000 apply to both. In addition, the procedure for transfer is the same for both.

5.1.4 Return on capital

Loan capital gives a fixed return (interest) on the investment, payable even if no profits are made. Share capital gives an entitlement to a return on the investment (dividends) only if there are sufficient profits. The higher the risk of the investment, the greater the return required to attract investors. The equity shareholders will require a greater return than lenders as they run greater risks than those lending money to a company if there is a decline in profits or insolvency. Thus a company may rely more heavily on loan capital. The ratio between fixed return capital (eg loans) and variable return capital (eg shares) is called gearing. The greater the proportion of fixed return capital, the higher the gearing. Gearing at too high a level will result in investors requiring a higher return to compensate for the risk of insolvency.

At the Bar, company borrowing on debentures is most commonly met in the context of the provision of security, although other issues can arise from time to time.

5.2 What are debentures?

5.2.1 Definition

The term 'debenture' is defined in the following way by CA 2006, s 738:

In the Companies Acts 'debenture' includes debenture stock, bonds and other securities of a company, whether or not constituting a charge on the assets of the company.

Obviously, this is an inclusive definition. It covers both secured and unsecured loans, the word 'securities' in the definition being used in its commercial sense of a document evidencing a loan. In *Levy v Abercorris Slate and Slab Co* (1887) 37 ChD 260, a case on the Bills of Sale Act (1878) Amendment Act 1882, Chitty J said:

> In my opinion a debenture means a document which either creates a debt or acknowledges it, and any document which fulfils either of these conditions is a 'debenture'.

In fact, the word 'debenture' is used in two senses. One is the wide meaning considered previously, which covers any document acknowledging a company's indebtedness. In this meaning it does not matter whether the indebtedness is secured or not (*Lemon v Austin Friars*

Investment Trust Ltd [1926] Ch 1). The second use of the term is to describe loan contracts as described at **5.3.2**, and their derivatives, which are considered at **5.3.3** to **5.3.8**.

5.2.2 Debenture documents

There may be a single debenture (eg to a bank to secure an overdraft), a series of debentures in identical form all ranking for repayment *pari passu* (eg a number of individual loans to the company) or debenture stock which is a single debt in which each lender has a holding of a specified value (eg through an offer to the public where a loan is raised from a large number of lenders). The loan contract must (for debenture stock) and may (for a series of debentures) take the form of a debenture trust deed whereby trustees are appointed who are, in effect, the creditors of the company, but who hold as such for the true lenders, the beneficiaries of the trust, with the duty of enforcing the terms of the contract with the company and protecting the lenders' interests.

5.2.3 Standard terms of a debenture

The most important terms that a debenture may contain include the following:

(a) That the company pay capital and/or interest as specified.

(b) That if the company defaults in payment, the whole amount becomes repayable immediately.

(c) Giving the lender a fixed charge over fixed assets (see **5.3.1**).

(d) Giving the lender a floating charge over other assets, or a floating charge over the whole of the company's undertakings (note that the company can create a number of charges over the same property; see later for priority of such charges) (see **5.4**).

(e) That the company maintain the property subject to the charge (eg keep it repaired and insured).

(f) That the company maintains the value of the class of assets over which the floating charge has been granted at or above a certain level (to ensure there are sufficient assets to use to pay the debt if the company defaults).

(g) Specify the events which will cause crystallisation of the floating charge, for example failure to pay capital or interest as required by the debenture, or to keep the value of the assets at the level promised (see **5.5**).

(h) Specify the events which will entitle the chargee to enforce the charge and the methods by which this may be done. The two most common methods of enforcement are selling the assets subject to the charge, and appointing an administrator.

5.3 Categories of loan securities

5.3.1 Specific legal and equitable mortgages

Specific legal and equitable mortgages, if created by companies as security for their debts, have the same effect as mortgages created by individuals. The usual formalities on execution must be observed (see Law of Property Act 1925, ss 95, 86 and 136). A specific charge or mortgage gives the lender recourse against identified land or other assets owned by the company in the event of default on the loan, such as if payment of interest falls into arrears. Therefore, the terms of the mortgage will usually prohibit the company from dealing with the charged assets without the lender's permission, and will require the company to maintain and insure those assets.

5.3.2 Debentures

Here we are considering the term 'debentures' in its narrower sense. They encompass all forms of loan contract between companies and lenders. They may be secured or unsecured. Security may be by fixed or floating (see **5.4**) charge. A company may issue either single debentures, for example to its bank, or a series of debentures. If a series of debentures is issued, it is usual for them to be issued on terms that they all rank *pari passu* (ie equally) in their rights to interest and repayment. An issue of debentures may sometimes be listed on the Stock Exchange.

Often when a series of debentures is issued, the company will enter into a trust deed whereby the interests of the debentureholders are represented by trustees. In this way the company can negotiate minor alterations in the terms of the debentures with the trustees, rather than having to negotiate with all the debentureholders individually. However, debenture certificates will be issued to all the debentureholders, in which the company will covenant to pay the loan and interest, so the debentureholders are creditors of the company in their own right.

5.3.3 Debenture stock

This is a development from the debenture trust deed. Here, the company covenants to repay the total loan with the trustees, with the effect that the trustees, and not the individual stockholders, are the creditors of the company. Any rights against the company are enforced by the trustees, the stockholders being restricted to having remedies against the trustees.

5.3.4 Loan stock and loan notes

These are rather like debenture stock, but whereas issues of debenture stock will be secured by fixed and/or floating charges, loan stock and loan notes are unsecured loans. Such unsecured loans are sometimes called unsecured notes or naked debentures. The difference between loan stock and loan notes is that loan notes are shorter term investments than loan stock, usually for periods up to ten years.

5.3.5 Income bonds

Generally, debentures provide for the payment of interest at a fixed rate, or at a stated rate above base or other fluctuating rate, regardless of whether profits are earned by the company. Income bonds are usually issued by companies in straitened financial circumstances, and provide for interest to be payable only out of profits.

5.3.6 Bearer debentures

Most debentures are issued in registrable form, and are transferable on sale by instrument of transfer in the same way as shares. Although very rare, a company may issue debentures in bearer form, which are negotiable instruments which may be transferred simply by delivery of the debentures. The holder of bearer debentures usually claims interest by sending coupons, which accompany the debentures, to the company on the due dates.

5.3.7 Convertibles

These are debentures which include in their terms a right to be surrendered to the company in return for shares. Unlike shares, debentures may be issued at a discount (eg debentures with a nominal value of £100 may be bought from the company for £80). If convertibles are issued at a discount, the terms of conversion must ensure that the conversion shares are not also issued at a discount (see **4.10.4** and *Mosely v Koffyfontein Mines Ltd* [1904] 2 Ch 108).

5.3.8 International bonds and Eurobonds

International bonds are securities issued by a borrower in a foreign country. They include foreign bonds, parallel bonds and Eurobonds. They are usually issued as bearer securities, but are sometimes registered securities. Some are convertible securities. The borrowers are large companies.

Foreign bonds, for example Yankee, Samurai and Bulldog bonds, are securities issued on a domestic capital market in the local currency by borrowers from abroad. Eurobonds are issued by foreign borrowers and are denominated either in US dollars, Canadian dollars, Japanese yen or in euros. They are underwritten and sold by international syndicates of financial institutions. Interest can accrue either on a fixed-rate basis or at a floating rate.

5.4 Floating charges

Specific charges were considered at **5.3.1**. A company is not restricted to giving fixed or specific charges, and can additionally give security by way of floating charge. A floating charge is a form of equitable charge on fluctuating assets. The distinction between the two types of security was described in the following way by Lord Macnaghten in *Illingworth v Houldsworth* [1904] AC 355, HL:

> A specific charge, I think, is one that without more fastens on ascertained and definite property or property capable of being ascertained and defined; a floating charge, on the other hand, is ambulatory and shifting in its nature, hovering over and so to speak floating with the property which it is intended to affect until some event occurs or some act is done which causes it to settle and fasten on the subject of the charge within its reach and grasp.

When the same case was before the Court of Appeal (sub nom *Re Yorkshire Woolcombers Association Ltd* [1903] 2 Ch 284), Romer LJ described the usual characteristics of a floating charge in the following way:

> I certainly do not intend to attempt to give an exact definition of the term 'floating charge', nor am I prepared to say that there will not be a floating charge within the meaning of the Act, which does not contain all of the three characteristics that I am about to mention, but I certainly think, that if a charge has the three characteristics that I am about to mention, it is a floating charge. (1.) If it is a charge on a class of assets of a company present and future; (2.) if that class is one which, in the ordinary course of the business of the company, would be changing from time to time; and (3.) if you find that by the charge it is contemplated that, until some future step is taken by or on behalf of those interested in the charge, the company may carry on its business in the ordinary way as far as concerns the particular class of assets I am dealing with.

Examples of floating charges include charges over a company's:

- Stock in trade from time to time.
- Book debts due to the company from time to time. Book debts are sums of money owed to the company, usually for goods or services supplied or work carried out. Sums due under loans may also be treated as book debts, as can sums due from the company's directors under any loan accounts with the company.
- Whole assets and undertaking for the time being.

Banks commonly take fixed charges and floating charges over the company's whole undertaking to secure overdrafts. It has been settled since the floating charge first emerged as a form of security that a charge 'on [the company's] undertaking' prima facie extends to all property which may become the property of the company as well as to the property at the date of the charge: see *Re Panama, New Zealand, and Australian Royal Mail Co* (1870) LR 5 Ch App 318. This is so even if the property covered by the charge is not expressed in the debenture as being 'present and future'—this will be taken as read: *Re Croftbell Ltd* [1990] BCC 781.

A charge will be held to be a floating charge if it is floating in nature. It is not a question of finding the intention of the parties, but of determining whether the rights created, as a matter of law, amount to a fixed or floating charge (*Smith v Bridgend County Borough Council* [2002] 1 AC 336). Lord Millett in *Agnew v Commissioner of Inland Revenue* [2001] 2 AC 710 said that the crucial feature is that a floating charge allows the chargor to control and manage the charged assets and withdraw them from the charged security without the chargee's consent. The same also applies in reverse, so that if the chargee is obliged to transfer charged money to the chargor with the chargee having no legal right to withhold payment until a default event, there is a floating charge (*Re F2G Realisations Ltd* [2011] 1 BCLC 313). In *Re Spectrum Plus Ltd* [2005] 2 AC 680 Lord Scott at [111] said the essential characteristic is that an asset under a floating charge is not finally appropriated as a security until the occurrence of some future event crystallising the charge. Accordingly, while the first two features mentioned by Romer LJ in the previous quotation are typical in many floating charges, they are not essential, and it is the third feature which is determinative of whether a charge is fixed or floating.

In *Agnew v Commissioner of Inland Revenue* [2001] 2 AC 710 it was held that deciding whether a charge is fixed or floating is a two-stage process. First, the court has to identify the rights and obligations created by the instrument. Secondly, the court must categorise the charge by reference to those rights and obligations, not by reference to the intention of the parties. Thus, in *Re Brightlife Ltd* [1987] Ch 200, Hoffmann J held that a charge over the company's 'book debts and other debts', although expressed to be a 'first specific charge', was a floating charge, because it related to fluctuating assets.

If the terms of a charge over book debts in favour of a bank create a blocked bank account, so that the chargor has no right to draw on the account until the debt on the account is discharged, the charge may well be fixed. If the terms of a charge over book debts in favour of a bank allow the chargor freedom to draw on its account, the charge will be floating even if described as 'fixed' in the charge document (*Re Spectrum Plus Ltd* [2005] 2 AC 680, and see also *Re Beam Tube Products Ltd* [2006] BCC 615).

During the currency of a floating charge, the company can continue its business in the usual way. Assets from the categories charged may be bought and sold. Indeed, unless the company has entered into a negative pledge (see **5.7**), it has the power to enter into further mortgages or charges affecting the categories of assets subject to the floating charge. When a floating charge crystallises, it is converted into a fixed security attaching to all the company's assets in the categories charged at the date of crystallisation, and also any such assets which it acquires thereafter.

5.5 Crystallisation of floating charges

At law, a floating charge will crystallise on the following events:

(a) Since 15 September 2003, when Enterprise Act 2002, s 250, was brought into effect, on the appointment of an administrator. Administration is discussed at **8.3**.

(b) On the commencement of the winding up of the company.

(c) On the company ceasing to carry on business. This particular crystallising event was accepted by Nourse J in *Re Woodroffes (Musical Instruments) Ltd* [1986] Ch 366, and was treated as beyond argument at first instance by Chadwick J in *Re Real Meat Co Ltd* [1996] BCC 254. It may be that the company ceasing business simply gives the lender grounds to appoint an administrator, and crystallisation takes place when the administrator is appointed.

Alternatively, the debenture itself may provide that certain events will cause the charge to crystallise. Such clauses fall into two categories:

(d) By intervention on the part of the lender, such as giving notice under an express power converting the charge into a fixed charge, as in *Re Brightlife Ltd* [1987] Ch 200.

(e) Automatic crystallisation, such as a term in the debenture providing for crystallisation on the company's assets falling below a specified level. Hoffmann J in *Re Brightlife Ltd* suggested that such a clause may be valid, but the matter is not yet settled. Automatic crysallisation may cause problems in cases where the crystallising event takes place without the knowledge of either or both parties.

5.6 Characteristics of debentures

5.6.1 Specific performance

In *South African Territories Ltd v Wallington* [1898] AC 309 it was held that the rule that an intending borrower cannot obtain specific performance of a contract of loan (because a loan can be raised elsewhere) applied to issues of debentures. This was reversed in 1907 by a provision now in CA 2006, s 740, that contracts to take up and pay for debentures may be enforced by specific performance.

5.6.2 Clogs on the equity of redemption

Secured (as opposed to unsecured) debentures are types of mortgage, and so are subject to the rule that provisions that clog or fetter the right of redemption are void (*Samuel v Jarrah Timber and Wood Paving Corporation Ltd* [1904] AC 323).

It has been held under this rule that a bonus or premium payable on redemption (eg where a debenture with a nominal value of £100 is purchased at par but provides that on redemption the holder is entitled to the nominal value plus, say, £20) constitutes a clog (*Re Rainbow Syndicate Ltd* [1916] WN 178).

Debentures may be made irredeemable, or redeemable only on a remote contingency, and still be valid by virtue of CA 2006, s 739, despite the usual rule that postponing the date of redemption of a mortgage for an excessive time is a clog on the equity of redemption.

5.7 Negative pledges

A negative pledge (sometimes called a restrictive clause) is a term in a debenture or other loan security by which the company undertakes not to create later charges ranking in priority to or *pari passu* with the present security. If the present loan is unsecured, the pledge is not to charge the company's assets at all. The purpose of the pledge is to prevent the company from watering down the lenders' security, or, in the case of unsecured loans, to prevent the company from giving priority to later lenders. A negative pledge in an unsecured loan is often reinforced by a further term limiting the amount of further indebtedness that may be incurred by the company.

Although such terms have contractual effect between the company and the lender, and may be enforced against the company while it is a going concern, it is quite likely that any breach by the company will not come to light until after the company becomes insolvent. The question then is whether the negative pledge has any effect on the subsequent charges.

If the pledge is contained in a secured debenture, it is an equitable restriction on the company's power to create later charges having priority to the first (*Rother Iron Works Ltd v Canterbury Precision Engineers Ltd* [1974] QB 1, CA per Russell LJ). It will therefore bind:

- a later chargee having notice of the pledge; and
- a later equitable chargee having no notice of the pledge if the equities between the first and second charges are equal.

Conversely, a later legal mortgagee for value with no notice, and a later equitable chargee with no notice with a stronger equitable claim than the first charge, would not be bound by such a pledge.

Where the pledge is contained in an unsecured loan, the lender has no interest in the company's assets other than the pledge, so the pledge will not constitute an equitable restriction on the company's power to create further charges, and will operate only contractually between the company and the original lender.

5.8 Avoidance of floating charges created before insolvency

Under IA 1986, s 245, certain floating charges created shortly before the onset of insolvency of the company are invalid. The 'onset of insolvency' is either:

- the date on which an administration application is made; or
- the date on which a copy of a notice of intention to appoint an administrator is filed with the court; or

- the date on which the appointment of an administrator takes effect; or
- the date of commencement of the winding up of the company (in compulsory winding up this is the date of presentation of the winding-up petition).

If the floating charge is given to a person connected with the company (such as directors, their spouses and employees), it is invalid if it is created within two years of the onset of insolvency. If given to anyone else, the period is one year. However, even if a floating charge is given to a person who is not connected with the company within the one-year period, the charge will only be invalidated if at the time the charge was given the company was unable to pay its debts or became unable to do so in consequence of the transaction.

A charge caught by IA 1986, s 245, is only invalidated to the extent that value (in money paid, goods or services supplied, or discharge or reduction of debts of the company) is not given for it at the same time as, or after, it is created (s 245(2)). This latter provision largely destroys the utility of the section, as illustrated by *Re Yeovil Glove Co Ltd* [1965] Ch 148, CA. The company gave its bank a floating charge to secure its previously unsecured overdraft of £68,000 less than a year before it went into liquidation. Before liquidation, the bank received £111,000 and paid out £110,000 on the company's accounts. Applying the rule in *Devaynes v Noble, Clayton's Case* (1816) 1 Mer 572 the court held that the £67,000 overdraft at the date winding up commenced was all new money received, so the charge was valid in full.

5.9 Registration of charges

There are two duties on companies regarding registration of charges. First, if a register of debentureholders is kept by the company, it must be kept at its registered office, and copies of all charges it creates must be kept there too. Fines are prescribed in default.

Secondly, most charges created over the company's assets must be registered at Companies House. Default may result in the security becoming void for certain purposes. In *Re Cosslett (Contractors) Ltd* [1999] 1 BCLC 205 a charge was void against an administrator for want of registration, but that did not invalidate contractual rights which were not a security and which did not require registration.

For charges created before 6 April 2013, the system of registration can be found in the CA 2006, ss 860–877. Those provisions have been repealed and replaced by CA 2006, ss 859A–859Q for charges created on or after 6 April 2013 (Companies Act 2006 (Amendment of Part 25) Regulations 2013, (SI 2013/600), reg 6).

5.9.1 Registration of charges at Companies House

Under the pre-2013 system there was a list of charges that had to be registered at Companies House contained in CA 2006, s 860(7). This included fixed charges on land and interests in land, floating charges on a company's property or undertaking and various other charges such as charges on uncalled share capital and charges on goodwill. Under the post-2013 system, all charges have to be registered unless they are exempted by CA 2006, s 859A(6), see **5.9.2**.

Registrable charges under both the pre- and post-2013 systems must be registered within 21 days from the day on which the charge was created (CA 2006, s 870; CA

2006, s 859A(4)). There are detailed rules on when a charge is treated as created in CA 2006, s 859E. For example, a charge created in a deed that takes effect on execution and delivery, is treated as created after it is executed by all the parties to the instrument (s 859E(2)) and delivered (s 859D(1)).

A company that creates a registrable charge must (for pre-2013 charges, by CA 2006, s 860(1), and for post-2013 charges by CA 2006, s 859D), deliver to the Registrar of Companies:

(a) a statement of particulars relating to the charge;

(b) a certified copy of the instrument (if any) by which the charge is created or evidenced; and

(c) the prescribed fee.

Prescribed particulars include the name and number of the company, the date of creation of the charge, the names of the persons in whose favour the charge was created, whether it is a floating charge, whether it includes a negative pledge (see **5.7**) and short details of the assets or property charged (CA 2006, s 869(4); CA 2006, s 859D(1), (2)). There are similar requirements in respect of debentures (see CA 2006, ss 863–865 and CA 2006, s 859B)).

Registration may be effected by the company or any other person interested in the charge (CA 2006, s 860; CA 2006, 859A(2)). This is useful, because while there are fines payable by the company and its officers if it fails to register a charge, it is the chargee who stands to lose its priority through non-registration who has the greatest practical incentive to ensure a charge is duly registered.

If at a later stage the loan is repaid fully or in part, or if the property charged is released from the charge, a memorandum of satisfaction or of release may be registered at Companies House to record that fact (CA 2006, s 872; CA 2006, s 859L).

5.9.2 Exemption from registration

With effect from 6 April 2013, under CA 2006, s 859A(6), the following charges are exempted from registration:

(a) A charge in favour of a landlord on a cash deposit given as security in connection with the lease of land;

(b) a charge created by a member of Lloyd's; and

(c) a charge excluded from the application of this section by or under any Act of Parliament.

An example within (c) is a 'security financial collateral arrangement' under the Financial Collateral Arrangements (No 2) Regulations 2003, SI 2003/3226. These are exempted from the registration requirements in what is now the CA 2006, s 859A (reg 4(4) of the 2003 Regulations). The exemption gives effect to European Parliament and Council Directive 2002/47/EC, and is intended to remove formalities such as registration in respect of security arrangements between a company providing and a company taking collateral (such as cash or financial instruments) to secure financial obligations owed by the company providing the collateral. To come within the exemption the collateral arrangement must involve some form of dispossession. An arrangement that merely gives the collateral taker administrative or practical control over the collateral is insufficient to come within the exemption from registration (*Re F2G Realisations Ltd* [2011] 1 BCLC 313).

5.9.3 Effect of non-registration

If a company creates a registrable charge, but fails to register it, the charge is by virtue of CA 2006, s 874(1)/CA 2006, s 859H, void as a security on the company's property or undertakings against:

(a) a liquidator of the company;
(b) an administrator of the company; or
(c) a creditor of the company.

Avoidance of a charge under CA 2006, s 874(1) or 859H, does not invalidate any payment obligation secured by the charge, and when a charge is avoided the money secured becomes immediately payable (s 874(3)/s 859H(4)). Further, a chargee with a charge which is void for want of registration is able to apply to the court for relief in the form of an extension of the period allowed for registration (CA 2006, s 859F) or an order to rectify the register (CA 2006, s 873 or CA 2013, s 859M).

5.9.4 Rectification of the register of charges

On an application under CA 2006, s 873(2), or CA 2006, s 859F or 859M, the court has the power to order that the period allowed for registration of a charge be extended, or that any omission or mis-statement in the registered documents be rectified. Such an order may be made, by virtue of s 873(1), 859F(2) or 859M(2), if the court is satisfied:

(a) that the failure to register the charge before the end of the period allowed for registration, or the omission or mis-statement of any particular relating to the charge or in a memorandum of satisfaction:
    (i) was accidental or due to inadvertence or to some other sufficient cause, or
    (ii) is not of a nature to prejudice the position of creditors or shareholders of the company; or
(b) that on other grounds it is just and equitable to grant relief.

An omission of registrable particulars can only be cured by an application for rectification under what is now s 859M, and cannot be cured by asking the court to insert the missing particulars by way of contractual interpretation (*Cherry Tree Investments Ltd v Landmain Ltd* [2013] 1 BCLC 484). The underlying guide to the exercise of the power to rectify under ss 873, 859F and 859M is whether for any reason it would be just and equitable to do so (*Re Braemar Investments Ltd* [1988] BCLC 556). In deciding whether there is any prejudice to relevant parties through late registration, a key question is whether a person has entered into substantial unexecuted transactions with the company who might have been affected by knowledge of the charge had it been registered. In *Confiance Ltd v Timespan Images Ltd* [2005] 2 BCLC 693 the court rectified the register to allow registration of a first charge out of time, with the effect that it took priority over a second charge which had been registered in time. The main reason was that the second charge was in favour of a director of the company, who had breached his duty to register the first charge, and could not as a result register his second charge in good faith knowing of the outstanding first charge.

Relief may be granted on such terms and conditions as seem to the court to be just and expedient (ss 873(2), 859F(3) and 859M(3)).

5.10 Priorities

The basic rules for determining the priorities (ie which creditor gets paid first) between charges appear to be as follows:

(a) The charge created first is paid first.

(b) A floating charge does not become fixed until crystallisation, so a later fixed charge will have priority if created before crystallisation of an earlier floating charge.

(c) Debentures issued in a series may, by their terms, rank *pari passu*.

(d) An unregistered charge may be void under CA 2006, s 874 or 859H.

(e) An unregistered charge will only be void as against a subsequent charge if complete particulars of the second charge are either duly registered within 21 days after it is created, or before full particulars are delivered of the first charge.

(f) An unregistered charge is not void against a later charge if the later charge is expressly subject to the first.

(g) Where an administrator is appointed on behalf of the holders of debentures secured by a floating charge, the administrator must pay unsecured preferential debts in priority to the sums secured by the debentures (IA 1986, s 40).

5.11 Administrative receivers and administrators

Debentures invariably contain terms that if the company defaults in the payment of the principal or interest the lender may appoint an administrator. An administrator's function is to realise the assets charged for the benefit of the debentureholders. Very often, the terms of debentures allow the debentureholders to appoint a receiver and manager. Such a person has wider powers, with the intention that the possibility of preserving the company as a going concern be explored. Where such a person is appointed by or on behalf of the holders of debentures secured by a floating charge over the whole or substantially the whole of the company's undertaking, the appointment will have been by the holder of a qualifying floating charge, with the result that the administration provisions in the IA 1986, Sch B1 apply.

Receivership is considered in further detail at **8.2** and administration at **8.3**.

6

Decision making

6.1 Introduction

The members together own the company and therefore have the right to decide how it should be run. They must, however, act in accordance with the articles of association that have been adopted for the company. Shareholders' decisions have to be made in shareholders' meetings, and the normal rule is that motions are carried by simple majority. Initially this will be by a show of hands of those present, though there is usually provision for taking a poll under which the normal rule is that each share carries one vote.

In addition, every private company must have at least one director, and every public company must have at least two directors. The articles provide for their appointment, removal, powers and procedure at board meetings.

6.2 Distribution of powers

6.2.1 Delegation of powers to directors

It is invariably recognised that it is impracticable for the members to meet regularly for the purpose of making decisions on the day-to-day running of commercial companies. The invariable practice is therefore for the articles to provide for the delegation of most decision-making powers to the company's directors.

Thus both the Model Articles for Private Companies Limited by Shares ('Model Articles Private Companies') and the Model Articles for Public Companies ('Model Articles Public Companies') provide that, 'subject to the articles, directors are responsible for the management of the company's business, for which purpose they may exercise all the powers of the company' (reg 3). This is very similar but not identical to 1985 Table A, reg 70. The current Model Articles also provide that members may by special resolution direct the directors to take or refrain from taking specified action (reg 4). Thus very wide management powers are delegated to the directors who must exercise those powers as a board (ie collectively) unless they are empowered to sub-delegate (as they are by Model Articles reg 5 Private Companies and reg 5 Public Companies and 1985 Table A, reg 72). The reserve power given by reg 4 to the shareholders is only available for specified purposes as passed by special resolutions, and is not a general reserve of power to the members.

As a general rule, once members have delegated powers to directors, the members cannot simultaneously exercise those powers (see *Automatic Self-Cleansing Filter Syndicate Co Ltd v Cunninghame* [1906] 2 Ch 34 and *Salmon v Quin and Axtens Ltd* [1909] 1 Ch 311). This principle is the subject of much debate and can cause difficulties, particularly when the directors' and members' views as to how the company should be managed and the business run differ.

6.2.2 Powers retained by members

The wide management power delegated to the directors under the Model Articles and 1985 Table A, reg 70, is subject to the following restrictions.

(a) *Provisions of the Act* The Companies Acts specifically require certain (constitutional) powers to be exercised by the members, for example alteration of articles (CA 2006, s 21(1)), and voluntary liquidation of the company (IA 1986, s 84). In addition, CA 2006, s 168, empowers the members to remove directors by ordinary resolution and this power can be exercised by the members even if it has also been delegated to the board.

(b) *Provisions of the memorandum and articles* The articles themselves may specifically give powers to the members, for example to appoint directors (Model Articles reg 17(1)(a) Private Companies and reg 29(a) Public Companies; reg 17(1)(a) and 1985 Table A, reg 73); or to declare dividends (Model Articles reg 30 Private Companies and reg 70 Public Companies and 1985 Table A, reg 102) (although these are very qualified powers).

(c) *Direction by special resolution (Model Articles and reg 4)* In the 1948 Table A the general delegation article is reg 80, which read 'subject to such regulations being not inconsistent with the aforesaid regulations or provisions as may be prescribed by the company in general meeting'. This was held not to be effective in empowering the members to instruct the directors as to the manner in which they should exercise delegated powers. The general academic view on 1985 Table A, reg 70, which said management by the directors was 'subject ... to any directions given by special resolution ...', enabled members, without withdrawing the powers from the directors, to give directions by special resolution as to how those powers should be used. Model Articles, reg 4, makes it absolutely clear that shareholders can, by special resolution, direct the directors to take or refrain from taking, any action, and so can override how directors exercise their powers.

6.2.3 Constitutional limits on directors' powers

The directors must exercise their powers within the constitution (limits set in the articles), the law (provisions of the Companies Acts) and for the benefit of the company as a whole (see **7.3**). The exercise of their powers outside these limitations is an abuse of their power and unauthorised, although the members may ratify most acts which are not illegal. However, even where the directors are exercising their powers within the limits set but contrary to the view of the majority of the members, the members may exercise some control over the directors by removing one or more of them (ordinary resolution: CA 2006, s 168), altering the articles and removing the power (special resolution: CA 2006, s 21(1)) or (under the Model Articles or 1985 Table A) by direction by special resolution. However, any such removal, alteration or direction will not invalidate any prior act and will operate only as to future actions.

6.2.4 Delegation to managing director

Many companies adopt articles of association permitting delegation of day-to-day management powers to a managing director. The Model Articles reg 5 Private Companies and reg 5 Public Companies allow the directors to delegate any of their powers to such person as they think fit. 1985 Table A, reg 72, specifically allowed the directors to delegate their powers to a managing director.

The actual powers of a managing director depend on the wording of the articles and the terms of any delegation of powers (*Smith v Butler* [2012] 1 BCLC 444). It is most common to delegate powers over commercial decisions and the day-to-day running of the company's business to a managing director. It was unlawful for a managing director with delegated powers of that nature to go further and purport to dismiss or suspend the chairman of the company (*Smith v Butler* [2012] 1 BCLC 444).

6.3 Directors' duties

Directors are in a powerful position in that they will run the company and control its assets. In addition, most articles delegate the power to directors to call and set the agenda for general meetings. They therefore owe various duties including a duty of good faith to the company. These duties are considered in more detail in **Chapter 7**.

6.4 Board meetings

The division of powers within a company will be laid down in its articles, but it is usual for the power to manage the company's business to be conferred on the directors. The number of directors to be engaged by the company may also be dealt with in the articles (no provision in the Model Articles but a requirement of at least two by 1985 Table A, reg 64). However, the articles cannot provide for less than one director for private companies or two directors for public companies (CA 2006, s 154).

Where a company has more than one director, the principle is that the directors must act collectively as a board either at directors' meetings or by directors' written resolution (eg see Model Articles Public Companies, reg 7). The articles will govern the basic procedure relating to board meetings, but it is usual for the articles to allow the directors discretion to make rules as to how to regulate their proceedings (Model Articles reg 16 Private Companies and reg 16 Public Companies and 1985 Table A, reg 88). The degree of formality encountered in practice varies widely. However, subject to reasonable departures, directors can normally expect any established practice in their company to continue until a change is agreed.

6.4.1 Calling meetings

There may be regular weekly or monthly board meetings, or the next meeting may be fixed at the end of business at each meeting. The articles usually allow any director to call a meeting (Model Articles reg 9 Private Companies and reg 8 Public Companies and 1985 Table A, reg 88).

6.4.2 Notice

Subject to the practice in the company, generally directors are entitled to advance notice of meetings. A director objecting to short notice must object at the meeting, failing which the courts will not interfere (*Browne v La Trinidad* (1887) 37 ChD 1, CA). Usually there is no requirement that notice be given in writing. The Model Articles reg 9(4) Private Companies and reg 8(4) Public Companies provide that notice need not be given to directors who waive their entitlement and 1985 Table A, reg 88, provides that it is unnecessary to give notice to directors who are absent from the UK.

6.4.3 Quorum

A quorum is the minimum number of voting members who must be present for a meeting to be competent to transact business. Model Articles reg 11 Private Companies and reg 10 Public Companies allow this to be fixed by the directors, but it must never be less than two and, unless otherwise fixed it is two. 1985 Table A, reg 89, makes similar provision but does not require it never to be less than two. *Hood Sailmakers Ltd v Axford* [1997] 1 WLR 625 deals with the situation where one of two directors purports to transact business while the other director is out of the country. Articles of association of many companies provide that it is unnecessary to give notice of board meetings to directors who are abroad (see **6.4.2** and 1985 Table A, reg 88), and fix the quorum at two (see reg 89). It was held that the quorum requirement takes precedence, with the result that a director cannot evade its requirements simply by waiting until the other director leaves the country. In companies where the quorum is two, business transacted at 'board meetings' by one director while the other director is abroad is therefore invalid.

6.4.4 Chairman

Regulation 12 in Model Articles Private Companies and Model Articles Public Companies and 1985 Table A, reg 91, allow the directors to appoint one of their number to be the chairman of the board and to preside at meetings.

6.4.5 Disclosure and conflict of interest

As fiduciaries, directors have a duty not to allow their own personal interests to conflict with their duty to the company. The CA 2006 now includes detailed rules both as to the duties owed and disclosure by directors of their interests. This is discussed further at **7.5**.

6.4.6 Voting

Subject to the articles, proposals are carried by a simple majority. In the event of a tie, the articles may give the chairman a second casting vote (Model Articles Private Companies, reg 13 and Model Articles Public Companies, reg 14 and 1985 Table A, reg 88).

The interrelation of a number of these rules can be illustrated by *Barron v Potter* [1914] 1 Ch 895. The company's articles of association laid down that the quorum for board meetings was two. The company had two directors, Barron and Potter. They fell out, and Barron refused to attend any meetings with Potter. One day, Potter intercepted Barron as Barron alighted from a train at Paddington Station. While they were walking along the platform Potter said, 'I want to see you, please'. Barron replied, 'I have nothing to say to you'. Potter then said, 'I formally propose that we add the Reverend Charles Herbert, Mr William George Walter Barnard and Mr John Tolehurst Musgrave as additional directors to the board of the British Seagumite Co Ltd [the company]. Do you agree or object?' Barron replied, 'I object and I object to say anything to you at all'. Potter concluded, 'In my capacity as chairman I give my casting vote in their favour and declare them duly elected. That is all I want to say. I thank you. Good day.'

Warrington J pointed out that it is of course possible to hold a board meeting anywhere and under any circumstances, provided those present consent to the proceedings being regarded as a board meeting. On the facts Potter knew all along that Barron would not discuss the company's affairs with him. Accordingly, it was held that although Potter was present at the 'board meeting' at Paddington Station, Barron was not. The meeting was therefore inquorate, and the new directors were not validly appointed.

6.4.7 Minutes

CA 2006, s 248, requires the company to record minutes of all proceedings at board meetings. If authenticated by the chairman at that meeting or the next, the minutes are evidence of the proceeding (CA 2006, s 249). The company must keep the minutes for ten years and failure to comply results in an offence being committed by every officer in default. However, the company owes no duty to disclose minutes of its board meetings to its shareholders. In contrast, shareholders are entitled to inspect the minutes of general meetings: see **6.7**.

6.5 Communication between company and members

The CA 2006 includes provisions to facilitate electronic communication between the company and members as this is clearly much more efficient and becoming widely used generally in industry.

Section 1144 of the CA 2006 and Schs 4 and 5 enable communication between the company and its members by hard copy or electronic form. Schedule 4 enables communication with the company by sending or supplying documents and information to the company in hard copy, electronic form or other agreed form of communication and contains detailed provisions as to the requirements for valid communication. Schedule 5 enables the company to communicate with its members by sending or supplying documents and information in hard copy, electronic form, website or other agreed form of communication and contains detailed provisions as to the requirements for valid communication. A member is entitled to require the company to provide a hard copy of any electronic communication and this must be supplied by the company free of charge within 21 days of receipt of the request (s 1145).

6.6 Decision making by members

6.6.1 Differences between private and public companies

Shareholders must act collectively and decisions of members are those taken by voting on resolutions. Prior to the CA 2006, this generally required companies to call general meetings, although there was an exception for private companies. Under the CA 2006, private and public companies are treated very differently. The Companies (Shareholders' Rights) Regulations 2009, SI 2009/1632, introduced the concept of a 'traded company', basically any company admitted to trading on a regulated market. Thus, it will include public companies which trade on, for example, the London Stock Exchange but few private companies, as most are prohibited from offering their shares to the public (an exception is private unlimited companies). The regulations amend provisions in the CA 2006 to include specific provisions for 'traded companies' similar to the provisions for public companies but with some differences.

In recognition that private companies are likely to be small concerns which operate more informally than public companies, the CA 2006 enables private companies to operate without calling formal meetings and to use the written resolution procedure set out in the CA 2006 instead (see Part 13, ch 2). Public companies must make decisions by voting on resolutions at general meetings.

The CA 2006, Part 13, ss 281–361, deals first with basic provisions about resolutions and voting, then with private companies and then the additional requirements for public and quoted companies. It is generally expressly provided in the relevant sections relating to the sending or providing of information or documents such as notice of meetings, resolutions, statements, requisitions etc discussed later that this can be done either in paper form or electronically and, when by the company, via a website. Where appropriate, the provisions include detailed requirements to be fulfilled to ensure valid communication and certainty as to date of receipt.

6.6.2 Types of resolutions

Both private and public companies make decisions by passing resolutions which must be passed in accordance with the provisions of the CA 2006 to be valid (s 281). There are two types of resolution:

(a) *Ordinary resolution* This means a resolution passed by a simple majority, whether as a written resolution or at a meeting (s 282).

(b) *Special resolution* This means a resolution passed by a majority of not less than 75 per cent, whether as a written resolution or at a meeting (s 283).

The concept of extraordinary resolutions is not carried forward to the CA 2006. Section 281(3) provides that where a resolution is required, but the type of resolution is not specified, an ordinary resolution will be required unless the articles require a higher majority. Where the CA 2006 requires an ordinary resolution, the articles may not require a higher majority. The CA 2006 requires special resolutions for those more important constitution decisions such as alteration of the articles (s 21). Most decisions will therefore be by ordinary resolution.

6.6.3 Types of shareholders' meetings

There are three types of shareholders' meetings:

(a) *Annual general meetings* These must be held by all public companies within six months of their financial year end (CA 2006, s 336). All members may attend, and the purpose of such meetings is to inform members of the company's activities and performance, debate issues and pass resolutions binding on the members and the company. However, information and debate are often non-existent, and annual general meetings are frequently over in a matter of minutes. The usual matters that fall to be considered at the annual general meeting include consideration of the accounts, fixing the auditors' remuneration, election or re-election of directors, declaring dividends and approval of the minutes of the last meeting. Private companies are not required to hold AGMs but may do so.

(b) *General meetings* These are general meetings (open to all members) other than annual general meetings.

(c) *Class meetings* These are meetings of individual classes of shareholders. Attendance must be restricted to members of the class, unless there is unanimous consent that others may attend. The purpose of such meetings is to approve variations in class rights, compromises and arrangements affecting the class etc.

6.6.4 Written resolutions by private companies

This procedure may be used by private companies except to pass a resolution to remove a director (CA 2006, s 168) or remove an auditor (s 510) before expiration of his or her period or term of office (s 288). These decisions must be by resolution in a general meeting (or AGM if one is held).

6.6.4.1 Directors' resolutions

Directors proposing a written resolution must send a copy to all eligible members together with a statement informing the member how to signify agreement and the date by which the resolution must be passed if it is not to lapse (s 291). This date must not be more than 28 days after the circulation date unless the articles provide otherwise (s 297). Section 289 provides that eligibility is fixed on the day the resolution is circulated and s 290 provides that the circulation date is the date on which copies are sent or submitted to members. Section 291 also allows companies to pass round a document/email rather than sending out copies where this would not cause undue delay.

6.6.4.2 Members' resolutions

Members holding 5 per cent of the total voting rights (or lower if specified in the articles) may require the company to circulate a written resolution together with a statement of not more than 1,000 words on the subject matter of the resolution. The company must circulate the written resolution and statement to all eligible members within 21 days of receipt of the request together with a statement informing the member how to signify agreement and the date by which the resolution must be passed if it is not to lapse (s 293). This date must not be more than 28 days after the circulation date unless the articles provide otherwise (s 297). The members requiring the circulation must pay the expenses of having it done unless the company resolves otherwise (s 294). The court, on application by the company or aggrieved person, may relieve the company of the requirement to circulate the statement (s 295).

6.6.4.3 Passing resolutions

Members signify their agreement to written resolutions when the company receives from them or someone acting on their behalf an authenticated document identifying the resolution and indicating agreement to it (s 296). Agreement is ineffective if signified after 28 days (or such other period as specified in the articles) (s 297).

A written resolution will be valid if it is passed by members representing the requisite majority holding voting rights (simple majority for ordinary resolution and 75 per cent for special resolution). Every member has one vote per share. Where there is no share capital, every member has one vote (s 284).

6.6.5 Company meetings

Company meetings are called both as a means of information transmission and discussion and for passing resolutions. The provisions on meetings apply equally to private and public companies. Public companies must call annual general meetings and must pass resolutions at meetings (subject to the acquiescence principle—see **6.6.5.4**). Private companies may do so.

A resolution passed at a general meeting is valid if passed in accordance with the provisions of the CA 2006 and any additional requirements in the articles regarding notice and the holding and conduct of the meeting (s 301).

6.6.5.1 Calling and notice of meetings

Section 302 of the CA 2006 empowers directors to call general meetings and primary responsibility lies with them to call meetings. They will also generally determine the business to be conducted including the resolutions to be passed at the meeting. Occasionally, a company will send circulars to its members in advance of a meeting to explain the purpose of, or issues or arguments relating to, the resolutions proposed at a meeting. Where this is done, the circular must give a fair, candid and reasonably full explanation of the purpose for which the meeting is called (*CAS (Nominees) Ltd v Nottingham Forest FC plc* [2002] 1 BCLC 613). A failure to do so may be relied upon in proceedings for unfair prejudice (see **Chapter 13**).

However, members may feel that directors are not calling sufficient meetings, are manipulating the agenda for their own purposes or are generally unhappy with the management of the company and wish to challenge the directors. The CA 2006 gives members three rights to assist:

(a) *Right to require directors to call general meeting* Members holding 5 per cent of voting rights may require the directors to call a general meeting under s 303. The request must state the general nature of the business to be dealt with at the meeting and may include the text of a resolution to be moved at the meeting. Section 304 requires the directors to call a general meeting with 21 days of receipt of the request to be held not more than 28 days after the date of the notice convening the meeting. Section 305 empowers the members to call the meeting at the company's expense if the directors fail to call a meeting in accordance with s 304.

(b) *Right to require company to circulate statement* Members holding the requisite voting rights may also require the company to circulate a statement of up to 1,000 words with respect to a matter referred to in a proposed resolution or business to be dealt with at a meeting. The requisite holding for such requisition is 5 per cent of the voting rights or 100 members with voting rights each of whom had paid up at least £100. The voting rights must relate to the resolution or matter about which the statement is made (s 314). The company must then circulate the statement in the same manner and at the same time, or as soon as reasonably practicable after it gives notice of the meeting. The members must pay the cost of the circulation unless the company resolves otherwise or the request is in respect of an annual general meeting of a public company and it is received by the company before the end of the financial year preceding the meeting (s 316).

(c) *Rights re public company annual general meetings* Sections 338–340B contain provisions enabling members to require circulation of resolutions for AGMs of public companies which are similar to those set out in point (b).

Sections 307–313 of the CA 2006 set out the provisions on notice which provide:

(a) Notice must be given to every member and director in the case of a public company annual general meeting of at least 21 days, and in the case of all other general meetings of public and private companies of at least 14 days.

(b) Shorter notice may be given if agreed by the requisite majority of members with voting rights. For private companies this is 90 per cent and for public companies it is 95 per cent.

(c) The notice must state the time, date and place of the meeting and the general nature of the business to be dealt with at the meeting (this latter requirement being subject to provisions in the articles).

(d) The notice must also specify the intention to propose any resolution as a special resolution and contain the text of the proposed special resolution (s 283(6)). The resolution may then only be passed as a special resolution (ie by 75 per cent majority).

(e) Resolutions requiring special notice (eg to remove a director under s 168 of the CA 2006) must be given to the company at least 28 days before the meeting and the company must give members notice of the resolution at the same time as it gives notice of the meeting unless that is not practicable in which case it must give at least 14 days' notice.

6.6.5.2 Conduct of meetings

Business conducted and resolutions passed at meetings are only valid if the meeting is quorate. A quorum for a single-member company is one person which may be a proxy or corporate representative. A quorum for other companies is two persons. Subject to the articles, neither a proxy nor a corporate representative count towards a quorum for companies with more than one member (s 318).

The chairman of the meeting will usually be a member of the board of directors, although s 319 allows any member to be elected as chairman of a general meeting by resolution passed at the meeting.

In the first instance, votes are usually taken on a show of hands. Each member attending in person has one vote, regardless of the number of shares each holds. This can produce a distorted picture, and a poll may be demanded. On a poll, subject to the articles, each share carries one vote.

The articles will usually prescribe how a poll may be demanded. The Model Articles for both Private Companies and Public Companies and 1985 Table A allow, *inter alia*, the chairman of the meeting or at least two members to demand a poll. Different articles may make different provision, but cannot deny a poll if demanded by at least five members or members representing at least 10 per cent of the voting rights in the company (CA 2006, s 321).

In the event of a tie, the articles may (as in 1985 Table A, reg 50) give the chairman an additional, casting vote. Neither the Model Articles Private Companies or Public Companies make such provision.

Section 320 provides that on a show of hands, the chairman's declaration and an entry of such declaration in the minutes that a resolution has been passed or not passed or passed by a particular majority is conclusive proof of the fact. The articles may give the chairman power to appoint scrutineers and decide how and when the result is to be declared (eg Model Articles Public Companies, reg 37(2) and 1985 Table A, reg 49).

6.6.5.3 Proxies

Sections 324–330 of the CA 2006 contain provisions on proxies. Section 324 provides that every member of a company is entitled to appoint a proxy.

A proxy is a person appointed by a member to attend a meeting in place of the member. The word is also used to describe the document making the appointment.

All notices calling meetings must contain a reasonably prominent statement that members may appoint proxies (s 325). Proxy forms are often incorporated into notices calling meetings. A member may give a proxy complete discretion over how to use the member's votes, or may give specific instructions on individual resolutions. A proxy must vote in accordance with their instructions (CA 2006, s 324A). Usually the company's articles will restrict proxies to voting on a poll, but proxies may join in a demand for a poll (s 329).

Usually, proxy forms are required by the articles to be received by the company in advance of the meeting. If this period of advance notice were particularly long, few members could avail themselves of the procedure. Accordingly, articles requiring proxy forms to be lodged more than 48 hours in advance of the meeting are void (s 327).

6.6.5.4 Acquiescence principle

Section 281(4) of the CA 2006 preserves the common law acquiescence/assent principle. This provides that if all members knew of and acquiesced in a decision, they and the company are bound. Although this principle was originally subject to the necessity of showing that they had all met, this would appear no longer to be the case (*Re Duomatic Ltd* [1969] 2 Ch 365; *Wright v Atlas Wright (Europe) Ltd* [1999] 2 BCLC 301; *Euro Brokers Holdings Ltd v Monecor (London) Ltd* [2003] 1 BCLC 506). Although the agreement may be express, implied, verbal or by conduct, nothing short of objectively established unqualified agreement will suffice (*Schofield v Schofield* [2011] 2 BCLC 319).

6.7 Records

Records of minutes of proceedings at general meetings and all resolutions passed otherwise than at general meetings must be kept for ten years, and copies made available to members (ss 355–359).

6.8 Deadlock

It happens from time to time that companies are unable to hold effective meetings. This may occur, for example, where a company's articles of association require meetings (whether of the directors or shareholders) to have a quorum of at least two persons; the company has only two directors and shareholders; and one of them refuses to attend meetings. The same thing may happen through the death or disappearance of some of the original members. The problem should not arise where, through differing rules on quorums or differing membership, it is possible to have effective board or shareholders' meetings, as further shares may be issued or directors appointed as appropriate.

Where a company is truly unable to hold effective meetings, an application may be made to the court under the CA 2006, s 306.

> (1) *This section applies if for any reason it is impracticable—*
>
> (a) *to call a meeting of a company in any manner in which meetings of that company may be called, or*
>
> (b) *to conduct the meeting in the manner prescribed by the articles or this Act.*
>
> (2) *The court may, either of its own motion or on the application—*
>
> (a) *of any director of the company, or*
>
> (b) *of any member of the company who would be entitled to vote at the meeting,*
>
> *order a meeting to be called, held and conducted in any manner the court thinks fit.*
>
> (3) *Where such an order is made, the court may give such ancillary or consequential directions as it thinks expedient.*
>
> (4) *Such directions may include a direction that one member of the company present at the meeting be deemed to constitute a meeting.*
>
> (5) *A meeting called, held and conducted in accordance with an order under this section is deemed for all purposes to be a meeting of the company duly called, held and conducted.*

The section empowers the court to order a company meeting for the purpose of passing resolutions, for example to appoint new directors, and to direct that if the applicant alone attends, the meeting shall nevertheless be deemed to constitute a 'meeting'.

On an application under CA 2006, s 306, the first question is whether it is impracticable to call a meeting. This generally requires evidence of steps taken to call meetings, without success. The next question is whether the court's discretion should be exercised in favour of the application. Where the purpose of seeking an order under s 306 is a proper one, such as to enable the majority shareholder to exercise his or her right to remove and appoint directors, the discretion may be properly exercised in favour of granting the order (*Union Music Ltd v Watson* [2003] 1 BCLC 453). On the other hand, if the power to block decisions through non-attending is construed as a class right or substantive right, the order should be refused. In *Re Woven Rugs Ltd*

[2002] 1 BCLC 324 the minority shareholders, who held 40 per cent of the shares, refused to attend meetings of a company whose articles required two for a quorum. The court made an order under s 306 with a direction allowing a quorum of one, because there was no prior agreement that the minority would have a place on the board, and there was no unfairness in ordering a meeting, even though its purpose was to replace the minority director.

In *Re Sticky Fingers Restaurant Ltd* [1991] BCC 754, the company had two directors who also held all its issued shares (66 and 34 each). The minority shareholder was complaining of unfair prejudice (for which, see **Chapter 13**) and had issued a petition against the majority shareholder. The majority shareholder wanted to appoint extra directors, but the minority shareholder, who feared he would lose his directorship, refused to attend meetings, which were ineffective through lack of a quorum. It takes some time for unfair prejudice petitions to be dealt with, so the court made an order convening a meeting under the section, on the application of the majority shareholder, adding provisos that any new directors appointed would first undertake pending the resolution of the petition:

(a) not to vote to dismiss the minority shareholder from his directorship; and

(b) not to vote for any alteration in the constitution or capital of the company.

In *Harman v BML Group Ltd* [1994] 1 WLR 893 the Court of Appeal refused to make an order under the section in a deadlocked company. An unfair prejudice petition was pending. The court accepted that that did not preclude the making of an order convening a meeting, but decided its existence was a relevant factor to be taken into account. Dillon LJ said it was not the court's function to require cross-undertakings from the parties to ensure the company's business was conducted along sensible lines. That was a matter for the company's advisers. However, the most important factor was that the effect of the proposed order under what is now s 306 was to override the objecting shareholder's class rights which enabled him to exercise a right of veto, which was held to be an improper use of s 306.

For similar reasons, the application under what is now s 306 was refused in *Ross v Telford* [1998] 1 BCLC 82, CA. Mr Ross, who was one of two 50 per cent shareholders in a company called Linkside, wanted to hold a meeting to ratify proceedings brought by Linkside against a bank. The second shareholder was another limited liability company, PLB, whose shares were held equally by Mr Ross and Mrs Telford. In effect, therefore, Mr Ross held 75 per cent of the shares in Linkside. However, Mr Ross and Mrs Telford had previously been married to each other, and in ancillary relief proceedings they had been awarded equal beneficial interests in Linkside. Linkside's articles provided for a quorum of two, and in the absence of someone to represent PLB it was impossible to have effective meetings. It was held that s 306 is a procedural section, and is not designed to shift the balance of power between equal shareholders, who must be taken to have agreed that either of them could block decisions by non-attendance. Nourse LJ said that in these circumstances there is no jurisdiction to make an order under s 306, alternatively, the court would exercise its discretion against making an order. It is different where a company has two shareholders with unequal numbers of shares. In such a case the majority shareholder is entitled to exercise his or her ordinary voting rights to appoint and remove directors. Where that right is being frustrated by the non-attendance of the minority shareholder the court may exercise its discretion under s 306 to break the deadlock (*Smith v Butler* [2012] 1 BCLC 444).

6.9 Members' rights against directors

If the members wish to remove or criticise the directors they must resolve to do so at a general meeting or an AGM. However, most articles will delegate the power to call meetings and set the agenda to the directors. The CA 2006 therefore gives members the statutory right to require the directors to call a general meeting (s 303).

However, if a minority of shareholders wish to remove or criticise the directors, even if they have the requisite shareholding to require a general meeting to be called or a resolution put to an AGM, they must still have sufficient votes to carry the resolution (simple majority for ordinary resolution; 75 per cent majority for special resolution). Further, the members may ratify, by majority vote, most breaches of duty. If shareholders wish to sue directors or former directors, the board of directors, if capable of acting, has sole control of the litigation (*Breckland Group Holdings Ltd v London and Suffolk Properties Ltd* [1989] BCLC 100; *Mitchell and Hobbs (UK) Ltd v Mill* [1996] 2 BCLC 102). There are also the restrictions on shareholder claims under the rule in *Foss v Harbottle* (see **11.5.1**). In practical terms, shareholders wishing to sue directors therefore need to gain control of the board of directors.

6.10 Appointment and removal of directors

Shareholders' primary function in the management of their companies is in hiring and firing the directors. This is buttressed by CA 2006, s 168:

> (1) *A company may by ordinary resolution at a meeting remove a director before the expiration of his period of office, notwithstanding anything in any agreement between it and him.*
>
> (2) *Special notice is required of a resolution to remove a director under this section or to appoint somebody instead of a director so removed at the meeting at which he is removed ...*
>
> (5) *This section is not to be taken—*
>
> (a) *as depriving a person removed under it of compensation or damages payable to him in respect of the termination of his appointment as director or of any appointment terminating with that as director, or*
>
> (b) *as derogating from any power to remove a director which may exist apart from this section.*

Special notice of the resolution is required by CA 2006, s 168(2), which means that notice of the intention to move it must be given to the company at least 28 days before the meeting (s 312).

Where notice is given of a proposed resolution for removal under s 168(2), the director must be informed and given an opportunity to protest. CA 2006, s 169, provides:

> (1) *On receipt of notice of an intended resolution to remove a director under section 168, the company must forthwith send a copy of the notice to the director concerned.*
>
> (2) *The director (whether or not a member of the company) is entitled to be heard on the resolution at the meeting.*
>
> (3) *Where notice is given of an intended resolution to remove a director under that section, and the director concerned makes with respect to it representations in writing to the company (not exceeding a reasonable length) and requests their notification to members of the company, the company shall, unless the representations are received by it too late for it to do so—*

(*a*) *in any notice of the resolution given to members of the company state the fact of the representations having been made; and*

(*b*) *send a copy of the representations to every member of the company to whom notice of the meeting is sent (whether before or after receipt of the representations by the company).*

There is no need to circularise defamatory representations. Instead, s 169(5) provides that an application can be made to the court for an order declaring that there is no need to send the representations out.

6.11 Exercise 2

RE: AT YOUR SERVICE LIMITED

INSTRUCTIONS TO COUNSEL

Counsel is instructed on behalf of Miss Catherine Anne Barton, of 6 University Mews, Cambridge, CB4 8RT, a director of and shareholder in the above-named company. The company was incorportated on 14th September 1984. Its capital consists of 100 fully paid up £1 ordinary shares. 60 are held by Miss Barton, and 40 are held by Miss Amanda Louise Simpson, who is also the second director and company secretary. Since its incorporation the company has carried on the business run by Miss Barton and Miss Simpson as a recruitment agency. This business was set up as a joint venture, and, until July 2009 the two women were the only people employed by the company.

The company trades from its registered office at 53 College Road, Cambridge, CB1 4LN, and its clients are drawn from the area around Cambridge. In the spring of last year matters turned sour between the two women over questions of how the business should be run. In July Miss Simpson orally informed our client that she would be leaving at the end of the week and would be starting her own business in Lincoln. Since that time Miss Simpson has severed all links with the company, and has not visited its premises or communicated with our client in any way. It is understood that Miss Simpson now devotes herself full time to her new business in Lincoln.

It has been quite impossible for Miss Barton to run the business single-handed, and she has taken on a Miss Deborah Welsh of 12 Parkside Road, Cambridge, CB4 3LR to perform the duties previously undertaken by Miss Simpson. Ideally, it is desired that Miss Simpson should be replaced as a director by Miss Welsh. However, subject to Counsel's advice, on a practical level this cannot be done. The company does have registered articles, but they are silent on the question of meetings etc. Under Table A of the 1948 Act two people are required to form a valid meeting (both of directors and shareholders), and as Miss Simpson will have nothing to do with the company at present meetings to elect new directors cannot be held. Relevant extracts from Table A are enclosed.

Counsel is therefore asked to advise on any appropriate steps to be taken and to draft any necessary documents.

Counsel is instructed to advise and draft any necessary documents.

Relevant regulations from Table A (Companies Act 1948)

General Meetings

49. The directors may, whenever they think fit, convene an extraordinary general meeting, and extraordinary general meetings shall also be convened on such requisition, or, in default, may be convened by such requisitionists, as provided by Section 132 of the Act. If at any time there are not within the United Kingdom sufficient directors capable of acting to form a quorum, any director or any two members of the company may convene an extraordinary general meeting in the same manner as nearly as possible as that in which meetings may be convened by the directors.

Notice of General Meetings

50. An annual general meeting and a meeting called for the passing of a special resolution shall be called by twenty-one days' notice in writing at the least, and a meeting of the company other than an annual general meeting or a meeting for the passing of a special resolution shall be called by fourteen days' notice in writing at the least. The notice shall be exclusive of the day on which it is served or deemed to be served and of the day for which it is given, and shall specify the place, the day and the hour of meeting and, in case of special business, the general nature of that business, and shall be given, in manner hereinafter mentioned or in such other manner, if any, as may be prescribed by the company in general meeting, to such persons as are, under the regulations of the company, entitled to receive such notices from the company:

Provided that a meeting of the company shall, notwithstanding that it is called by shorter notice than that specified in this regulation, be deemed to have been duly called if it is so agreed—

(a) in the case of a meeting called as the annual general meeting, by all the members entitled to attend and vote thereat; and

(b) in the case of any other meeting, by a majority in number of the members having a right to attend and vote at the meeting, being a majority together holding not less than 95 per cent in nominal value of the shares giving that right.

Proceedings at General Meetings

53. No business shall be transacted at any general meeting unless a quorum of members is present at the time when the meeting proceeds to business; save as herein otherwise provided two members present in person or by proxy shall be a quorum.

68. The instrument appointing a proxy shall be in writing under the hand of the appointer or of his attorney duly authorised in writing, or, if the appointer is a corporation, either under seal, or under the hand of an officer or attorney duly authorised. A proxy need not be a member of the company.

69. The instrument appointing a proxy and the power of attorney or other authority, if any, under which it is signed or a notarially certified copy of that power or authority shall be deposited at the registered office of the company or at such other place within the United Kingdom as is specified for that purpose in the notice convening the meeting, not less than 48 hours before the time for holding the meeting or adjourned meeting, at which the person named in the instrument proposes to vote, or, in the case of a poll, not less than 24 hours before the time appointed for the taking of the poll, and in default the instrument of proxy shall not be treated as valid.

Proceedings of Directors

98. The directors may meet together for the despatch of business, adjourn, and otherwise regulate their meetings, as they think fit. Questions arising at any meeting shall be decided by a majority of votes. In case of an equality of votes, the chairman shall have a second or casting vote. A director may, and the secretary on the requisition of a director shall, at any time summon a meeting of the directors. It shall not be necessary to give notice of a meeting of directors to any director for the time being absent from the United Kingdom.

99. The quorum necessary for the transaction of the business of the directors may be fixed by the directors, and unless so fixed shall be two.

7 Directors

7.1 Introduction

7.1.1 Position of directors

Every private company must have at least one director and every public company at least two (CA 2006, s 154). Directors are usually in a powerful position as wide management powers are generally delegated to them by the articles. This division of power between members and directors was discussed at **6.2**. This chapter will cover the appointment of directors in outline, their position and duties to the company, action which can be taken if they are in breach of their duties and disqualification under the Company Directors Disqualification Act 1986.

7.1.2 Who is a director?

There is no comprehensive definition of a director. CA 2006, s 250, states that it 'includes any person occupying the position of director, by whatever name called'. The test is therefore one of function not title, and the terms 'manager', 'governor' etc may sometimes be used. On the other hand, the fact that an employee is called the marketing director will not make that person a director in law. The directors of a company will be those people who take part in board meetings of the company. They will be *de jure,* or legally appointed, directors if their details have been registered at Companies House.

7.1.2.1 *De facto* directors

The definition in CA 2006, s 250, is wide enough to cover persons who have not been registered as such, but who have acted as though they were directors. There is no single decisive test for when a person will be treated as a *de facto* director, because what is required will depend on the circumstances and the nature of the duty under consideration (*Secretary of State for Trade and Industry v Tjolle* [1998] 1 BCLC 333). Nevertheless, those who assume to act as directors and who thereby exercise the powers and discharge the functions of a director, whether they are validly appointed or not, will be treated as accepting the responsibilities of the office (*Re Hydrodam (Corby) Ltd* [1994] 2 BCLC 180). The crucial question is whether a person has assumed the duties of a director (*Re Idessa (UK) Ltd* [2012] 1 BCLC 80). In relation to alleged breach of fiduciary duty, a person is a *de facto* director if they were part of the company's governing structure *(Fayers Legal Services Ltd v Day* (unreported) 11 April 2001). In relation to alleged liability under IA

1986, s 212, for misfeasance by an officer of the company, the question is whether they were in a position to prevent damage to the creditors of the company by taking proper steps to protect their interests (*Revenue and Customs Commissioners v Holland* [2010] 1 WLR 2793 at [39]).

7.1.2.2 Shadow directors

In addition, the CA 2006 applies certain provisions to any person not actually appointed as a director but who is a 'shadow director'. This is defined in CA 2006, s 251, as 'a person in accordance with whose directions or instructions the directors of the company are accustomed to act'. However, a person is not deemed to be a shadow director by reason only that the directors act on advice given by him or her in a professional capacity. It is not clear exactly who may be caught by the 'shadow director' provision. It would appear from the decision in *Re Unisys Group Ltd (No 2)* [1994] BCC 166 to require a 'regular course of conduct' by the board or governing majority acting in accordance with such directions. A single incident of acting on the instructions of an outsider is not enough (*Secretary of State for Trade and Industry v Becker* [2003] 1 BCLC 555). In *Re a Company (No 005009 of 1987)* [1989] BCLC 13 it was said that it was arguable that where a company was managed in accordance with a bank's instructions to avoid the appointment of an administrative receiver by the bank, the bank was acting as a shadow director, although the allegation was abandoned at trial (*Re MC Bacon Ltd* [1990] BCLC 372). See also *Secretary of State for Trade and Industry v Deverell* [2001] Ch 340.

7.1.3 Appointment

The documents delivered to the Registrar of Companies on incorporation must include particulars of first directors and their signed consent to act (CA 2006, s 12). These people will be named in the articles or appointed by the subscribers. Subsequent appointment is regulated by the articles. Under the Model Articles Private Companies, reg 17, and Public Companies, reg 20, a director may be appointed by ordinary resolution or by the directors. The position is the same under 1985 Table A; by ordinary resolution (reg 78) and by the directors (reg 79). A new director's consent to act will be filed with the Registrar of Companies. For the appointment to be valid it is necessary that the person appointed give informed consent to the appointment (*Re CEM Connections Ltd* [2000] BCC 917).

The articles may also set out when directors must retire. Small private companies' articles may provide that the directors remain in office indefinitely, for example the Model Articles Private Companies contains no provision for retiring. The Model Articles Public Companies, reg 21, and 1985 Table A, regs 73–77, contain provisions for retirement by rotation. They also provide that any director appointed by the directors must retire at the next AGM (although they are also eligible for re-election (Model Articles Public Companies, reg 21 and 1985 Table A, reg 79)). Under 1985 Table A, reg 84, a managing director does not retire by rotation. There is no equivalent provision in the Model Articles Public Companies.

Generally anyone (including a company), can be a director, and a director need not be a member of the company unless the articles contain a share qualification clause (now rare). An individual who is a director of a company which is a corporate director of the company in question is not, without more, a *de facto* director of the company in question (*Revenue and Customs Commissioners v Holland* [2010] 1 WLR 2793). To prevent abuse of the use of corporate directors, at least one director of every company must be a natural person (CA 2006, s 155).

Under the CA 2006 there is no longer any maximum age limit for directors. However, a new minimum age of 16 is introduced by CA 2006, s 157. Section 158 enables the Secretary of State to make regulations providing for exceptions.

7.1.4 Directors' contracts

A director is an officer of the company (CA 2006, s 1173(1)). As an officer the director may be paid director's fees. Under the Model Articles Private Companies, reg 19, and Public Companies, reg 23, these fees are determined by the directors. Under 1985 Table A, reg 82, these are set by the company by ordinary resolution.

A director may also be an employee, for example if he or she also acts as managing director. As such he or she will have a contract of service like any other employee. The articles usually provide that the appointment as employee and the terms of the service contract are fixed by the board (Model Articles Private Companies, reg 19, and Public Companies, reg 23, and 1985 Table A, reg 84). A potential conflict of interest arises where the director concerned is a member of the board making the appointment or determining the terms of the service contract. See further on this at **7.5**. To prevent abuse by the board CA 2006, s 188, provides that a company may not agree a provision under which the guaranteed term of a director's employment is or may be longer than two years during which it cannot be terminated by notice by the company unless the contract is first approved by ordinary resolution in general meeting. A copy of the proposed agreement must be available for 15 days before the meeting and at the meeting. Failure to obtain the required agreement results in the service contract being deemed to contain a term enabling the company to terminate on reasonable notice. A company must keep available for inspection a copy of every director's service contract with the company at the company's registered office or place specified in regulations (s 228). Section 227 defines service contract extensively and includes contracts of service and contracts for services.

7.2 Directors as agents of the company

7.2.1 Common law

The company cannot act on its own; it must act through the agency of humans. Employees will be agents for the company. In addition, the directors who act on the company's behalf will do so as agents of the company and the company will be bound by acts for which the agent has actual or apparent authority.

Actual authority was defined in *Freeman and Lockyer v Buckhurst Park Properties (Mangal) Ltd* [1964] 2 QB 48 as 'a legal relationship between principal and agent created by a consensual agreement to which they alone are parties'. Such actual authority may be express or implied:

(a) Express, if given by express words, for example when a board of directors authorises a director to contract on behalf of the company.

(b) Implied, from the conduct of the parties, for example when a board appoints a managing director (see **6.2.4**) the implication is that he or she may do all things which fall within the scope of that office, see *Hely-Hutchinson v Brayhead Ltd* [1968] 1 QB 549.

Apparent authority is the authority which is perceived by others based on a representation of such authority by someone who has actual authority and which is relied on, see again *Freeman* (discussed in the previous paragraph). The actual authority of the board is determined by the articles which invariably delegate very wide management powers to them and empower them to sub-delegate (see **6.2.1**). It is usual for the board to delegate extensive authority to a managing director. A managing director will therefore also have fairly extensive apparent authority. More limited authority may also be delegated to other directors who have specific remits, for example a finance director may have authority to act on behalf of the company in financial matters.

However, the scope of the apparent authority of a single director (who is not the managing director) is probably fairly limited. The principal role of a director is to attend board meetings and vote on resolutions (ie be part of the decision-making process). The exact scope of such a director's authority to act as agent of the company is open to question. One view is that even an executive director is not invested with any apparent authority to act on the company's behalf (see *George Whitechurch Ltd v Cavanagh* [1902] AC 117). This may have changed with time and the position may now be that while a non-executive director will have no apparent authority to bind the company, an executive director will have apparent authority to transact business on behalf of the company within a specific area.

7.2.2 Statutory protection

As the articles are public documents, the common law was that persons dealing with the company had notice of any limitation on the actual authority of directors or the right to delegate. Such persons therefore could not rely on the principles of apparent authority to bind a company by acts which were in fact outside the actual authority of the directors or the managing director as set out in the company's articles. However, provisions in successive Companies Acts have given protection to outsiders entering into transactions with companies.

CA 2006, s 40, which largely restates CA 1985, ss 35A and 35B, continues to give this protection:

> *(1) In favour of a person dealing with a company in good faith, the power of the directors to bind the company, or authorise others to do so, is deemed to be free of any limitation under the company's constitution.*
>
> *(2) For this purpose—*
>
> *(a) a person 'deals with' a company if he is a party to any transaction or other act to which the company is a party,*
>
> *(b) a person dealing with a company—*
>
> *(i) is not bound to enquire as to any limitation on the powers of the directors to bind the company or authorise others to do so,*
>
> *(ii) is presumed to have acted in good faith unless the contrary is proved, and*
>
> *(iii) is not to be regarded as acting in bad faith by reason only of his knowing that an act is beyond the powers of the directors under the company's constitution.*
>
> *(3) The references above to limitations on the directors' powers under the company's constitution include limitations deriving—*
>
> *(a) from a resolution of the company or of any class of shareholders, or*
>
> *(b) from any agreement between the members of the company or of any class of shareholders.*

> (4) *This section does not affect any right of a member of the company to bring proceedings to restrain the doing of an action that is beyond the powers of the directors. But no such proceedings lie in respect of an act to be done in fulfilment of a legal obligation arising from a previous act of the company.*
>
> (5) *This section does not affect any liability incurred by the directors, or any other person, by reason of the directors' exceeding their powers.*
>
> (6) *This section has effect subject to—*
>
> *section 41 (transactions with directors or their associates), and*
>
> *section 42 (companies that are charities).*

Section 41 applies to transactions the validity of which depends on s 40 and provides that where a company enters into such a transaction and the parties to the transaction include a director of the company or person connected with such a director, the transaction is voidable at the instance of the company. Irrespective of whether it is avoided, the director or connected person and any director who authorised the transaction is liable to account for any gain made or indemnify the company for any loss suffered.

Note that s 40 uses the word 'directors' (ie plural) and thus may not protect an outsider where a single director acts on behalf of the company without actual or apparent authority.

Contracts entered into by a company may be made in writing under its common seal, or on behalf of the company by a person acting under its express or implied authority (s 43). The alternative allows a company to enter into an oral contract. Where a document has to be executed by a company, this is done by affixing its seal, or if the document is to be signed without the use of its seal, by two authorised signatories or by one director in the presence of a witness who attests the signature (s 44). A document that purports to be entered into by a company without using the company's seal must have two signatures on behalf of the company as provided by s 44, failing which it is ineffective (*Hilmi & Associates Ltd v 20 Pembridge Villas Freehold Ltd* [2010] 1 WLR 2750, and see also *Williams v Redcard Ltd* [2011] 2 BCLC 350).

Where a transaction is entered into by the directors in obvious breach of their fiduciary duties to the company, and where the third party knows of the circumstances (even if it does not know that those circumstances are a vitiating factor), the transaction will be unenforceable by the third party on account of it being beyond the actual or ostensible authority of the directors (*Criterion Properties plc v Stratford UK Properties LLC* [2004] 1 WLR 1846). In *Knopp v Thane Investments Ltd* [2003] 1 BCLC 380, the articles of the company provided that the remuneration of the directors was to be fixed by the shareholders. In contravention, the two directors approved each other's service agreement in a board meeting. It was held the directors had no authority to do this, and the service agreements were never validly entered into.

A director may himself be a person 'dealing with a company' within the meaning of s 40, but where the director is also the chairman of the company, he will not be able to rely on any mistake he might make as to whether a directors' meeting is quorate or whether decisions made at the meeting are otherwise valid (*Smith v Henniker-Major and Co* [2003] Ch 182).

7.2.3 Defective appointment—statutory protection

Finally, one should be aware of CA 2006, s 161, which states:

> (1) *The acts of a person acting as a director are valid notwithstanding that it is afterwards discovered—*
>
> (a) *that there was a defect in his appointment;*

(b) *that he was disqualified from holding office;*

(c) *that he had ceased to hold office;*

(d) *that he was not entitled to vote on the matter in question.*

(2) *This applies even if the resolution for his appointment is void under section 160 (appointment of directors of public company to be voted on individually).*

This will not validate acts of a director where there was no appointment at all (as opposed to a defective one)—*Morris v Kanssen* [1946] AC 459.

7.2.4 Other agents of the company

It is important to note that agency is not confined to directors. A company secretary has apparent authority to bind the company to contracts relating to the administrative affairs of the company: *Panorama Developments (Guildford) Ltd v Fidelis Furnishing Fabrics Ltd* [1971] 2 QB 711. An employee who was not a director, but whose job title was 'Director of PSU Sales', was held in *SMC Electronics Ltd v Akher Computers Ltd* [2001] 1 BCLC 433 to have actual authority to enter into a commission-sharing agreement on behalf of his company with another company. In any event, he had implied authority to enter into the agreement because it was ordinarily incidental to his duties.

7.3 Directors' duties: general

7.3.1 To whom owed

Directors in practice control the company, and its success or failure largely depends on them. They are fiduciaries and owe duties of good faith. There are potentially a number of individuals or bodies to whom the directors might owe duties—the company, the members, the employees, the creditors. However, the general rule is that the directors owe their duties to the company as a whole. This has traditionally been used to mean the shareholders as a collective body including present and future shareholders.

The traditional view is that directors owe no general duty to individual members (*Percival v Wright* [1902] 2 Ch 421; *Peskin v Anderson* [2001] 1 BCLC 372) although there may be circumstances which do give rise to such a duty, for example where they are authorised to act as agents for particular shareholders (*Allen v Hyatt* (1914) 30 TLR 444). There are a number of cases on the duty of directors to shareholders, largely dealing with advising on takeover bids (see *Gething v Kilner* [1972] 1 WLR 337; *Heron International Ltd v Lord Grade* [1983] BCLC 244; *Dawson International plc v Coats Patons plc* (1989) 5 BCC 405). The role of employees will, with European influence, become greater but no duty is owed to individual employees. Recent decisions show that directors have duties to creditors as a class when the company is approaching insolvency (*Lonrho Ltd v Shell Petroleum Co Ltd* [1980] 1 WLR 627; *Winkworth v Edward Baron Development Co Ltd* [1986] 1 WLR 1512 and *Brady v Brady* [1989] AC 755 and see **7.3.4**). Note also IA 1986, s 214 (wrongful trading, see **8.6.3**) and CDDA 1986 (see **7.8**).

7.3.2 Codification in Companies Act 2006

Under the CA 2006, directors' existing common law and equitable duties are codified and placed on a statutory footing. Section 170(3) states that the statutory duties under the CA 2006 are based on, and have effect in place of, certain common law rules and equitable principles. Regard has to be had to existing common law rules and equitable principles in interpreting and applying the general duties (s 170(4)).

The statutory duties continue to be owed to the company and not to individual shareholders. Section 178 also makes it clear that the statutory duties under the CA 2006 are fiduciary duties, with the exception of the duty to exercise care, skill and diligence, which remains a duty in tort.

The statutory duties apply to all directors of a company. Some of the statutory provisions are expressed to apply even to former directors of the company (s 175 on conflicts of interest and s 176 on the duty not to accept benefits from third parties), although they may only apply to former directors 'subject to any necessary adaptations' (see s 170(2)). The statutory duties also apply to shadow directors to the same extent as the corresponding common law or equitable principles (s 170(5)); therefore if an existing common law or equitable rule applied to a shadow director, then the corresponding statutory rule will also apply, but not otherwise.

Under the CA 2006, directors have to comply with seven specific duties:

(a) to act in accordance with the company's constitution (s 171);

(b) to promote the success of the company (s 172);

(c) to exercise independent judgement (s 173);

(d) to exercise reasonable care, skill and diligence (s 174);

(e) to avoid conflicts of interest (s 175);

(f) not to accept benefits from third parties (s 176);

(g) to declare any interest in transactions or arrangements with the company (ss 177 and 182).

7.3.3 Duty to act within powers and for a proper purpose (CA 2006, s 171)

Section 171 of the CA 2006 provides that a director *must* act in accordance with the company's constitution (defined by s 257 to include the articles, decisions taken in accordance with the articles and other decisions taken by the members, or a class of them, if they can be regarded as decisions of the company), and must only exercise powers for the purposes for which they are conferred.

Directors must exercise their powers for proper purposes. The directors must decide how to exercise their powers but may only do so for the purposes for which the powers were given. Many of the cases on the improper use of powers are on the issue of shares, in particular where directors issue shares to prevent a takeover bid which might oust them from power. The traditional view has been that shares are issued to raise capital and any other purpose is a collateral purpose. Where the power may be exercised for a variety of reasons it is the substantial or dominant purpose which is important (*Howard Smith Ltd v Ampol Petroleum Ltd* [1974] AC 821). A different situation arose in *Criterion Properties plc v Stratford UK Properties LLC* [2004] 1 WLR 1846, where a director entered into a contract on behalf of his company on extremely onerous terms which had the effect of crippling the company. The purpose of the contract was to make the company an unattractive proposition for a predatory investor, but this was held to be an improper purpose, and the transaction was set aside. Where a power is used for a collateral or improper purpose the directors are acting in an unauthorised manner and the company may not be bound. Note, however, the general agency rules, and also CA 2006, s 40, by which the company may be bound (see **7.2**).

Even where the company is bound, however, the directors will have acted in breach of their duty to the company and will be liable to it. The company may, however, generally ratify the directors' actions (*Bamford v Bamford* [1970] Ch 212). Such ratification will not be effective if there is a fraud on the minority (see **11.5.3.2**) or possibly where the breach of duty prejudices the interest of creditors when the company is insolvent (*West Mercia Safetywear Ltd v Dodd* (1987) 4 BCC 30).

7.3.4 Promoting the success of the company

Section 172(1) of the CA 2006 provides that a director *must* exercise his duties in a way that he considers, in good faith, would be most likely to promote the success of the company for the benefit of the members as a whole.

This replaces the duty to act bona fide in the interests of the company as a whole, an area on which there is a vast amount of case law which has established that the test is subjective, that is, provided directors act lawfully and bona fide in what they consider to be the interests of the company and not for a collateral purpose the court will not interfere. The lack of any reasonable ground for being a benefit to the company may be sufficient for the court to interfere and find lack of good faith (*Shuttleworth v Cox Brothers and Co (Maidenhead) Ltd* [1927] 2 KB 9). Where the act or omission under challenge has resulted in a substantial detriment to the company, the director has a harder task in persuading the court that he or she honestly believed it was in the company's interests (*Regentcrest plc v Cohen* [2001] 2 BCLC 80). However, mere incompetence is not a breach of fiduciary duty (*Extrasure Travel Insurances Ltd v Scattergood* [2003] 1 BCLC 598), although it may amount to negligence (see **7.4**).

The duty under s 172 also promotes the principle of 'enlightened shareholder value' which was one of the aims of the CA 2006. In debates on the Bill, Lord Goldsmith, then Attorney-General, stated:

> What is success? The starting point is that it is essentially for the members of the company to define the objective they wish to achieve. Success means what the members collectively want the company to achieve. For a commercial company success will usually mean long-term increase in value. For certain companies, such as charities and community interest companies, it will mean the attainment of the objectives for which the company has been established (see Department of Trade and Industry compilation of ministerial statements on duties of company directors, June 2007).

The decision as to what will promote the success of the company is one for the director's good faith and judgement. In exercising this duty, a director *must* have regard (amongst other things) to the factors laid down in s 172(1) namely:

(a) The likely consequences of the decision in the long term.

(b) The interests of the company's employees.

(c) The need to foster the company's business relationships with suppliers, customers and others.

(d) The impact of the company's operations on the community and the environment.

(e) The desirability of the company maintaining a reputation for high standards of business conduct.

(f) The need to act fairly as between the members of the company.

The Explanatory Notes to the CA 2006 make it clear that it will not be sufficient to pay lip service to the factors. Although there is no guidance in the Act as to the weight to be given to each of these factors, Margaret Hodge, then Minister of State for Industry and the Regions, stated 'The decisions taken by the directors and the weight given to the factors will continue to be a matter for his (ie the director's) good faith judgment' (see Department of Trade and Industry compilation of ministerial statements on duties of company directors, June 2007). There has been much debate about whether board minutes will have to record consideration of these factors. Margaret Hodge has stated 'The clause does not impose a requirement on directors to keep records, as some people have suggested, in any circumstances in which they would not have to do so now.'

The duty is also subject to any enactment or rule of law which requires directors in certain circumstances to consider or act in the interests of creditors of the company (eg where the company is insolvent or threatened with insolvency—s 172(3)). This applies where the company is insolvent, of doubtful solvency or on the verge of insolvency. It is a duty to have regard to the interests of the creditors as a class (*GHLM Trading Ltd v Maroo* [2012] 2 BCLC 369). A director is required to have paramount regard to the interests of creditors when acting on behalf of an insolvent company (*Re Capitol Films Ltd* [2011] 2 BCLC 359). This involves a duty to consider the separate interests of the company and its creditors, as distinct from the interests of other group companies or other companies the director might be interested in.

7.3.5 Duty to exercise independent judgement (CA 2006, s 173)

Section 173 of the CA 2006 requires a director to exercise independent judgement (within the limits of his or her authority as conferred by the company's constitution). This will not prevent a director from exercising a power to delegate, provided that this is permitted by the company's constitution. It also does not prevent a director from relying on advice or work of others and in some circumstances failing to take appropriate advice may be a breach of duty. However, the final judgement must be the director's responsibility (see statement of Lord Goldsmith in Department of Trade and Industry compilation of ministerial statements on duties of company directors, June 2007).

7.4 Duty of care and skill

7.4.1 Common law

Case law established a fairly low standard of care and skill below which directors might be liable. The standard of care was subjective with the result that a director with little skill was judged by a standard which would reasonably be expected of a person with that level of knowledge or experience (*Re City Equitable Fire Insurance Co Ltd* [1925] Ch 407).

Although there were comparatively few negligence claims that were successful, a director might be liable in negligence for leaving signed blank cheques with another director (*Dorchester Finance Co Ltd v Stebbing* [1989] BCLC 498) or for delegating a task to an employee who was unfit for the responsibilities delegated (*Cohen v Selby* [2001] 1 BCLC 176, where the claim failed on a pleading point). In addition, a director who was also an employee, for example a managing director, had the implied duty to exercise reasonable care and skill.

7.4.2 Companies Act 2006, s 174

CA 2006, s 174, requires a higher standard of care and mirrors the test in the IA 1986, s 214, for wrongful trading. It requires a director of a company to act:

(a) with the reasonable care and skill and diligence which would be exercised by a reasonably diligent person with both the general knowledge, skill and experience that may be expected of a person carrying out the functions carried out by a director in relation to the company; and

(b) the general knowledge, skill and experience that the director actually has. In exercising reasonable care, skill and diligence, it seems likely that the directors will have to take account of the factors set out in s 172 (see **7.3.4**).

Like the common law, this statutory duty is not a fiduciary duty (see CA 2006, s 178). However, common law negligence cases are no longer good law. Cases on the IA 1986, s 214, and the Company Directors Disqualification Act 1986 (see **7.7.3**) are the best guides on this new standard.

The duty includes:

(a) understanding and attending to the company's affairs: at common law directors were not bound to give continuous attention to the affairs of the company (*Re City Equitable Fire Insurance* [1925] Ch 407). Under s 174 each director probably has a duty to understand the company's business, the level of understanding being more general for non-executive than executive directors (*Lexi Holdings plc v Luqman* [2008] 2 BCLC 725) and to keep informed about the company's affairs (*Re Westmid Packing Services Ltd* [1998] 2 All ER 1240);

(b) supervising officials to whom duties delegated: at common law directors were justified in trusting an official to whom duties were properly delegated to perform such duties honestly. Regulation 5 of the Model Articles for both Private Companies and Public Companies allows the directors to delegate power conferred on them to such persons as they think fit. This could include other directors or employees. The extent to which there is now a duty to supervise such persons will depend on the context.

7.5 Conflict of interest

7.5.1 The common law

Case law established that directors must not put themselves in a position where their personal interests conflict with their duty to the company. This 'no conflict of interest' rule manifested itself in a number of sub-rules.

7.5.1.1 Directors as fiduciaries—the basic rules

(a) No Conflict of Interest Rule
Directors as fiduciaries must not put themselves in a position where their personal interests conflicted with their duty to the company. There is substantial case law on this.

(b) Profits from Position as Director

Directors as fiduciaries were also not allowed to profit from their position and held any such profit on trust for the company. They were liable where they actively diverted opportunities away from the company to themselves (*Cook v Deeks* [1916] 1 AC 554—contract so diverted) or even where they had acted honestly and openly and the benefit was not diverted from the company (*Regal (Hastings) Ltd v Gulliver* [1967] 2 AC 134—directors made a profit on shares which the company was not in a position to take up and they were held liable to account to the company even though they had acted bona fide throughout). The actual limits on the duty to account were not clear, particularly where a former director pursued opportunities after leaving the company or the company (through the board) decided not to pursue the opportunity (see *Industrial Development Consultants Ltd v Cooley* [1972] 1 WLR 443 and *Island Export Finance Ltd v Umunna* [1986] BCLC 460).

Liability is strict in the sense that it does not depend on whether the director was fraudulent or had a corrupt purpose (*Premier Waste Management Ltd v Towers* [2012] 1 BCLC 67). The principle recognises the primacy of the interests of the company which the director is trusted not to betray. Cases where a director becomes involved in the business of a competitor are fact-specific, and it is not an invariable rule that there is always a breach of the no-profit rule (*In Plus Group Ltd v Pyke* [2002] 2 BCLC 201). In this case the defendant had remained as a director of the claimant company, but was excluded from management, the claimant had ceased paying him and the loans he had made to the claimant had not been repaid. It was held that this was an exceptional case where there was no breach of fiduciary duty despite the defendant having formed a new company in competition with the claimant, which had obtained substantial amounts of work from one of the claimant's former customers.

If there had been a breach, the company could ratify the transaction and permit the director to retain the profit by unanimous consent of all the members or possibly by ordinary resolution in general meeting. In *Regal (Hastings) Ltd v Gulliver* it was stated that the directors could have protected themselves by obtaining a resolution in general meeting. However, in *Cook v Deeks* such attempted ratification was held to be ineffective. The standard explanation to reconcile these two cases was that in *Cook v Deeks* the directors were diverting opportunities away from the company and not acting bona fide whereas in *Regal (Hastings) Ltd v Gulliver* they were not diverting assets and were acting bona fide. This has been said to be the difference between ratifiable and non-ratifiable breaches. Where the breaches were ratifiable it would appear that the directors could exercise their votes as members (see *North-West Transportation Co Ltd v Beatty* (1887) 12 App Cas 589). The articles could also permit the directors to retain such profits as did 1985 Table A, reg 85.

7.5.1.2 Contracts with the company

Where a director entered into a contract with the company, it was voidable by the company even where it was made on fair terms after full disclosure (*Aberdeen Railway Co v Blaikie Brothers* (1854) 1 Macq 461). However, the right to rescind could be lost by delay, affirmation or the intervention of third party interests. In addition, the members could ratify the contract after full disclosure, such ratification being by ordinary resolution in general meeting, at which the director concerned could vote as a member (*North-West Transportation Co Ltd v Beatty* (1887) 12 App Cas 589).

The strict rule could be relaxed by the articles. 1985 Table A, regs 85 and 86, allowed a director who had disclosed the nature and extent of any material interest to have a service contract with the company and to be a party or otherwise interested in transactions generally with the company and to retain any benefit derived. General notice could be given, for example where a director is a partner in a firm which dealt with the company on a regular basis. The director concerned could not be counted in the quorum nor vote on the transaction except in very limited circumstances (see regs 94 and 95). CA 1985, s 317, imposed a statutory duty on directors in any event to declare the nature of any interest at the first meeting at which the contract was proposed or when the director's interest first arose (if later). Again general notice would suffice. (However, disclosure had to be to the board and not a committee of the board: *Guinness plc v Saunders* [1988] BCLC 43.) There could be a breach of s 317 even where the director had not made a conscious decision to conceal the information that ought to have been disclosed (*J.J. Harrison (Properties) Ltd v Harrison* [2001] 1 BCLC 158). Failure to comply with this section rendered the director liable to a fine. The better view is that an infringement of s 317 did not in any way vitiate the contract affected by the non-disclosure (*MacPherson v European Strategic Bureau Ltd* [1999] 2 BCLC 203).

7.5.2 Companies Act 2006

7.5.2.1 Conflict of interest (CA 2006, s 175)

CA 2006, s 175, deals with the position regarding directors avoiding conflicts with the company's interests. However, s 175(3) provides that it does not apply to a conflict of interest arising in relation to a transaction or arrangement with the company. Thus directors contracting with their company will not be caught by this section. These situations are covered by CA 2006, ss 177 and 182 (see **7.5.2.3**) and CA 2006, s 190 (see **7.5.3**).

Section 175(1) provides that a director must avoid situations in which he has or can have a direct or indirect interest that conflicts or possibly may conflict with the company's interests. Section 175(2) provides that this applies in particular to the exploitation of property, information and opportunity (whether or not the company could take advantage of the property, information or opportunity). However, s 175(4)(a) provides that the duty is not infringed if the situation cannot reasonably be regarded as likely to give rise to a conflict of interest. Finally, s 175(7) makes clear that the duty includes a conflict of interest and duty and a conflict of duties.

Section 175 would appear to include, but not be confined to, those cases dealing with profits obtained from the position of director. It is very similar to the pre-CA 2006 case law which includes cases dealing with exploitation of property, information and opportunity (see previously). However, the inclusion of the words 'or possibly may conflict' may result in a wider interpretation of the duty than under the existing case law. It is not clear how this provision will be interpreted given the duty in s 176 not to accept benefits from third parties (see **7.5.2.2**).

Under CA 2006, s 175(4)(b), the duty is not infringed if the matter has been authorised by the directors. Section 175(5) allows such authorisation by directors in private companies provided nothing in the company's constitution invalidates this and in public companies where the constitution includes a provision enabling it. Section 175(6) makes it clear that the director with the conflicting interest will not count in any requirement as to the quorum of the meeting or the votes agreeing to authorisation. Thus, provided the constitution allows authorisation by directors, ratification or consent of the members is no longer required.

7.5.2.2 Duty not to accept benefits from third parties (CA 2006, s 176)

By CA 2006, s 176, a director must not accept any benefit from a third party which is conferred by reason of his being a director, or his doing (or not doing) anything as a director, unless the acceptance of the benefit could not reasonably be regarded as likely to give rise to a conflict of interest. Third parties are defined in s 176(2) to exclude the company, or its holding company or subsidiaries and s 176(3) excludes benefits conferred by the director's service contract.

There is no provision which enables the directors to authorise acceptance of benefits which otherwise would be a breach of this duty (contrast with s 175 discussed previously), but s 180(4) preserves the ability of the members to give such authorisation.

The Guidance to the Act states that '[t]his section codifies the rule prohibiting exploitation of the position of director for personal benefits'. However, it also makes clear that s 175 covers the position where 'a director makes a profit in the course of being a director, in the matter of his directorship, without the knowledge or consent of his company'. Section 179 also states that except as otherwise provided, more than one of the general duties may apply in any given case. Given that directors will be able to authorise matters which potentially come within s 175 but not those within s 176, there is likely to be substantial dispute as to what each covers. Alternatively it may be that it will be common to plead breach of both duties in a wide variety of circumstances.

7.5.2.3 Contracts/transactions under CA 2006, ss 177 and 182

Under the CA 2006, the duty to avoid a conflict of interest in s 175 does not apply to transactions with the company. Instead, directors must disclose the nature and extent of their interest, direct or indirect, in such transactions to the other directors. The requirement for disclosure to the board in CA 1985, s 317, is repeated in the CA 2006. However, it is covered in two different sections.

Existing transactions or arrangements are dealt with in s 182, which provides: 'where a director of a company is in any way, directly or indirectly, interested in a transaction or arrangement that has been entered into by the company, he must declare the nature and extent of the interest to the other directors in accordance with this section'. The declaration must be made as soon as is reasonably practicable (s 182(4)). Section 183 makes it an offence for a director to fail to comply with this requirement.

Proposed transactions or arrangements are dealt with in s 177, which provides: 'if a director of a company is in any way, directly or indirectly, interested in a proposed transaction or arrangement with the company, he must declare the nature and extent of that interest to the other directors'. The declaration must be made before the company enters the transaction (s 177(4)). There is no equivalent provision to s 183 making failure to disclose an offence. However, s 178 provides that the remedies for breach of ss 171–177 are the same as would apply under the common law rules and equitable principles.

Breach of CA 1985, s 317, was also an offence and generally regarded as not giving rise to civil liability. The position under s 177 and s 182 is not particularly clear. However, given the wording of s 183 and s 178 and the general presumption that there is no civil liability for breach of a statutory duty which carries criminal penalties, it is arguable that civil remedies are available for breach of s 177, but not for breach of s 182.

Detailed requirements as to how the declaration of interest should be made under both s 177 and s 182 are set out in s 184 and s 185. The Model Articles Private Companies (reg 14) and Public Companies (reg 16) make detailed provisions about the right of the director to participate in any directors' meeting involving an actual or proposed transaction or arrangement in which the director is interested.

7.5.3 Substantial property transactions

Section 190(1) of the CA 2006 provides that a company may not enter into an arrangement under which a director of the company or of its holding company, or a person connected with such a director, acquires or is to acquire from the company or the company acquires or is to acquire from the director (directly or indirectly), a substantial non-cash asset unless the arrangement has been approved by a resolution of the members of the company (and by s 190(2) the holding company where appropriate) or is conditional on such approval being obtained. It was held in *NHB v Hoare* [2006] EWHC 73 (Ch), a case under the previous provisions in CA 1985, s 320, that a formal resolution of the shareholders is not necessary to approve a substantial property transaction if all the shareholders who have the right to attend and vote at a general meeting unanimously assent to the transaction. This is an application of the *Duomatic* principle (see **6.6.5.4**).

Section 191 explains that an asset is a substantial asset if its value is 10 per cent of the company's asset value and is more than £5,000 or if it exceeds £100,000. The value of the asset will be the true market value or the worth of the property to the director or connected person (*Micro Leisure Ltd v County Properties and Developments* [2000] BCC 872). This value is determined by reference to the statutory accounts. Whether an asset is substantial is determined at the time the arrangement is entered into.

Section 190(5) provides that an arrangement involving more than one non-cash asset or one of a series involving non-cash assets, shall be treated as involving a non-cash asset of value equal to the aggregate value involved in the transaction or series. See also *Ultraframe (UK) Ltd v Fielding* [2005] EWHC 1638 (Ch) where the court considered a number of transactions to determine whether they were 'non cash assets' for this purpose.

The definition of 'connected person' under CA 1985, s 346, included spouses, children, companies where the directors control 20 per cent of the votes, partners etc. This has been extended (see CA 2006, ss 252 and 253 which replace CA 1985, s 346).

Sections 192–194 set out exceptions to s 190 which include permitting intra-group transactions, distributions on winding up and to directors in their capacity as members. Section 190(6) also provides that the s 190(1) requirement does not apply to transactions which relate to entitlements under directors' service contracts or payments for loss of office as defined in s 215 (which require approval of members under s 217).

If the resolution is not obtained the transaction is voidable by the company unless restitution is no longer possible, the company has been indemnified for loss or damage suffered, rights acquired bona fide for value without actual notice of the contravention would be affected or the arrangement is within a reasonable period affirmed by the company in general meeting. In addition, the director or connected person and any director who authorised the arrangement is liable to account for any gain or indemnify the company for any loss or damage (CA 2006, s 195). A wide effect has been given to this provision (*Duckwari plc v Offerventure Ltd (No 2)* [1999] BCC 11). The measure of the indemnity was dealt with in subsequent proceedings reported at [1999] BCC 11 at 22.

7.5.4 Loans, quasi-loans and credit transactions

Under CA 1985, a company was not able to make a loan to a director. This was subject to a number of exceptions. Under the CA 2006, there is no longer any general prohibition on loans to directors. However, if the company does wish to grant a loan to a director, it needs to obtain shareholder approval (ss 197–214).

All companies require members' approval for loans or giving guarantees or providing security in connection with a loan to a director by the company or its holding company (s 197(1)). Public companies and private companies associated with a public company also require members' approval for loans, guarantees and security to connected persons and for quasi-loans (eg agreeing to pay the director's credit card on condition that the director will later repay the company) and credit transactions (eg hire purchase or conditional sale) made for a director or person connected to a director of the company or its holding company (ss 198, 200 and 201). The provisions set out detailed requirements as to disclosure and obtaining approval. Section 203 requires members' approval for related transactions which covers arrangements under which another person enters a transaction which would have required approval had it been entered into by the company.

Sections 204–209 contain exceptions setting out expenditure which does not require approval. These include expenditure on company business (s 204), on defending proceedings (s 205), in connection with regulatory action or investigation (s 206) and exceptions for minor and business transactions (s 207), intra-group transactions (s 208) and money lending companies (s 209).

If a company contravenes s 197, 198, 200 or 201 the arrangement is voidable by the company unless restitution is no longer possible, the company has been indemnified for any loss suffered or rights acquired by a bona fide purchaser for value without notice would be affected. In addition, the director or connected person and any director who authorised the transaction is liable to account for any gain or indemnify the company for any loss or damage (s 213). (Note that all loans, quasi-loans or credit transactions with directors must be disclosed in the company's annual accounts.)

Where there is a dispute over whether drawings on a director's loan account are legitimate, the burden of proof rests with the director, who also has a duty to explain what has happened to the company's property in his or her hands (*GHLM Trading Ltd v Maroo* [2012] 2 BCLC 369).

7.5.5 Interests in shares or debentures

7.5.5.1 Common law

Directors are in the best position to acquire information which may be used unfairly in dealing in the company's securities. At common law it is a breach of the director's duty to use such information and any profit acquired will be held on trust for the company (*Regal (Hastings) Ltd v Gulliver* [1967] 2 AC 134, see **7.5.1.1**). However, directors owe no such duty to individual shareholders and will not be liable to account to them if they buy shares from them without disclosing, for example, a potential takeover bid which will increase their value (*Percival v Wright* [1902] 2 Ch 421) although they may be liable if they are acting as agents for the shareholders (*Allen v Hyatt* (1914) 30 TLR 444).

7.5.5.2 Insider dealing

Under the Criminal Justice Act 1993, s 52, an individual with 'insider' information who deals with shares, debentures and other price-affected company securities on a regulated market (such as the London Stock Exchange) is guilty of an offence punishable by a fine and/or imprisonment for up to seven years. There are also offences where 'insiders' encourage others to deal with price-affected securities or disclose 'inside' information to others otherwise than in the proper performance of their duties. 'Inside' information must relate to particular securities rather than securities in general. It must not have been made public and must be likely to have a significant effect on the price of the securities in question (CJA 1993, s 56). To be an 'insider' a person must know that the relevant information is 'inside' information and that it comes from an inside source, that is, that it was obtained directly or indirectly from a director, employee or shareholder in the company, or through a person having access to the information by virtue of that person's employment, office or profession (CJA 1993, s 57).

A number of defences are set out in CJA 1993, s 53. These include the defendant not expecting to make a profit on account of the information used being price-sensitive, and reasonable belief that others taking part in the deal would not be prejudiced due to wide disclosure of the information. The CJA 1993 merely renders the person guilty of an offence. It does not make the transaction void or unenforceable.

7.6 Consequences of breach of duty

Where a director is in breach of a duty to the company, there are a number of possible consequences.

7.6.1 Removal as an officer and dismissal as an employee

A director may be removed from office by the board where the articles so provide. 1985 Table A, reg 81, provides that a director shall vacate office if absent without permission of the directors from meetings of directors for more than six consecutive months and the board so resolves. There is no equivalent provision in the Model Articles Private Companies or Public Companies.

CA 2006, s 168, provides that a company may by ordinary resolution remove a director before the expiration of his or her period of office, notwithstanding anything in any agreement between the company and the director.

Where a director is removed from office any contract of service, for example as managing director, is terminated (1985 Table A, reg 84). The director may therefore have a claim for wrongful or unfair dismissal unless the terms of the service contract are observed and/or the behaviour warrants summary dismissal. There is no equivalent provision in the Model Articles Private Companies or Public Companies. However, reg 5 allows the directors to revoke any delegation of powers in whole or part or alter its terms and conditions.

7.6.2 Proceedings against the director

Section 178 of the CA 2006 provides that proceedings can be brought against a director for breach of duty in exactly the same way as under the existing law, and for the same remedies, including damages, restoration of the company's property, an account of profits made by a director and rescission of a contract if a director has failed to disclose his interest in it. The cases fall into three categories over whether there is a constructive trust against the director (*FHR European Ventures LLP v Mankarious* [2013] 3 All ER 29). There will be if the director has come into possession of property beneficially owned by the company, or where the director has acquired property using an opportunity belonging to the company. There will be no constructive trust, and therefore only a personal rather than a proprietary claim, in any other type of case (*Sinclair Investments (UK) Ltd v Versailles Trade Finance Ltd* [2012] Ch 453).

A claim may be brought to obtain an injunction to restrain an actual or threatened breach of duty or claim damages for breach of duty or an account of profits received in breach of duty. Generally it is thought that an equitable allowance (for which, see *Boardman v Phipps* [1967] 2 AC 46) should not be granted in favour of a director in respect of the work done in exploiting a business opportunity diverted in breach of fiduciary duty (*Guinness plc v Saunders* [1990] 2 AC 663). However, in practice the court will order the director to account for the profits properly attributable to the breach of fiduciary duty, taking into account the expenses connected with those profits and a reasonable allowance for the overheads (but not necessarily a salary for the director), together with an account of other benefits derived from the diverted business (*CMS Dolphin Ltd v Simonet* [2001] 2 BCLC 704). The claim will be brought by the company which means that a resolution to institute proceedings must be passed either at a board meeting or in a general meeting.

7.6.3 Relief from liability

Under the CA 2006 shareholders will continue to be able to ratify a director's conduct which amounts to negligence, default, breach of duty or breach of trust (s 239). At common law this could be done by ordinary resolution unless the articles required a higher majority or unanimity. This has now been put on a statutory footing, see ss 239(2) and 281(3). Under the common law directors could generally use their votes as shareholders in general meetings, although there were limits on this use in such circumstances (see *Cook v Deeks* [1916] 1 AC 554 and *Daniels v Daniels* [1978] Ch 406, and fraud on the minority, see **11.5.3.2**). However, the CA 2006 provides that directors and those connected with them may not use their own votes as members to pass any resolution which seeks to ratify any breach of duty on their part (s 239). See s 252 for the definition of 'connected person', which is wider than the definition of 'connected person' under the CA 1985.

A company is not permitted to exempt or indemnify a director against a breach of duty, and any such provision is void (CA 2006, s 232). The provisions in CA 1985 which enabled a company to indemnify its directors in respect of proceedings brought by third parties and to purchase and maintain insurance for the benefit of a director are restated in CA 2006, ss 232–234. However, the provisions in the CA 2006 are wider because they also enable a company to indemnify a director in relation to liability incurred in connection with the company's activities as trustee of an occupational pension scheme (s 235). Shareholders are also given the right to inspect and request a copy of the third party indemnity or pension scheme indemnity provisions (s 238). In addition, as one of the exceptions to the requirement in respect of loans, guarantees etc (see **7.5.4**) the company may provide a director with funds to meet legal costs in defending criminal or civil proceedings as set out in s 205, provided the terms are that the loan will be repaid in the event that he is convicted, judgment is given against him or the court refuses him relief.

CA 2006, s 1157, empowers the court in any proceedings for negligence, default, breach of duty or breach of trust against an officer of a company to grant relief in whole or in part from such liability on such terms as it thinks fit. Such relief may be granted where it appears to the court that the officer has acted honestly and reasonably and, having regard to all the circumstances, ought fairly to be excused. A belief that the conduct was not unlawful, that the benefit to the director was modest and the nature of the relationships between the director and the other individuals concerned, did not provide grounds for granting relief under s 1157 in *Premier Waste Management Ltd v*

Tower [2012] 1 BCLC 67. Relief is not available where directors are liable for wrongful trading under IA 1986, s 214 (*Re Produce Marketing Consortium Ltd* [1989] 1 WLR 745).

7.7 Liability of directors of insolvent companies

7.7.1 Fraudulent and wrongful trading

The IA 1986, ss 213 and 214, provide that directors can be made to contribute to the company's assets where there has been fraudulent trading (s 213) or wrongful trading (s 214). These provisions are considered at **8.6.2** and **8.6.3.**

7.7.2 Re-use of company names

The IA 1986, s 216, provides that where a company has gone into insolvent liquidation, directors and shadow directors are prohibited from using the company's name, or a similar name which might suggest an association with the company, for five years. A person who breaches this provision commits an offence and will be personally liable for the debts of the new business trading under the prohibited name.

7.8 Company Directors Disqualification Act 1986

7.8.1 Power to disqualify

The CDDA 1986 empowers the court to disqualify a person from being a director, liquidator, administrator, receiver or manager or in any way, directly or indirectly, being concerned or taking part in the promotion, formation or management of a company for the period specified in the order. The court *may* make an order where a person:

(a) Is convicted of an indictable offence in connection with a company (s 2—maximum 15 years).

(b) Is in persistent default of the filing requirements under the companies legislation (ss 3 and 5—maximum five years).

(c) On the winding up of a company, appears to be guilty of fraudulent trading under CA 2006, s 993, or of any fraud or breach of duty (s 4—maximum 15 years).

(d) Is found to be unfit by the court after a BIS investigation (s 4—maximum 15 years).

(e) Is ordered to contribute to the company's assets on liquidation under IA 1986, s 213 or s 214 (fraudulent or wrongful trading) (s 10—maximum 15 years).

These provisions apply to directors and shadow directors (see **7.1.2**).

The court *must* make an order if satisfied that a person was a director of an insolvent company (ie it went into liquidation when unable to pay its debts, an administrative receiver is appointed or an administration order is made) and his or her conduct makes him or her unfit to be concerned in the management of a company (s 6—minimum two years, maximum 15 years). Schedule 1 contains matters which the court shall have regard to in determining whether the conduct makes the person unfit. These include breach of duty, misapplication or retention of company property, responsibility for defrauding creditors or insolvency. An objective standard of 'probity and competence' is applied. Misconduct must be serious before a disqualification order can be imposed. A proper degree of delegation and division of responsibility by the board is permissible, but not a total abrogation of responsibility.

Selling the company's plant just before ceasing to trade in a way which deprived the company of VAT on the sale was not sufficiently incompetent to justify a disqualification order in *Secretary of State for Trade and Industry v Walker* [2003] 1 BCLC 363. Trading while insolvent is not enough to render directors unfit, whereas trading while insolvent with no reasonable prospect of paying creditors can be (*Secretary of State for Trade and Industry v Creegan* [2002] 2 BCLC 99). Trading while the company is insolvent when the directors know or ought to know that its position is unlikely to improve, failing to get any or any further accountancy advice and paying themselves excessive remuneration, can render directors unfit (*Re Amaron Ltd, Secretary of State for Trade and Industry v Lubrani (No 2)* [2001] 1 BCLC 562). Whether a director who follows the incorrect advice of professional advisers is unfit is a matter of degree. In some cases the director will not be unfit, and in others, particularly where the director abrogates all responsibility, it is simply something to take into account in mitigation (*Re Bradcrown Ltd, Official Receiver v Ireland* [2001] 1 BCLC 547). Failure to supervise colleagues or insist on proper and systematic production of timely information which resulted in a high level of indebtedness to the Crown rendered a director unfit in *Secretary of State for Trade and Industry v Thornbury* [2007] EWHC 3202 (Ch). Pursuing a deliberate policy of non-payment of one category of debt, owed whether to the Crown or trade creditors, if carried on for a lengthy period, will usually result in a finding of unfitness (*Re Structural Concrete Ltd* [2001] BCC 578). The court can take into account the director's performance in the disqualification proceedings in deciding whether he is unfit (*Secretary of State for Trade and Industry v Reynard* [2002] 2 BCLC 625). If conduct below the required standard is proved, the court has a duty to impose a period of disqualification, even if the director has recognised past errors and is presently fit to act (*Re Landhurst Leasing plc* [1999] 1 BCLC 286).

The court *must* also make a disqualification order if a company has committed a breach of competition law and a director's conduct makes him unfit to be concerned in the management of a company (CDDA 1986, s 9A). In relation to competition disqualification orders, when considering whether a director is unfit the court must have regard to whether his conduct contributed to the breach of competition law, or if he ought to have known of the breach.

Concerted attacks on the procedure for disqualification applications based on alleged breaches of Arts 6, 8, 13 and 14 of the European Convention on Human Rights were rejected in *DC v United Kingdom* [2000] BCC 710, ECtHR and *WGS v United Kingdom* [2000] BCC 719, ECtHR.

7.8.2 Procedure

Applications under the CDDA 1986, ss 2, 3, 4, 6, 8A and 9A, must be made to a court having jurisdiction to wind up a company. In these cases, the person applying for the disqualification order must give at least ten days' notice to the defendant before making the application (CDDA 1986, s 16(1)). Failure to give the requisite notice does not prevent the court from hearing the application (*Secretary of State for Trade and Industry v Langridge* [1991] Ch 402). Except with the permission of the court, the application must be brought within two years after the company became insolvent (s 7(2)). Applications under ss 8 and 9B are made to the High Court.

Subsequent procedure is discussed at **2.5**. While the Secretary of State is under a duty to disclose relevant materials in his or her possession to the director, there is no specific duty on the Secretary of State to make investigations (*Secretary of State for Business, Innovation and Skills v Doffman* [2011] 1 BCLC 596).

7.8.3 Length of disqualification

Re Sevenoaks Stationers (Retail) Ltd [1991] Ch 164 was the first case to go to the Court of Appeal. The court set out guidelines for the length of the order under s 6: ten to 15 years for cases of utmost severity (eg where a director has been disqualified before), six to ten years for middle-ranking cases and two to five years for lesser cases. In addition, it stressed that the proper procedure must be followed in bringing cases, in particular, notice must be given to the director of the allegations made. It endorsed the approach that a disqualification order could be made where a director was not found to be dishonest but was incompetent or negligent to a 'very marked degree'. A variety of cases had indicated that the use of money owed to the Crown was more culpable than failure to pay commercial debts. The court stressed that failure to pay Crown debts does not automatically justify disqualification, and that the courts should not adopt some of the hard-and-fast tests suggested in earlier cases.

Raising £3 million worth of false invoices, combined with deliberately attempting to deceive Customs and Excise and giving voidable preferences, justified a 12-year disqualification in *Official Receiver v Doshi* [2001] 2 BCLC 235. Taking drawings of up to £0.5 million per annum while the company was insolvent, being at fault in allowing the company to trade while insolvent and to finance its business using Crown moneys, and using a second company as a phoenix to take over the insolvent company's business, when combined, also justified disqualification for 12 years (*Official Receiver v Stern (No 2)* [2002] 1 BCLC 119).

7.8.4 *Carecraft* procedure

Many disqualification cases are decided using a summary procedure known as the *Carecraft* procedure, from *Re Carecraft Construction Co Ltd* [1994] 1 WLR 172, where details of the procedure are described. See also PD DDP, para 13.

7.8.5 Disqualification undertakings

As an alternative to making an application for a disqualification order, the Secretary of State may accept an undertaking from a former director that he or she will not act as a director, receiver or be concerned in the promotion, formation or management of a company or act as an insolvency practitioner without the leave of the court for a specified period up to 15 years (s 1A, added by the Insolvency Act 2000, s 6). If disqualification proceedings are discontinued after the Secretary of State accepts a disqualification undertaking, the general rule is that the former director will pay the costs of the Secretary of State (PD DDP, para 28). The period of the undertaking may be reduced or ordered to cease on an application made to the court by the person giving the undertaking (CDDA 1986, s 8A, and see PD DDP, paras 29–34 for the procedure).

In relation to disqualification based on breach of competition law, disqualification undertakings may be accepted by the Office of Fair Trading or a specified regulator (CDDA 1986, s 9B, and see s 9E for the definition of 'specified regulator').

The Secretary of State has an unfettered discretion whether to accept an undertaking rather than applying for a disqualification order. It is usual, and a matter entirely at the discretion of the Secretary of State, for undertakings to be accepted with a schedule setting out the nature of the conduct that made the director unfit (*Re Blackspur Group plc (No 3), Secretary of State for Trade and Industry v Davies (No 2)* [2002] 2 BCLC 263).

7.8.6 Interrelation with criminal proceedings

As discussed at **7.8.1**, the criminal courts can make disqualification orders of up to 15 years where a director is convicted of an indictable offence in connection with a company. While a prosecution is proceeding, it is generally inappropriate to stay a civil disqualification claim, see *Secretary of State for Trade and Industry v Crane* [2001] 2 BCLC 222. The making of a disqualification order by the criminal court does not operate as a bar to the making of a civil disqualification order on the application of the Secretary of State (*Secretary of State for Trade and Industry v Rayna* [2001] 2 BCLC 48, where it was said that the existence of a criminal disqualification order was unlikely to render a civil application an abuse of process).

7.8.7 Acting while disqualified

A person who acts in contravention of a disqualification order commits an offence and is personally liable for the debts of the company while so acting (ss 13 and 15). It is also an offence to act as a director etc while an undischarged bankrupt and personal liability is also incurred while so acting (ss 11 and 15).

7.8.8 Permission to act

A disqualified director can apply for permission to act (ss 1 and 17). Such applications are made either by issuing an application notice in existing disqualification proceedings, or by issuing a Part 8 claim form (see PD DDP, para 20). When considering such an application, Sir Richard Scott V-C in *Re Barings plc, Secretary of State for Trade and Industry v Baker (No 5)* [1999] BCC 960 said:

> the importance of protecting the public from the conduct that led to the disqualification order and the need that the applicant should be able to act as a director of a particular company must be kept in balance with one another. The court in considering whether or not to grant leave should, in particular, pay attention to the nature of the defects in company management that led to the disqualification order and ask itself whether, if leave were granted, a situation might arise in which there would be a risk of recurrence of those defects.

If there is no need to have the applicant as a director, even a small risk to the public would justify refusal of the application (*Shuttleworth v Secretary of State for Trade and Industry* [2000] BCC 204). Normally, permission is only granted subject to proper safeguards being in place to prevent a repeat of the abuse that led to the disqualification order. It is almost inconceivable that permission will be granted for a disqualified director to act as a one-man company (*Re Britannia Homes Centre, Official Receiver v McCahill* [2001] 2 BCLC 63). Ideally, the Secretary of State's application for a disqualification order and the former director's application for permission to act should come on for hearing one after the other. Invariably the applicant must pay the Secretary of State's costs, even if permission to act is granted (*Re TLL Realisations Ltd* [2000] BCC 998).

8 Insolvency

8.1 Introduction

8.1.1 Purpose of insolvency law

A significant proportion of the work undertaken by company law practitioners relates to corporate insolvency. As could be predicted, the amount of insolvency work increases in times of economic recession. 'Insolvency' as an expression has a number of different meanings in the law relating to corporate collapse. In broad terms a company may be said to be insolvent when it finds itself in the position of being unable to pay its debts as they fall due. However, this may describe a temporary, trivial cash flow difficulty, or a company with a sizeable business, but a history of incurring expenditure exceeding its income, or a situation where a company has incurred massive debts and is left with negligible assets and no hope of repaying what it owes.

The law relating to company insolvency seeks to achieve a number of objectives:

(a) to provide means by which companies in temporary financial difficulties can trade out of those difficulties without being killed off by overzealous creditors, while protecting the interests of the general body of creditors while this is happening;

(b) to provide means by which companies that cannot be saved are taken off the register and thereby cease trading;

(c) to ensure that the assets of insolvent companies are distributed in a fair and orderly manner (without an unseemly scramble to grab whatever can be salvaged from the wreckage);

(d) to provide means by which the causes of a company's collapse can be investigated, and by which any failure of those in control of the company to act properly can be investigated and if necessary penalised; and

(e) to ensure that those given the responsibility for getting in the assets of insolvent companies and making distributions to creditors do so honestly and are accountable.

8.1.2 Insolvency proceedings

Insolvency proceedings are governed by the Insolvency Act 1986 (IA 1986) and rules made thereunder. These are principally the Insolvency Rules 1986 (IR 1986). In addition, the Company Directors Disqualification Act 1986 (see **7.8**) is important as it provides for penalties on directors who have run their companies into insolvency in disregard of the interests of the creditors of their companies.

A creditor faced with a company that has not paid its debts has a number of options:

(a) If the creditor has been able to obtain security for the indebtedness from the company, it may seek to enforce its security. This is done typically either by selling the assets comprising the security, or by appointing a receiver or administrator.

(b) To apply to the court for an administration order. This is an order under which an administrator is appointed by the court to formulate and put into operation a recovery plan, which is aimed at enabling the company to pay its debts.

(c) Seek a voluntary arrangement, that is, an agreement with creditors as to how debts will be paid.

(d) Wind up or liquidate the company, which will ultimately dissolve it.

8.1.3 Cross-border jurisdiction

Cross-border jurisdiction in insolvency proceedings involving EU countries is governed by Regulation 1346/2000 (OJ 2000 L160/1) on insolvency proceedings, which has direct effect. The main insolvency proceedings must be commenced in the Member State where the debtor has its main interests. This is assessed as at the time when a request is made for the opening of the insolvency proceedings, rather than the time when the insolvency proceedings are formally issued (*Staubitz-Schreiber* (Case C-1/04) [2006] BCC 639). The preamble says this should correspond to where the company conducts the administration of its interests on a regular basis, and is presumed to be where the company's registered office is located, in the absence of proof to the contrary (art 3(1)). The location of a company's centre of main interests is assessed by comparing the scale and importance of a company's activities in the two competing jurisdictions (*Re Ci4net.com Inc* [2005] BCC 277). If a company's main interests are carried on somewhere other than its registered office, its centre of main interests is where the functions of its head office are carried on (*Re Lennox Holdings plc* [2009] BCC 155).

Commencing main proceedings in one Member State prevents the courts in any other Member State having jurisdiction (*French Republic v Klempka* [2006] BCC 841). Any judgment in main proceedings in the court first seised will be recognised in all the other Member States (art 16). If an interested party wishes to challenge the jurisdiction of the court first seised, this must be done using the procedures of that court (*Eurofood IFSC Ltd* (Case C-341/04) [2006] BCC 397).

Amendments made to the domestic insolvency legislation following the coming into force of Regulation 1346/2000, combined with the direct effect of the Regulation itself, mean that the various procedures available under the IA 1986 can be used in respect of a company registered abroad, provided its centre of main interests is in the UK. In addition to compulsory winding up, this includes making orders confirming a creditors' voluntary winding up (*Re TXU Europe German Finance BV* [2005] BCC 90) and the making of administration orders (*Re BRAC Rent-A-Car International Inc* [2003] 1 WLR 1421). Secondary proceedings may be commenced in parallel in a Member State where the debtor has an establishment, but limited to the assets located in that State. An 'establishment' is defined as any place of operations where the company carries out non-transitory economic activity with human and physical resources (art 2(h)). This is designed to allow English insolvency procedures where a foreign company has an English branch. Where a company has subsidiaries in different countries, each set of insolvency proceedings in respect of the different companies in the group is 'main proceedings', and the concept of 'secondary proceedings' has no application (*Klempka v ISA Daisytek SA* [2003] BCC 984, unaffected by the appeal reported at [2006] BCC 841).

Where insolvency proceedings are commenced against company A under Regulation 1346/2000 on the basis that the centre of its main interests is (say) in France, company B can only be joined to those insolvency proceedings if its main interests are also within that country. Otherwise joinder would circumvent the requirements of the Regulation (*Rastelli Davide e C Snc v Hidoux* (Case C-191/10) [2013] 1 BCLC 329).

By art 1(2), the Regulation does not apply to insolvency proceedings concerning insurance undertakings, credit institutions, investment undertakings which provide services involving the holding of funds or securities for third parties, or collective investment undertakings.

8.2 Receivership, IA 1986, ss 28–49 and IR 1986, Part 3

Receivership is one of the principal ways in which a chargeholder may enforce his or her charge. The debenture will usually give debentureholders the power to appoint a receiver. However, if it does not, the court has power to appoint a receiver on the application of the debentureholders in certain circumstances including default in payment of the debt.

The principal effects of the appointment of a receiver are:

(a) directors' powers over the charged assets are suspended;

(b) floating charges crystallise;

(c) notice of the appointment must be given to the Registrar of Companies and put on all the company's documents and its websites (IA 1986, s 39; giving notice to outsiders that the company is in financial difficulty).

The principal duty of the receiver is to take control of the assets subject to the charge and pay off the debentureholders having due regard to the rights of others under IA 1986. Thus the order of priority is:

(a) Fixed chargeholders (who may realise the assets subject to their charge).

(b) Preferential creditors (who will be paid out of money subject to floating charges if there are insufficient other funds to pay them). These creditors are set out in Sch 6 as amended by the Enterprise Act 2002, s 251, and include occupational and state pension scheme contributions, employees' pay (four months or £800 per employee) and holiday pay.

(c) Floating chargeholders.

(d) Ordinary unsecured creditors.

To enable the receiver's principal duty to be carried out, the receiver is given certain powers in the debenture, for example to sell the assets subject to the charge. However, if appointed under a floating charge over the whole or substantially the whole of the company's undertaking, the receiver will be an administrator (see **8.3.3.3**) and will have all the powers set out in the debenture plus those in IA 1986, so far as consistent with the debenture. These powers were very wide and included the power to carry on the business of the company (Sch B1, para 59). This power is particularly important where the physical assets of the company are not of much value and there is a possibility of trading the company out of financial difficulty or 'hiving down' (by creating a new company, selling the viable parts of the business to the new company in exchange for shares in the new company and then selling the shares in the new company to a willing buyer; the new company thereby having the assets but not the liabilities of the old company).

The receiver is not concerned with ordinary unsecured creditors as they rank below any secured creditor.

8.3 Administration orders, IA 1986, s 8 and Sch B1 and IR 1986, Part 2

8.3.1 Nature of administration

A description of what happens on the appointment of an administrator was given by Mocatta J in *George Barker (Transport) Ltd v Eynon* [1973] 1 WLR 462:

> The appointment of [an administrator] by the debenture-holders does not end the legal life of the company; the company is so to speak anaesthetised, but the [administrator] may carry on business on its behalf. The legal persona of the company will continue to subsist until liquidation and the company in the case of the most successful [administrations] may be restored to full conscious activity when the anaesthetic is no longer applied after the debts owing to the debenture-holders have been paid.

Of course, many administrations are not so successful, and the company is soon put into liquidation.

8.3.2 Pre-Enterprise Act 2002

Administration orders were inspired by the success of receivers and managers (more recently called administrative receivers) prior to the IA 1986 in turning round or hiving down companies. It was a procedure whereby a court-appointed administrator had much the same (and in fact greater) powers than an administrative receiver. The procedure was replaced with effect from 15 September 2003 when the Enterprise Act 2002, s 248, was brought into force. The current procedure is discussed at **8.3.3**.

8.3.3 Administration under the Enterprise Act 2002

Under the Enterprise Act 2002, ss 248–250, there is a unified procedure, set out in IA 1986, Sch B1, governing administrators appointed:

- by an administration order made by the court;
- by the holder of a floating charge; and
- by the company itself.

8.3.3.1 Proper purpose test

The purpose behind administration is to achieve one of the three objectives set out in the IA 1986, Sch B1, para 3(1), which are either:

(a) to rescue the company as a going concern;

(b) to achieve a better result for the company's creditors as a whole than would be likely if the company were wound up. This will not be satisfied if administration will merely achieve no worse an outcome than a winding up (*Auto Management Services Ltd v Oracle Fleet UK Ltd* [2008] BCC 761); or

(c) to realise company property in order to make a distribution to one or more secured or preferential creditors (para 3(1)(c)). This third purpose is only permissible if the administrator thinks it is not reasonably practicable to achieve either of the other two purposes, and only if it will not unnecessarily harm the interests of the creditors of the company as a whole (para 3(4)).

These statutory purposes do not include seeking administration in place of an existing receivership with a view to getting a better price for the company's assets where it is feared the receiver may be in the process of selling those assets at an undervalue (*Doltable Ltd v Lexi Holdings plc* [2006] 1 BCLC 384). Conversely, a willingness on the part of the applicant to provide funds to the company to investigate potential claims available to the company which would otherwise be abandoned made it likely that an administration would provide a better outcome for the benefit of creditors than a liquidation in *Re Logitext UK Ltd* [2005] 1 BCLC 326. An administration order was also made in *Re British American Racing (Holdings) Ltd* [2005] BCC 110, where a sale of the company's interest in a subsidiary by an administrator was much simpler and quicker than a sale through a divided board, and so would produce a better result for the company's creditors as a whole.

The appointment of an administrator is not permitted if the company is already in administration (para 7) or in liquidation (para 8).

8.3.3.2 Administration orders

Administration orders can principally be applied for by the company, its directors and creditors (para 12(1)). An alleged creditor will not have standing to seek an administration order if the debt is disputed on substantial grounds. This is the same as the test used in relation to standing to present a winding-up petition (see **9.6.3**: *Thunderbird Industries LLC v Simoco Digital UK Ltd* [2004] 1 BCLC 541). Notification must be given to interested parties (para 12(2)).

An administration order can be made if the court is satisfied that the company is, or is likely to become, unable to pay its debts, and if making an order is reasonably likely to achieve one of the para 3 purposes of administration (see **8.3.3.1**) (para 11). 'Reasonably likely' in para 11 does not mean on the balance of probabilities, but that there is a real prospect (*Auto Management Services Ltd v Oracle Fleet UK Ltd* [2008] BCC 761).

8.3.3.3 Administrator appointed by floating chargeholder

An administrator may alternatively be appointed by the holder of a qualifying floating charge (para 14(1)). A floating charge 'qualifies' if it states that Sch B, para 14, applies, or if it purports to empower the holder to appoint an administrator or a person who would be an administrative receiver. A person holds a qualifying floating charge if he or she holds one or more debentures which together, or together with secured charges, relate to the whole or substantially the whole of the company's property (para 14(3)). Before appointing an administrator the holder of a qualifying floating charge must give at least two business days' written notice to the holder of any prior floating charge, or the prior chargee must consent in writing. An appointment can only be made at a time when the qualifying floating charge is enforceable (para 16), and cannot be made if there is a provisional liquidator or administrative receiver in office (para 17). Notice of the appointment must be filed in court together with a statutory declaration (para 18).

8.3.3.4 Administrator appointed by the company

An administrator can be appointed by the company or its directors (para 22). However, this is not permitted within 12 months of a previous administration or moratorium under IA 1986, Sch A1 (paras 23 and 24), nor if a petition to wind up has been presented, or if an administration application has not been disposed of, or if an administrative receiver is in post (para 25). The applicant must give five days' notice to persons entitled to appoint an administrator under a qualifying floating charge (para 26). The para 26 notice together with a statutory declaration in the prescribed forms must be filed at court, and once the administrator is appointed, notice of the appointment and a statement from the administrator setting out his or her consent to act and the purpose of the administration must also be filed (para 27).

8.3.3.5 Effect of administration

An administrator is an officer of the court (para 5) and must be a qualified insolvency practitioner (para 6). The administrators will normally be those nominated by the applicant, and it is not appropriate to hold a head count of creditors before deciding who should be appointed (*Re World Class Homes Ltd* [2005] 2 BCLC 1).

A petition for winding up is dismissed on the making of an administration order, and is suspended if the administrator is appointed by a floating chargee (para 40). The making of an administration order results in the vacation of office of any administrative receiver (para 41). While in administration, there is a moratorium on resolutions for winding up and orders for winding up and appointing administrative receivers (paras 42 and 43(6A)). Forfeiture by landlords, taking steps to enforce any security, and repossession of goods in the company's possession under a hire-purchase agreement are only permitted with the consent of the administrator or the court's permission (para 43). Permission to commence proceedings is only granted if the circumstances are exceptional (*AES Barry Ltd v TXU Europe Energy Trading Ltd* [2005] 2 BCLC 22).

8.3.3.6 Progress of administration

Administrators must exercise their functions in the interests of the company's creditors as a whole (para 3(2)) and as quickly and efficiently as is reasonably practicable (para 4). The administrator must make a statement setting out proposals for achieving the purpose of the administration, which must be sent out to creditors accompanied by an invitation to an initial creditors' meeting (paras 49 and 51). The meeting may approve or modify the proposals (but only with the administrator's consent) (para 53). If the meeting disagrees, the administrator reports to the court (para 55) which may decide that the administration shall cease, adjourn, make an interim order, make an order to wind up the company or any other order. The appointment lasts for 12 months, although this can be extended by the court (and, for up to six months by the consent of all secured creditors or, in certain circumstances, 50 per cent of preferential creditors) (paras 76 and 78). While an extension cannot be granted after the expiry of the administrator's office (para 77(1)(b)), an extension can be granted provided the application is filed before the expiry date even if the hearing is thereafter (*Re TT Industries Ltd* [2006] BCC 372).

In cases where the administrator thinks that the secured creditors will be paid in full and a distribution will be made to the unsecured creditors, the administrator may file a conversion notice under para 83 to move the administration to a creditors' voluntary liquidation. In such a case the administration ends, and the voluntary liquidation commences, on the date the conversion notice is registered by the Registrar of Companies

(*Re Globespan Airways Ltd* [2013] 1 WLR 1122). If the administrator thinks the company has no property, he or she can send notice to the Registrar of Companies, which terminates his or her appointment. Three months after registration of the notice the company is deemed to be dissolved (para 84). Dissolving the company under para 84 is appropriate in cases where the court has made a direction allowing distributions to creditors under para 65 (see **8.3.3.7**), when after such distributions there are no assets left (*Re GHE Realisations Ltd* [2006] BCC 139, disapproving *Re Ballast plc* [2005] 1 WLR 1928).

8.3.3.7 Management during administration

The administrator may do anything necessary or expedient for the management of the affairs, business and property of the company (para 59(1)). He or she has the powers specified in IA 1986, Sch 1 (para 60), and may remove and appoint directors (para 61). He or she is obliged to take custody or control of all the company's property (para 67), and to manage its affairs, business and property in accordance with the proposals as approved at the creditors' meeting (para 68). In the period before their proposals are approved by the creditors, administrators are permitted to sell the assets of the company without seeking directions from the court (*Re Transbus International Ltd* [2004] 2 BCLC 550). Business documents must state the name of the administrator and that the company's affairs are being managed by him or her (para 45). The administrator may apply to the court for directions, and may make distributions to creditors (paras 63 and 65). A direction may be made for the distribution of assets to non-preferential unsecured creditors provided this is in the best interests of the company's creditors as a whole (*Re GHE Realisations Ltd* [2006] BCC 139).

8.4 Voluntary arrangements, IA 1986, ss 1–7, IR 1986, Part 1 and Insolvency Act 2000, ss 1–2

These provisions enable companies to make binding agreements with creditors. Provided the company is not in liquidation or administration, its directors may make a proposal for a composition in satisfaction of its debts or for a scheme of arrangement of its affairs (IA 1986, s 1(1)). Detailed requirements for the proposal are set out in IR 1986, r 1.3. A proposal for a CVA is made by the liquidator or administrator where the company is in liquidation or administration (s 1(3)). Where it is the directors of the company who intend to make the proposal for a CVA, provided the company is a small company and meets the eligibility criteria in Sch A1, paras 2 to 4, the directors can take steps to obtain a moratorium for the company (IA 1986, s 1A). To do this various documents have to be filed at court (Sch A1, para 7), and the moratorium comes into effect when these documents are filed (para 8(1)). During the moratorium various restrictions apply, such as a prohibition on winding-up petitions, resolutions for winding up, applications for administration, appointments of administrative receivers and re-entry by landlords (para 12). The moratorium ends with the meetings of creditors summoned under para 29, or, if the nominee fails to call meetings, 28 days after it starts (para 8(2), (4)). The moratorium can be extended by the meeting of creditors under para 32. Detailed provisions for the progress of CVAs taking advantage of the use of a moratorium are to be found in Sch A1.

In a proposal for a CVA where there is no moratorium, an insolvency practitioner will be appointed as the 'nominee', who must be provided with a statement of affairs and any other information he or she requires. The nominee will submit a report to the court on whether the proposal has a reasonable prospect of being approved and implemented (s 2(1)). If the report is favourable, the nominee convenes meetings of creditors and shareholders. A three-quarters majority is required at the creditors' meeting (calculated according to the amount owed to each creditor: IR 1986, rr 1.17 and 1.19), whereas a simple majority is required at the shareholders' meeting (r 1.20). If approved, the composition or scheme takes effect as if made at the creditors' meeting. A copy of the chairman's report of the meetings must be filed at court and sent to the Registrar of Companies (r 1.24). A composition or scheme will also take effect if approved by the creditors but rejected by the members. If this happens, a member will be allowed to apply to the court, which can make any order it thinks fit (IA 1986, s 4A).

An application can in any event be made to the court under IA 1986, s 6, challenging the decisions made at the creditors' and members' meetings. The court can revoke or suspend the decisions, or make directions for further meetings, on the ground that the scheme or composition unfairly prejudices the interests of a creditor or member or that there was some irregularity in either of the meetings. Whether there is unfair prejudice depends on all the circumstances of the case, taking into account the alternatives available and the practical consequences of the decision to confirm or reject the CVA (*Mourant & Co Trustees Ltd v Sixty UK Ltd* [2011] 1 BCLC 383). In assessing this the court often considers 'vertical' and 'horizontal' comparisons. A vertical comparison compares the outcomes for creditors provided by the proposed CVA against the outcome in a winding up. A horizontal comparison looks at how different categories of creditor are treated by the CVA. In doing this there is no absolute rule that all creditors must be treated in the same way.

There may be an irregularity for the purposes of IA 1986, s 6, where the proposal fails to disclose offers to purchase the company's business, as this may prevent the creditors reaching an informed decision (*Re Trident Fashions plc (No 2)* [2004] 2 BCLC 35). Even if there is such an irregularity, the court will only revoke the CVA if it is likely the creditors would have rejected it if given full information.

If a CVA is approved, it binds every person who was entitled to vote at the creditors' meeting, including creditors and members who were not actually given notice of the meetings (s 5). It gives rise to a form of statutory contract between the company and those creditors. The position of creditors outside a CVA (eg creditors whose debts are not admitted by the chairman at the creditors' meeting) was considered in *Oakley Smith v Greenberg* [2005] 2 BCLC 74. On the facts it was held they should be treated in the same way as unsecured creditors under the CVA.

The CVA will be administered by a 'supervisor', and it is the duty of the directors to do everything necessary for giving the supervisor possession of the assets included in the arrangement (IR 1986, r 1.23). Once transferred, such assets become subject to a trust in favour of the CVA creditors, even if the CVA subsequently fails (*Re Zebra Industrial Products Ltd* [2005] BCC 104). If the CVA requires the supervisor to carry on the business of the company or realise its assets, the supervisor must keep accounts and records of his or her dealings (r 1.26A). On completion of the CVA, the supervisor sends written notice and a report on all his or her dealings to the creditors and members bound by the CVA. The notice and report also have to be sent to the Registrar of Companies and to the court (r 1.29).

8.5 Liquidation, IA 1986, Parts IV and VI and IR 1986, Part 4

This is the ultimate sanction against a company which fails to pay its debts as it will dissolve the company. Liquidation can be voluntary (ie the company resolves to liquidate) or compulsory (the court orders that it be liquidated). Either way the effect is the same; a liquidator is appointed to realise the assets and pay off the debts. Once this task has been completed, a return is made to the Registrar of Companies and the company is dissolved and removed from the register of companies (IA 1986, s 205).

8.5.1 Voluntary liquidation, IA 1986, ss 84–116 and IR 1986, Part 4

This commences by a resolution of members in general meeting and will be a members' or creditors' liquidation. If the directors swear a statutory declaration of solvency (ie that the company will be able to pay its debts in full within a specified period not exceeding 12 months (s 89)) it will be a members' voluntary liquidation in which the creditors play no part. The liquidator is appointed by the members and reports to them.

If the directors are not prepared to swear a statutory declaration, it will be a creditors' voluntary liquidation in which the creditors will play a role. A meeting of creditors will be called within 14 days of the resolution being passed and they will appoint a liquidator (if members nominated a different person the creditors' nominee will act). The liquidator will report to a liquidation committee which is composed of representatives of members and creditors, a maximum of five of each.

If the directors make a statutory declaration without reasonable grounds for their opinion that the company will be able to pay its debts, they commit an offence, and if the company does not pay its debts within the stated period, they are presumed to have had no reasonable grounds for their opinion (s 89). Hence the incentive for the directors to ensure that the declaration is accurate.

8.5.2 Compulsory liquidation, IA 1986, ss 117–162 and IR 1986, Part 4

This is commenced by the presentation of a petition to the court by the company (rare), the directors, any creditor(s) (most frequent) or member(s) (s 124). To obtain an order, one of the grounds set out in s 122 must be proved, which includes the ground that the company is unable to pay its debts. By s 123 a company is deemed to be unable to pay its debts if:

- a statutory demand for a debt exceeding £750 has been served on the company and not paid, secured or compounded within three weeks;
- execution of a judgment debt is unsatisfied;
- the court is satisfied that the company is unable to pay its debts as they fall due.

Compulsory liquidation is considered in greater detail in **Chapter 9**, and guidance on presenting winding-up petitions in court is given in **Chapter 10**.

8.5.3 Effect of liquidation, IA 1986, ss 175–219 and 230–246 and IR 1986, Part 4

The effects of the making of an order or passing of a resolution to wind up a company are largely the same. A liquidator is appointed, the company must cease business except as necessary to wind up, all floating charges crystallise, the directors' powers cease and are assumed by the liquidator and all invoices, letters etc must show that the company is being wound up. The liquidator takes control of the assets, realises them and pays off the debts in the order of priority under IA 1986, which is basically:

- fixed chargeholders (who may realise the assets subject to their charge);
- preferential creditors;
- floating chargeholders;
- unsecured creditors;
- payments due to members (eg unpaid declared dividends);
- return of capital to members; and
- distribution of any surplus to members in accordance with their rights.

8.5.4 Invalid transactions

Section 245 of the IA 1986 provides that a floating charge is invalid, except insofar as consideration is given for it, if given within a specified period before the onset of insolvency (defined as the commencement of liquidation or presentation of petition for an administration order). The period depends on whether the charge was given to a connected person (defined in ss 249 and 435 to include directors, their relatives and companies under their control), in which case it is two years; or unconnected persons, in which case it is one year. In addition, if the charge was given to an unconnected person it must be shown that at the time the charge was granted the company was unable to pay its debts or became so as a result of the charge.

Section 238 empowers the court to set aside a transaction at an undervalue (ie where the company makes a gift or receives consideration significantly less than that provided by the company), unless it was made in good faith on reasonable belief that it would benefit the company. A genuine sale of assets by the company to a shareholder will not be set aside even if objectively the company has made a bad bargain and so has sold the asset at an undervalue (*Progress Property Co Ltd v Moorgarth Group Ltd* [2011] 1 WLR 1). Where there are linked transactions, the 'consideration' will be the value received by the company from the transactions as a whole, see *Phillips v Brewin Dolphin Bell Lawrie Ltd* [2001] 1 WLR 143, HL. The transaction may be set aside if it was made within two years of the onset of insolvency provided that at the time of the transaction the company was unable to pay its debts or became unable to do so as a result of the transaction (presumed if the transaction was with a connected person).

Section 239 empowers the court to set aside preferences, that is, any transaction whereby the company puts a creditor in a better position in the event of the company's insolvency than he or she would otherwise have been, provided the company was influenced by a desire to prefer the creditor (this is presumed if the preference was given to a connected person) and the preference was given within six months of insolvency (if to an unconnected person) or two years (if to a connected person).

Under IA 1986, ss 423–425, a transaction at an undervalue may be set aside if it can be shown that the purpose of the transaction was to put assets beyond the reach of creditors, or to prejudice creditors' interests in some other way. A transaction is at an undervalue if:

- it is by way of gift, or otherwise made in return for no consideration;
- the transaction is entered into in contemplation of marriage; or
- the consideration is significantly less than the value of the consideration provided by the company.

There is no time limit for setting aside such transactions. The principal difficulty is in proving the prohibited purpose of the transaction.

8.6 Personal liability in liquidation

8.6.1 Summary remedy against delinquent directors

Under IA 1986, s 212, if on the winding up of a company it appears that an officer or person concerned in the management, promotion or formation of the company has misapplied and retained or become accountable for company property and been guilty of any misfeasance or breach of duty to the company, the court may compel him or her to repay, restore or account for the property or pay compensation for the breach. Liability under s 212 is imposed on persons who are in a position to prevent avoidable harm to the company's creditors (*Revenue and Customs Commissioners v Holland* [2011] 1 WLR 2793, SC). A sole director of a company that is the sole corporate director of the company being wound up will not be liable under s 212 if all his or her acts are held to be attributable to his or her role as a director of the corporate director rather than the company being wound up (*Revenue and Customs Commissioners v Holland*). A corporate director is a different legal person to the company being wound up.

8.6.2 Fraudulent trading

Under IA 1986, s 213, where on the winding up of a company it appears to the court that the company has been carried on with intent to defraud creditors, it may declare any persons knowingly parties to it liable to contribute to the company's assets. Section 213 is most commonly used against directors. It does not apply to employees who are merely carrying out orders, but it can be used against persons not in managerial or controlling roles within the company if they were involved in, and assisted and benefited from, an offending business or one which was carried on in an offending way (*Re Bank of Credit and Commerce International SA, Banque Arabe Internationale d'Investissement SA v Morris* [2001] 1 BCLC 263). Actual dishonesty on the part of the defendants must be shown (*Re Patrick and Lyon Ltd* [1933] Ch 786). This provision was taken from an existing provision in CA 1985 which had little success because of the difficulty in proving the necessary intent.

8.6.3 Wrongful trading

Under IA 1986, s 214, the court may declare a director to be liable to contribute to the company's funds if there has been wrongful trading. There are four issues in establishing liability:

(a) that the company went into insolvent liquidation;

(b) that at some point before the commencement of the winding up a director knew, or ought to have concluded, that there was no reasonable prospect that the company could avoid insolvent liquidation;

(c) that the respondent was a director at the time; and

(d) that the director had failed to take every step he or she ought to have taken to minimise the potential loss to creditors.

The burden of proof on the first three issues is on the liquidator, and the burden of proof on the fourth issue is on the director (*Re Idessa (UK) Ltd* [2012] 1 BCLC 80). The standard in judging the facts which the director ought to have known, the conclusions reached and steps taken is that of a reasonably diligent person having the knowledge, skill and experience of that director and that which might reasonably be expected of a person carrying out the same functions as the director. Thus the test is both objective and subjective. It is important not to invoke hindsight, and to give proper regard to the difficult choices which often confront directors when deciding whether to continue trading and on what basis (*Re Idessa (UK) Ltd*). However, conduct that might be justifiable when the company is solvent might be wholly inappropriate at a time when the company is of doubtful solvency (*Roberts v Frohlich* [2011] 2 BCLC 625). According to *Re Produce Marketing Consortium Ltd* [1989] 1 WLR 745, a director is to be treated as possessing information which was capable of being ascertained had the company fulfilled its statutory duties and which the director ought to have ascertained. The directors were found liable and ordered to contribute £75,000. While s 213 applies to any person party to the fraudulent trading, s 214 applies only to directors, although shadow directors (those on whose instructions the board is accustomed to act, see **7.1.2.2**) are included.

8.7 Fixing and approval of the remuneration of appointees

Practice Statement: The Fixing and Approval of the Remuneration of Appointees [2004] BCC 912 sets out the procedure on applications to set or vary remuneration to insolvency practitioners for performing their functions under the IA 1986. The objective of the practice statement is to ensure that remuneration is fair, reasonable and commensurate with the nature and extent of the work properly undertaken by the appointee in any given case (para 3.2). Applications are usually dealt with by a registrar or district judge (para 4.1). Detailed guidance on the evidence to be adduced is contained in para 5.2.

9

Compulsory winding up

9.1 Introduction

Liquidation (or winding up) is the process whereby a company's business, assets and liabilities are terminated, realised and distributed, after which the company is dissolved and ceases to exist. Liquidations fall into two categories: voluntary and compulsory. Voluntary liquidations fall into two sub-categories: members' voluntary liquidations and creditors' voluntary liquidations. A members' voluntary liquidation is initiated by a solvent company's shareholders, the directors making a declaration of solvency (that after full inquiry they are of the opinion that the company will be able to pay its debts in full within a specified period not exceeding 12 months). A creditors' voluntary liquidation is also initiated by the shareholders, but the directors have not made a declaration of the company's solvency. The liquidator will usually be appointed by the company's unsecured creditors (as opposed to the shareholders in a members' voluntary liquidation).

A compulsory liquidation, on the other hand, is commenced by a petition being presented to the court, usually by an unpaid creditor. Petitions may also be presented by the company, its directors, and contributories (which broadly means those persons, such as holders of partly paid shares, who are liable to contribute to the assets of the company in the event of it being wound up: IA 1986, s 79). Compulsory winding up is a form of hostile litigation, generally resorted to by unpaid creditors as a means of recovering unpaid debts, with the threat of dissolution if the company does not pay.

The major practitioner text on winding up of companies is *Applications to Wind Up Companies*, Derek French, 2nd edn (OUP, 2008).

9.2 Superseding voluntary winding up with compulsory winding up

In *Re Gordon and Breach Science Publishers Ltd* [1995] BCC 261 the company was in voluntary liquidation. It was alleged that the controllers of the company had arranged to pay certain favoured creditors at the expense of the rest. Companies associated with the debtor company claimed they were owed substantial sums, and voted, it was alleged, to have a liquidator appointed in the voluntary liquidation who would view matters in a way favourable to the debtor company. It was held that even though the voluntary liquidation was well advanced, a substantial independent creditor was entitled to an order for the compulsory liquidation of the company, because such a creditor is entitled to have an independent investigation of the company's affairs. See also *Re Inside Sports Ltd* [2000] BCC 40.

9.3 Grounds for compulsory winding up

9.3.1 Statutory grounds for winding up

The grounds on which a company may be compulsorily wound up are set out in IA 1986, s 122(1), as follows:

A company may be wound up by the court if—

(a) the company has by special resolution resolved that the company be wound up by the court,

(b) being a public company which was registered as such on its original incorporation, the company has not been issued with a trading certificate under section 761 of the Companies Act 2006 (requirement as to minimum share capital) and more than a year has expired since it was so registered,

(c) it is an old public company, within the meaning of Schedule 3 to the Companies Act 2006 (Consequential Amendments, Transitional Provisions and Savings) Order 2009,

(d) the company does not commence its business within a year from its incorporation or suspends its business for a whole year,

(e) [repealed]

(f) the company is unable to pay its debts,

(fa) at the time at which a moratorium for the company under section 1A comes to an end, no voluntary arrangement approved under Part I has effect in relation to the company,

(g) the court is of the opinion that it is just and equitable that the company should be wound up.

Further, by IA 1986, s 124A, the Secretary of State may present petitions to wind up companies in certain circumstances where it is in the public interest for this to be done.

Ground (g), that it is just and equitable that the company be wound up, is often met in the context of giving relief to disgruntled minority shareholders, and will be considered in more detail in **Chapter 12**. The ground most commonly relied on is ground (f), that the company is unable to pay its debts.

9.3.2 Debts

'Debts' for the purpose of IA 1986, s 122(1)(f), are liquidated amounts owed by the company, but include contingent and prospective liabilities (future liabilities). Although there is an extended definition of the word 'debt' in IR 1986, r 13.12 (discussed at **9.9.3.3**), that applies at the later stage after a winding-up order is made, or after a company enters into voluntary liquidation.

An obligation to pay the costs of civil proceedings was regarded as being a 'debt' for these purposes even before costs were assessed in *Tottenham Hotspur plc v Edennote plc* [1994] BCC 681. If the contract under which a liability arises requires a demand for payment (eg guarantees in the nature of collateral debts), there will be no subsisting 'debt' until the sum is demanded. A statutory demand (see **9.3.3**, para (a)) will not amount to such a demand (*TS & S Global Ltd v Fithian-Franks* [2008] 1 BCLC 277).

9.3.3 Presumptions of inability to pay debts

Four statutory presumptions of inability to pay debts are contained in IA 1986, s 123(1), (2), namely where:

(a) The company owes a debt exceeding £750 and the creditor has served a statutory demand for the debt by leaving the statutory demand at the company's registered office, and the company neglects to pay or to secure or compound for it to the creditor's satisfaction within 21 days. Statutory demands are governed by IR 1986, rr 4.2 and 4.4–4.6. A prescribed form must be used. It states the amount of the debt and interest, and how it was incurred, and warns that if payment or an acceptable proposal for payment is not made within 21 days after it is received, winding-up proceedings may be instituted.

As just stated, the statutory demand must be 'served' by 'leaving it' at the company's registered office. After some doubt, it now appears to be the case that it is sufficient if the demand is posted to the registered office: see *Re a Company (No 008790 of 1990)* [1992] BCC 11, disapproving *Re a Company* [1985] BCLC 37. However, there are no presumptions as to the fact and date of service if the Post Office is used, so delivery has to be proved or admitted. It is probable that the rules on giving notice and the supply of documents in IR 1986, rr 12A.1–12A.5 do not apply to service of statutory demands, because 'leaving' a statutory demand is different from 'given, delivered or sent', the phrase used in r 12A.1(1). IR 1986, rr 12A.16–12A.20 on service of court documents also do not apply, because statutory demands are not court documents.

A winding-up petition can be validly based on a statutory demand claiming the wrong amount, provided the statutory demand is sufficiently clear and provided there is still an indisputable debt above the statutory minimum of £750: *Re Tweeds Garages Ltd* [1962] Ch 406.

(b) Judgment has been entered against the company, and execution on that judgment has been returned unsatisfied in whole or in part.

(c) It is proved to the satisfaction of the court that the company is unable to pay its debts as they fall due (IA 1986, s 123(1)(e)). The phrase 'fall due' means 'become due', and includes, if known, the company's future liabilities (*Re Cheyne Finance plc* [2008] BCC 182 at [49]–[70]) falling due in the reasonably near future. What constitutes the reasonably near future depends on the circumstances of the case and the nature of the company's business *(BNY Corporate Trustee Services Ltd v Eurosail-UK 2007-3BL plc* [2013] 1 WLR 1408).

The circumstances surrounding the non-payment of a debt may justify the inference that the company is unable to pay its debts as they fall due. A series of dishonoured cheques may be good evidence to justify this inference. Further, the mere failure to pay a debt is of itself evidence of inability to pay where the debt is due, an invoice has been sent and the company has not advanced reasons for non-payment: *Re Taylor's Industrial Flooring Ltd* [1990] BCC 44, CA. Consequently, it is not always necessary to serve a statutory demand before issuing a winding-up petition based on non-payment of a debt. However, care must be taken before petitioning on this basis. If it later transpires there was a genuine dispute over the petition debt, not only will the petition be dismissed, but indemnity-basis costs and even wasted-costs orders may be imposed (see *Re a Company (No 006798 of 1995)* [1996] 1 WLR 491).

(d) It is proved to the satisfaction of the court that the value of the company's assets is less than its liabilities, taking into account its contingent and prospective liabilities (IA 1986, s 123(2)). This is a 'balance-sheet' test. It requires the court to make a judgement, determined on the balance of probabilities, on whether the company had insufficient assets to meet its current and future liabilities, making proper allowance (discounting for contingencies and deferment) for its prospective and contingent liabilities (*BNY Corporate Trustee Services Ltd v Eurosail-UK 2007-3BL plc* [2013] 1 WLR 1408). This subsection does not come into operation every time a company's assets fall below its liabilities. The court has to take a long-term view, and form a judgement based on commercial reality and fairness.

9.4 *Locus standi*

The following persons can present a winding-up petition (see IA 1986, ss 124–124C):

- the company;
- its directors;
- a creditor;
- a contingent or prospective creditor;
- a contributory (ie shareholder), subject to complying with IA 1986, s 124(2);
- various officials, for example the Secretary of State, the Financial Conduct Authority, official receivers and the Regulator of Community Interest Companies.

Section 124(2) is to the effect that to be entitled to petition as a contributory a shareholder must have held the shares for at least six out of the 18 months before presenting the petition, or must have been the original allottee of the shares, or they must have devolved on the petitioner through the death of a previous owner. Further, the courts have decided that the petitioner must have a financial interest in the winding up of the company. This will be satisfied either if the shares are partly paid (fairly rare in modern times) or if there is likely to be a surplus available for distribution to shareholders on a winding up of the company. The holder of fully paid shares in an insolvent company has no sufficient financial interest: *Re Rica Gold Washing Co* (1879) 11 ChD 36. The fact the petitioner holds a small proportion of the issued shares is not a bar to presenting a petition if the company is likely to be solvent (see *Bryanston Finance Ltd v de Vries (No 2)* [1976] Ch 63).

9.5 Procedure on the petition

9.5.1 The petition

The level of detail required to be set out in the petition depends on the nature of the case. For example, petitions presented by contingent creditors (which are relatively unusual) must contain material from which the court can infer the company is unable to pay its debts. General allegations in petitions presented by contingent creditors merely stating the grounds in the statute will be struck out as abuses of process: *Securum Finance Ltd v Camswell Ltd* [1994] BCC 434. On the other hand, petitions based on non-payment after service of a statutory demand, the failure to satisfy a judgment debt or non-payment of invoices, give little more than the basic details required by the prescribed form of petition. All petitions must follow IR 1986, Sch 4, Form 4.2.

The precedent in Figure 9.1 is an example of a winding-up petition based on a statutory demand. As mentioned in **2.1**, generally the High Court and county courts have concurrent jurisdiction, so the petitioner can choose which court to proceed in. The petitioner or someone concerned with or having knowledge of the matters giving rise to the petition must verify the petition with a statement of truth, which may be endorsed on the petition, or be in a separate document, such as a witness statement. Where the statement of truth is in a separate document, it must identify the petition, and specify the name and registered number of the company, the name of the petitioner and the court in which the petition is to be presented (IR 1986, r 4.12(3A)). The petitioner pays the £220 court fee for issuing the petition and the sum of £1,165 as security for the official receiver's fees. The petition and verifying statement of truth are filed in court, and the court allocates a case number to the petition and fixes a hearing date, which is endorsed on the petition. This is usually several weeks in advance, to provide sufficient time for service and advertisement.

Figure 9.1 Winding-up petition based on service of statutory demand

IN THE HIGH COURT OF JUSTICE No 1329 of 2014

CHANCERY DIVISION

COMPANIES COURT

IN THE MATTER of Woodcroft Kitchen Company Limited, Registered No: 9884321

AND IN THE MATTER of the Insolvency Act 1986

To Her Majesty's High Court of Justice
The petition of Rosewall Electricals Limited of 17 Commercial Road, Enfield, EN1 6DZ

1. Woodcroft Kitchen Company Limited, Registered No: 9884321 (hereinafter called 'the Company') was incorporated on the 20th day of May 1999 under the Companies Act 1985 as a company limited by shares.
2. The registered office of the Company is at 39 London Road, Potters Bar, Hertfordshire.
3. The nominal capital of the Company is £1,000 divided into 1,000 shares of £1 each. The amount of the capital paid up or credited as paid up is £200.
4. The principal objects for which the Company was established are to carry on business as retailers of kitchen furnishings and appliances and other objects stated in the memorandum of association of the Company.
5. The Company is unable to pay its debts. The Company is indebted to the Petitioner in the sum of £5,642.43 in respect of 19 XM–20 washing machines sold and delivered by the Petitioner to the Company on 28th of October 2013.
6. The Company is not an insurance undertaking; a credit institution; an investment undertaking providing services involving the holding of funds or securities for third parties; or a collective investment undertaking as referred to in Article 1.2 of the EC Regulation.
7. For the reasons stated in the statement of truth of Jennifer Williams filed in support hereof it is considered that the EC Regulation on Insolvency Proceedings will apply and that these proceedings will be main proceedings as defined in Article 3 of the EC Regulation.
8. A statutory demand was served on the company on 5th December 2013. More than 4 months have elapsed between the service of the statutory demand and the presentation of this petition for the reasons set out in the statement of truth of Jennifer Williams filed in support hereof.
9. In the circumstances it is just and equitable that the Company should be wound up.

The Petitioner therefore prays as follows:

(1) that Woodcroft Kitchen Company Limited, Registered No: 9884321 may be wound up by the Court under the provisions of the Insolvency Act 1986 or

(2) that such other order may be made as the court thinks fit.

Note: It is intended to serve this petition on the Company.

ENDORSEMENT

This petition having been presented to the court on the 24th of April 2014 will be heard at the Royal Courts of Justice, Strand, London WC2A 2LL on:

Date 25th of June 2014

Time 10.30 hours
(or as soon thereafter as the petition can be heard)

The solicitor to the petitioner is:
Messrs Thomas and Williams, of 28 Commercial Road, Enfield EN1 6DZ.
Telephone: 0208–609290.
Reference JBT.

9.5.2 Service

Service of the petition and verifying statement of truth is the responsibility of the petitioner (IPPD, para 1.3), and must generally be effected at the company's registered office: IR 1986, r 4.8(2). Permissible methods of service are set out in r 4.8(3), which provides:

Service of the petition at the registered office may be effected in any of the following ways—

(a) it may be handed to a person who there and then acknowledges himself to be, or to the best of the server's knowledge, information and belief is, a director or other officer, or employee, of the company; or

(b) it may be handed to a person who there and then acknowledges himself to be authorised to accept service of documents on the company's behalf; or

(c) in the absence of any such person as is mentioned in sub-paragraph (a) or (b), it may be deposited at or about the registered office in such a way that it is likely to come to the notice of a person attending at the office.

If service by any of these methods is not practicable, the petitioner may instead either:

- effect service at the company's last known principal place of business, under IR 1986, r 4.8(4); or
- make an application without notice to any other party supported by a witness statement for an order for substituted service under IR 1986, r 4.8(6), (7).

Service of the petition is proved by a certificate of service (CPR Form N215), which must be filed at least five business days before the hearing of the petition. The certificate of service must be sufficient to identify the petition served, and must give various details about the company and the proceedings as set out in IR 1986, r 4.9A. In particular it must specify the date of service and the method of service used (r 4.9A(2)(g), (h)). Any order for substituted service must be attached to the certificate: IR 1986, r 4.9A(3).

9.5.3 Advertisement

Winding up of a company obviously affects not only the company itself, but also its members and creditors. Shareholders and existing creditors may have their own views on whether the company should be wound up, and may wish to support or oppose the petition. Persons who may do business with the company in the future will be affected by IA 1986, s 127 (for which, see **9.8**), which will, subject to the court validating the transaction, avoid any disposal of the company's property after the presentation of the petition if a winding-up order is eventually made. All of these people need to be notified of the petition, and this is done by advertising it in the *London Gazette*.

By virtue of IR 1986, r 4.11(4)(b), the advertisement must appear not less than seven business days after service of the petition on the company and not less than seven business days before the hearing of the petition. Business days are all days apart from Saturdays, Sundays and bank holidays. These periods are to give the company sufficient time to pay or to seek an injunction (for which, see **9.6**) before the appearance of the potentially damaging advertisement, and to give other affected persons (shareholders and creditors) time to appear at the hearing.

In *Re Signland Ltd* [1982] 2 All ER 609, Slade J said:

> . . . the principal reasons why the rules have directed that advertisement shall take place not less than seven clear days after service on the company are (1) to give a company served with a winding-up petition the opportunity to discharge the debt in question, if it is undisputed, before advertisement takes place, with all the necessarily potentially damaging consequences to the company, and (2) to enable the company, if it wishes to dispute the debt, to apply to the court to restrain advertisement.

There is a prescribed form of advertisement, Form 4.6. Its contents are laid down by IR 1986, rr 12A.33(2), 12A.34 and 4.11(5) as follows:

12A.33(2) All notices published [in the Gazette] must specify insofar as it is applicable in relation to the particular notice—

(a) the name and postal address of the office-holder acting in the proceedings;

(b) the capacity in which the office-holder is acting and the date of appointment;

(c) either an e-mail address, or a telephone number, through which the office-holder may be contacted;

(d) the name of any person other than the office-holder (if any) who may be contacted regarding the proceedings;

(e) the number assigned to the office-holder by the Secretary of State; and

(f) the court name and any number assigned to the proceedings by the court.

12A.34 In addition to the information required by r 12A.33 a notice [in the Gazette] relating to a company must specify—

(a) the registered name of the company;

(b) its registered number;

(c) its registered office, or if an unregistered company, the postal address of its principal place of business;

(d) any principal trading address if this is different from its registered office;

(e) any name under which it was registered in the 12 months prior to the date of the commencement of the proceedings which are the subject of the Gazette notice; and

(f) any name or style (other than its registered name) under which—

(i) the company carried on business; and

(ii) any debt owed to a creditor was incurred.

4.11(5) In addition to the standard contents, the notice [in the Gazette under r 4.11(4)] must state—

(a) that a petition has been presented for the winding up of the company;

(b) in the case of an overseas company, the address at which service of the petition was effected;

(c) the name and address of the petitioner;

(d) the date on which the petition was presented;

(e) the venue fixed for the hearing of the petition;

(f) the name and address of the petitioner's solicitor (if any); and

(g) that any person intending to appear at the hearing (whether to support or oppose the petition) must give notice of his intention in accordance with Rule 4.16.

If the petition is not duly advertised in accordance with r 4.11, the court may dismiss it (r 4.11(6)). This power is used where the failure operates in a manner oppressive to the company, or where the circumstances are otherwise unsatisfactory. In most other cases, the court will allow an adjournment to enable proper advertisement to take place (*Secretary of State for Trade and Industry v North West Holdings plc* [1999] 1 BCLC 425). There have been cases where the petitioner has informed the company's bank and other creditors about the petition, or even issued a press notice about the petition, before the seven days after service have expired. It is clear that this does not constitute 'advertisement' of the petition within the meaning of r 4.11, which is restricted to advertisement in the *Gazette*, and consequently the court cannot dismiss the petition under r 4.11(6) in these circumstances (*Secretary of State for Trade and Industry v North West Holdings plc* [1999] 1 BCLC 425). Premature notification of a petition to creditors may, however, result in the petition being struck out in the court's inherent jurisdiction if the petitioner's conduct amounts to an abuse of process (*Re SN Group plc* [1994] 1 BCLC 319). In public interest petitions, if a provisional liquidator is appointed (see **9.7**), it is usually justifiable for the Secretary of State to issue a press notice once the order appointing the provisional liquidator is obtained. If there is any doubt, the court can be asked for directions about notifying other persons in advance of the advertisement in the *Gazette* (*Secretary of State for Trade and Industry v North West Holdings plc* [1999] 1 BCLC 425).

9.5.4 Certificate of compliance

A certificate in Form 4.7 must be filed five business days before the hearing. This proves due compliance with the rules on service and advertisement, and a copy of the advertisement must be filed with the certificate.

9.5.5 Dispute by the company

Winding up is not a suitable procedure for trying a disputed debt. If the company genuinely disputes the debt on which a petition is founded, it may:

(a) apply to strike out the petition; or

(b) apply for an injunction to restrain the petition (see **9.6**); or

(c) file a witness statement in opposition no less than five business days before the hearing under IR 1986, r 4.18 and argue that a winding-up order should not be made.

Defended petitions are referred to the judge and are considered in the Companies Court.

An example of a genuinely disputed claim was *Re a Company (No 00751 of 1992), ex p Avocet Aviation Ltd* [1992] BCLC 869. The company entered into an agreement with the creditor under which the creditor agreed to supply an aircraft undercarriage for £34,400. This sum was paid, but the creditor raised a second invoice for £44,109 for additional work done, relying on terms in its standard terms and conditions allowing it to make such a charge. The company immediately wrote back denying it had agreed to pay the supplementary charge, and denying it had knowledge of the standard terms or that they had been agreed. There was no previous course of dealing between the parties, and there was conflicting evidence of trade usage. Without serving a statutory demand, the creditor petitioned for the winding up of the company. This was held to be a case where there was a substantial dispute, so the petition was an abuse of process. In this case, and in the earlier case of *Re a Company (No 0012209 of 1991)* [1992] 1 WLR 351, it was also ordered that the creditor should pay the company's costs on the indemnity basis.

An unsuccessful petitioner may also find itself in further difficulty. If it is held that there was no rational basis for genuinely believing there was a proper basis for presenting the petition, that there were no reasonable grounds in law for presenting it, and that presentation of the petition was actuated by malice or improper motive, the company may bring separate proceedings claiming damages for the tort of malicious presentation of the petition (see *Partizan Ltd v O.J. Kilkenny and Co Ltd* [1998] 1 BCLC 157).

9.5.6 Supporting and opposing creditors

Any creditors or shareholders who wish to support or oppose the making of a winding-up order may appear at the hearing provided they first serve notice of their intention to appear on the petitioner's solicitors by 4 pm on the day before the hearing. The notice is in Form 4.9, and states whether the intention is to support or oppose the petition. A creditor giving notice must state the amount and nature of its debt. If notice is not given, a creditor can only appear if leave is granted to do so out of time.

On the day before the hearing the petitioner compiles a list in Form 4.10 of supporting and opposing creditors and contributories, which is provided for the court on the day of the hearing.

The court's practice is to allow the rationally supportable view of the majority of independent creditors to prevail. However, it is always possible for the majority view to be displaced in the circumstances of any individual case (see *Re Piccadilly Property Management Ltd* [2000] BCC 44).

9.5.7 The hearing

Disputed petitions are given special appointments. The bulk of undisputed petitions in the High Court are heard by the Companies Court Registrar in open court on Wednesdays. Under IA 1986, s 125(1), the court has power to dismiss the petition, adjourn the hearing conditionally or unconditionally, make any interim order, or any other order it thinks fit. Hearings are usually very short. Adjournments may be granted to allow time for advertisement or other steps required by the Insolvency Rules which have not been taken before the hearing, or to allow time for payment, or to allow the company time to propose a voluntary arrangement. Following an order adjourning the petition, unless the court orders otherwise, the petitioner must give notice of the order and the venue for the adjourned hearing to the company and to any creditors who have given notice under IR 1986, r 4.16 (see r 4.18A).

If the court is satisfied there is a properly presented petition by an undoubted creditor of a clearly insolvent company, a winding-up order will normally be made, unless there is a special reason why the company should not be wound up (*Re Lummus Agricultural Services Ltd* [2001] 1 BCLC 137). Opposition from other creditors only tends to carry much weight where the creditors are independent of the company. The views of secured creditors are usually accorded little or no weight, because they are protected to the value of their security (*Re Demaglass Holdings Ltd* [2001] 2 BCLC 633).

Where a majority of independent unsecured creditors have good reasons for opposing the proposed winding up, the court will carry out a balancing exercise, assessing the weight of the reasons for and against a winding up. Factors to be considered include whether the petitioner could be adequately protected by some other means, and the principle that ordinarily it is the duty of the court to order a winding up (*Re Demaglass Holdings Ltd* [2001] 2 BCLC 633). Guidance on the presentation of winding-up petitions can be found in **Chapter 10**.

9.5.8 Costs

If the petition is dismissed (typically because no one attends at the Wednesday hearing), the normal practice is for there to be no order as to costs. If an opposed petition is dismissed, costs usually follow the event, which means that the petitioner is usually ordered to pay the costs of the company. Where the petition is successful, the usual compulsory order includes payment of the petitioner's costs. There is no need for the advocate to make specific reference to costs in these circumstances, as they are included in the usual terms of the orders used by the court. The creditor is also usually entitled to its costs where the company buys off the petition by paying before it is heard (*Re Ryan Developments Ltd* [2002] 2 BCLC 792), although, as costs are discretionary, there is some scope for arguing that the petitioner's conduct was unreasonable in order to persuade the court to make some other costs order (*Holmes v Mainstream Ventures Ltd* [2010] 1 BCLC 651).

Where a winding-up order is made in an opposed petition, the costs of the company may be allowed as an expense of the petition under IR 1986, r 4.218(3)(h). This is appropriate where the opposition to the petition is in the best interests of the company, and provided those directing the company's opposition are not acting in their own self-interest (*Re Portsmouth City Football Club Ltd* [2013] 1 BCLC 572).

9.5.9 Substitution

Sometimes a petitioner does not see a petition through to obtaining a winding-up order. When this happens, another creditor may consider taking over the proceedings by asking for a substitution order. This is dealt with by IR 1986, r 4.19, which provides:

1. *This Rule applies where a person petitions and is subsequently found not entitled to do so, or where the petitioner—*
   - *(a) fails to advertise his petition within the time prescribed by the Rules or such extended time as the court may allow, or*
   - *(b) consents to withdraw his petition, or to allow it to be dismissed, consents to an adjournment, or fails to appear in support of his petition when it is called on in court on the day originally fixed for the hearing, or on a day to which it is adjourned, or*
   - *(c) appears, but does not apply for an order in the terms of the prayer of his petition.*
2. *The court may, on such terms as it thinks just, substitute as petitioner any creditor or contributory who in its opinion would have a right to present a petition, and who is desirous of prosecuting it. . . .*
3. *An order of the court under this Rule may, where a petitioner fails to advertise his petition within the time prescribed by these Rules, or consents to withdraw his petition, be made at any time.*

Where the court allows the substitution of a supporting creditor, the practice is to adjourn the petition to allow time for the petition to be amended to name the new petitioner and give details of the new petition debt, and for re-advertisement. Further notices from supporting and opposing creditors must, of course, be sent to the substituted creditor's solicitor.

9.5.10 Appeals and rescission

An appeal from a decision to wind up a company made by the Companies Court Registrar or a county court with winding-up jurisdiction lies to a single judge of the High Court (IR 1986, r 7.47(2)). Such an appeal is brought by filing an appellant's notice, and must be brought within 21 days after the decision in the lower court. Permission to appeal is required. The procedure on appeals is governed by IR 1986, r 7.49A, which imports the procedure from CPR, Part 52. A second appeal may be brought to the Court of Appeal, but only with permission of the Court of Appeal (Access to Justice Act 1999, s 55; CPR, r 52.13). An appeal in a disputed petition case from the decision of the judge is a first appeal, and lies to the Court of Appeal.

Further, every court having jurisdiction to wind up companies may review, rescind or vary any order it makes: IR 1986, r 7.47(1). An application to rescind must be made within five business days of the original order: r 7.47(4). Such an application will only be entertained if it is made by a creditor or a contributory, or by the company jointly with a creditor or contributory: *Re Mid East Trading Ltd* [1997] 3 All ER 481. The application must be supported by written evidence of assets and liabilities. If the winding-up order was made unopposed owing to some administrative error, such as some misunderstanding in briefing counsel, the application, if made promptly, may be dealt with on a statement by counsel of the circumstances (para 7.4). Otherwise the application will have to be further supported by written evidence setting out the circumstances.

On hearing an application to rescind a winding-up order the court may give permission for creditors who did not appear when the original order was made to be heard: *Re Dollar Land (Feltham) Ltd* [1995] BCC 740. The jurisdiction to rescind is exercised with great caution. The discretion should normally only be exercised if there has been a change of circumstances since the order was made, or if further evidence has been discovered which could not be adduced on an appeal (*Re Turnstem Ltd, Bhanderi v Customs and Excise Commissioners* [2005] 1 BCLC 388). Even if one of these conditions is satisfied, generally, a winding-up order will only be rescinded if the original petition debt has been or will be paid, if there is evidence the company is solvent in a general sense and if the official receiver is satisfied there is nothing requiring investigation and his costs can be paid. However, as made clear in *Re Dollar Land*, these are not invariable requirements.

9.6 Restraining winding-up proceedings

Injunctions restraining the prosecution of proceedings are recognised by the courts as being an extreme measure, but, given the commercial damage that usually results from the advertisement of winding-up petitions, it is also recognised that in suitable cases such injunctions can be granted. In fact, as mentioned at **9.5.5**, a company that finds itself the subject of unmeritorious winding-up proceedings can either apply to strike out or apply for an injunction if it wishes to stop further steps from being taken. Striking out can only be ordered after a petition has been presented, whereas it is possible to apply for an injunction on a *quia timet* basis to restrain the presentation of a petition. Otherwise, the results of the two options are similar, and it has been held that the principles to be applied are the same: *Re a Company (No 003079 of 1990)* [1991] BCC 683.

9.6.1 Procedure

Applications for *quia timet* injunctions are made by issuing an originating application in Form 7.1. After presentation of a petition, an ordinary application in those proceedings is made for an interim injunction. The application is brought in the court where the petition is or will be proceeding (IR 1986, r 4.6A). Being injunctions, they must be heard by a judge, see IPPD, para 3.2(3). A creditor who has in good faith served a statutory demand, and who undertakes not to present a petition based on it after being served with an application for an injunction to restrain such presentation, will usually also have to pay the costs of the application (*Re a Company (No 007356 of 1998)* [2000] BCC 214).

9.6.2 General principles

The jurisdiction to grant interim injunctions to restrain winding-up proceedings and the advertisement of the same derives from the court's inherent jurisdiction to prevent an abuse of its process. It is settled that the jurisdiction to grant such injunctions, whether *quia timet* or after presentation of the petition, is to be exercised with great caution, and only if there are clear and persuasive grounds. This situation is not governed by the principles in *American Cyanamid Co v Ethicon Ltd* [1975] AC 396, HL (for which, see BCP, paras 37.20—37.32). Instead, an injunction will only be granted if there is prima facie evidence that a petition will be an abuse of process: *Bryanston Finance v de Vries (No 2)* [1976] 1 Ch 63, CA (see BCP, paras 37.57 and 82.28–82.32).

9.6.3 Disputed debts

It has been said that a winding-up petition is not to be used as machinery for trying a common law claim: *Re Imperial Guardian Life Assurance Society* (1869) LR 9 Eq 44 at 450, per Sir William James V-C. Accordingly, where the petition debt is disputed by the company on not insubstantial grounds, the petition will be regarded as an abuse of process and an injunction may be granted. A further justification for this position is that if the debt is genuinely disputed the petitioner cannot be described as a 'creditor' and has no *locus standi* in the Companies Court, see *Mann v Goldstein* [1968] 1 WLR 1091, Ungoed-Thomas J.

What amounts to a genuine dispute as to liability on an alleged debt can give rise to difficult factual issues. Whether a dispute is 'substantial' turns on the quality of the evidence, not its quantity (*Re Claybridge Shipping Co SA* [1997] 1 BCLC 572, CA, where the evidence on the application extended to nine thick volumes of affidavits and exhibits). In this case a bank's petition was based on an alleged overdraft of about $30 million. The company alleged that the account had been manipulated by one of its directors acting in concert with one of the bank's employees in breach of what the company alleged was an altered mandate for operating the account. No mention of the defence had been given in a number of previous freezing injunction hearings; there was no documentary evidence to prove the new form of mandate contended for by the company; an accountancy expert had demonstrated that $15 million was, on any analysis, owing on the account; and the company was unable to demonstrate how it could contend that the account was not overdrawn. Despite the complexities, it was held that the debt was not disputed on substantial grounds.

An agreement between the company and the petitioner that an accepted debt may be paid by instalments is unenforceable for want of consideration moving from the petitioner, so will not constitute a substantial dispute warranting an injunction; see *Re Selectmove Ltd* [1994] BCC 349, CA. Apparent disputes are not simply accepted by the courts. In *MCI WorldCom Ltd v Primus* [2003] 1 BCLC 330 there were invoices in the name of a holding company to corroborate an argument that the contract was not with the party but its holding company. The court analysed the background facts and rejected the argument.

Conversely, in *Re a Company (No 003079 of 1990)* [1991] BCC 683, Ferris J held that an injunction can be granted despite the possibility that another creditor may seek to be substituted as the petitioner at the hearing, and in *MCI WorldCom Ltd v Primus* [2003] 1 BCLC 330 it was held that a petition would be struck out if there was a substantial dispute even if the company was otherwise shown to be insolvent.

9.6.4 Contingent debts

As indicated at **9.4**, a winding-up petition can be presented by a contingent creditor. The problem faced by a contingent creditor is finding a ground on which to petition, such as proving the company cannot pay its debts as they fall due. What a contingent creditor cannot do is to petition on the basis of an unsatisfied statutory demand (*JSF Finance and Currency Exchange Co Ltd v Akma Solutions Inc* [2001] 2 BCLC 307). As a contingent debt will only become due, if at all, in the future, it is premature to serve a statutory demand before the contingency occurs. If a contingent creditor nevertheless serves a statutory demand, the company should be entitled to an injunction limited to restraining the respondent from petitioning on the statutory demand: *Stonegate Securities Ltd v Gregory* [1980] 1 Ch 576, CA.

9.6.5 Cross-claims

It has been established for some time that an undisputed counterclaim amounting to a set-off in a sum exceeding the petition debt provides good grounds for granting an injunction. Conversely, where despite the existence of a counterclaim there is an undisputed balance owing to the petitioner exceeding the winding-up threshold, the petition will not be restrained: *Re Pendigo Ltd* [1996] BCC 608.

Where there is a disputed counterclaim exceeding the petition debt, until recently there was a great deal of confusion as to whether it would be right to grant an injunction. Cases like *Re FSA Business Software Ltd* [1990] BCLC 825 at first instance were to the effect that the discretion to grant an injunction should be refused where the cross-claim did not have the status of being a set-off. It was thought that the law was clarified by *Re Bayoil SA* [1999] 1 WLR 147, where it was held that an injunction could be granted (or a petition dismissed) where the company could point to a genuine and serious cross-claim against the petitioning creditor which it had not reasonably been able to litigate. Ward LJ pointed out that even if these elements were satisfied the judge still has a judicial discretion whether to grant the injunction (or dismiss the petition) and there may be special circumstances justifying the petition being allowed to proceed. Applying these principles, the court has regard to all the circumstances, and is not circumscribed by special rules, such as enforcement of adjudication decisions under the Housing Grants, Construction and Regeneration Act 1996 (see *A Practical Approach to*

ADR, 2nd edn (OUP, 2012), chapter 25). See *Shaw v MFP Foundations and Piling Ltd* [2010] 2 BCLC 85, where an order was made in favour of the debtor after service of a statutory demand to enforce an adjudicator's award where the debtor's case was that the adjudicator had been wrong, and that the creditor had been in repudiatory breach of the construction contract.

In *Re Bayoil SA* the petitioner sought to show special circumstances, in that the petition debt was based on a final and unappealable award, security had been given for the company's counterclaim, the company was of doubtful solvency and there was no real evidence that the petition debt could be paid. With the exception of the security, these points were regarded as being common in most cross-claim cases, and the addition of the security did not convert the case into a special one. The petition was dismissed. The existence of a CVA was not regarded as a special circumstance in *Re VP Developments Ltd, Penwith District Council v VP Developments Ltd* [2005] 2 BCLC 607, and the winding-up petition was dismissed. Special circumstances were found in *Atlantic and General Investment Trust Ltd v Richbell Information Services Inc* [2000] BCC 111, where the company had previously decided to wind itself up (but had not put this into action).

The most controversial issue is whether the third element in *Re Bayoil SA* is an essential requirement. In *Montgomery v Wanda Modes Ltd* [2002] 1 BCLC 289 it was said that it was not part of the *ratio decidendi* of *Re Bayoil SA* that the debtor must have been unable to litigate the cross-claim. In *Montgomery v Wanda Modes Ltd* the petition was dismissed simply on the ground that the debtor had a genuine and serious cross-claim exceeding the value of the undisputed debt. In *Popely v Popely* [2004] EWCA Civ 463 Jonathan Parker LJ said that the question of whether the company had been able to litigate its cross-claim was no more than an indication which might throw doubt on the genuineness of the cross-claim. This was affirmed by *Bolsover District Council v Dennis Rye Ltd* [2009] 4 All ER 1140, where it was held that while it is not fatal that the company may not have previously asserted, litigated or issued proceedings for the cross-claim unless it had a good excuse for not doing so, such a failure is part of the relevant circumstances in assessing the genuineness of the cross-claim.

In *Re a Company (No 006685 of 1996)* [1997] 1 BCLC 639 the petition was based on £80,000 in advertising fees said to be due under an oral contract for providing two-page inserts in a television guide. The company said in its affidavit that the agreement was for payment of £5,000 per issue, not the £10,000 per issue charged by the creditor. It was also alleged by the company that the agreement was for the adverts to be stapled into the guide, whereas the creditor only provided inserts, which it was said were significantly less effective as a marketing tool. Accordingly, the company claimed it had a substantial counterclaim for breach of contract exceeding the amount actually due. The court reaffirmed the principle that an injunction would only be granted if there was a genuine dispute based on substantial grounds. That was not the case here, as the allegations made by the company were not referred to in contemporaneous correspondence, and the creditor's invoices for £10,000 per issue were not objected to at the time. The injunction was refused.

If the cross-claim is a set-off, but does not exceed the amount of the petition debt, it is arguable that an injunction could still be granted if the balance is less than £750, the threshold for petitioning on a statutory demand (a point accepted by Lloyd J in *Greenacre Publishing Group v The Manson Group* [2000] BCC 11).

If the court finds that an alleged set-off lacks the substance necessary to constitute a genuine dispute, no injunction should be ordered. After such a finding it is contrary to principle to grant an injunction restraining advertisement of the petition pending resolution of common law proceedings dealing with the alleged set-off (*James Dolman and Co Ltd v Pedley* [2004] BCC 504).

9.6.6 Just and equitable petitions

Injunctions may be granted where the evidence establishes that the grounds alleged in the petition are bound to fail, for then the petition would be an abuse of process: *Charles Forte Investments Ltd v Amanda* [1964] 1 Ch 240, CA.

9.6.7 Exceptional cases

Dismissing petitions where the respondent company can show a substantial dispute may in certain circumstances cause undue difficulty to the petitioning creditor. In *Re Claybridge Shipping Co SA* [1997] 1 BCLC 572 Lord Denning MR pointed out the ease with which, under modern conditions, assets can be removed from the jurisdiction. There may also be significant or insurmountable difficulties in bringing ordinary proceedings against foreign companies, particularly those which might be amenable to freezing injunctions. In order to prevent foreign companies that trade in this country from frustrating their creditors in this way when things start going wrong, the courts will depart from the general rule that a disputed debt cannot form the basis of a creditor's petition. The former Master of the Rolls also said that a similar and more relaxed approach would be appropriate where the respondent company is English, but where the circumstances show there is a significant danger of its assets being put out of the reach of its creditors. In other words, there may be circumstances where winding up can be used in a similar way to freezing injunctions.

The *Claybridge Shipping* approach has been applied in exceptional cases where this is in the interests of justice because a petitioner is likely to be left without an effective remedy if the petition is struck out (see, eg, *Alipour v Ary* [1997] 1 WLR 534, CA). If there are exceptional circumstances the court will investigate the merits of a disputed debt, and, depending on the result, proceed to wind up the company. Examples identified in *Re GBI Investments Ltd* [2010] 2 BCLC 624 are where the dispute can be resolved without undue inconvenience, and the petitioner would lose its remedy altogether if the petition is struck out, and cases where the petitioner has at least a good arguable case on the petition debt and some injustice would occur if the petition is struck out. Ultimately, granting injunctions or striking out in these circumstances is a result of practice rather than law, and there is no doubt that the court retains a discretion to make a winding-up order even if there is a dispute over the petition debt (*Parmalat Capital Finance Ltd v Food Holdings Ltd* [2009] 1 BCLC 274, JCPC, per Lord Hoffmann).

9.6.8 Interrelation with summary judgment

Re Welsh Brick Industries Ltd [1946] 2 All ER 197 is an interesting case. A creditor brought an ordinary claim to recover a debt, and sought summary judgment. Unconditional leave to defend was granted. Not being prepared to wait for trial, the creditor petitioned to wind up the company on the ground it was unable to pay its debts. The company sought an injunction to restrain the petition. It was held by the Court of Appeal that the order on the summary judgment application did not establish there was a genuine dispute, and the winding-up court was entitled to consider the whole of the evidence. Although the order granting unconditional leave to defend would be taken into account, Lord Greene MR said the grounds justifying such an order could fall far short of a substantial ground of defence.

9.7 Provisional liquidator

Provisional liquidators may be appointed by the court at any time between the presentation of a winding-up petition and the disposal of the petition (IA 1986, s 135). Applications for the appointment of provisional liquidators are made in accordance with the procedure laid down by IR 1986, r 4.25, and must be supported by written evidence. Making such an appointment is a most serious step for the court to make, and will be justified according to *Revenue and Customs Commissioners v Rochdale Drinks Distributors Ltd* [2012] 1 BCLC 748 only if:

(a) there is a good prima facie case that a winding-up order will be made on the hearing of the petition; and

(b) in the circumstances of the case it would be right that a provisional liquidator should be appointed. This will most typically arise where there is a real risk the company's assets will be deliberately dissipated to frustrate future orders of the court.

A provisional liquidator's function is to maintain the status quo pending the determination of the petition, often by taking steps to preserve the company's assets.

9.8 Avoidance of dispositions after winding up

9.8.1 The statute

Section 127 of the IA 1986, provides:

> *(1) In a winding up by the court, any disposition of the company's property, and any transfer of shares, or alteration in the status of the company's members, made after the commencement of the winding up is, unless the court otherwise orders, void.*
>
> *(2) This section has no effect in respect of anything done by an administrator of a company while a winding-up petition is suspended under paragraph 40 of Schedule B1.*

The section only applies in respect of compulsory liquidations by the court and has no application in relation to voluntary liquidations. By IA 1986, s 129(2), a compulsory winding up is deemed to commence at the time of the presentation of the winding-up petition. The actual winding-up order, if made at all, will not be made until some weeks after the presentation of the petition. During that period, any disposals of the company's property are avoided by s 127, unless they are validated by the court. Some time is bound to elapse between presentation of the petition and service on the company. It is inevitable that persons dealing with the company will not become aware of the petition until some time later.

Creditors may well have traded in good faith with the company while unaware of the winding-up petition, but the effect of s 127 is to avoid the consideration given by the company. Once they have notice of the petition, third parties are likely to be unwilling to trade with the company. It is to offset these difficulties that the court is given power by the section to validate such dispositions of the company's property.

9.8.2 Policy of the section

In *Re Civil Service and General Store Ltd* (1887) 57 LJ Ch 119, Chitty J said the purpose of the then current section was to ensure that the company's unsecured creditors at the date of presentation of the petition were paid *pari passu*. In *Re Wiltshire Iron Co, ex p Pearson* (1868) LR 3 Ch App 443 Lord Cairns LJ said: 'This is a wholesome and necessary provision, to prevent, during the period which must elapse before a petition can be heard, the improper alienation and dissipation of the property of a company in extremis'. Lightman J in *Coutts and Co v Stock* [2000] 1 WLR 906 said that the section is 'designed to prevent the director of a company, when liquidation is imminent, from disposing of the company's assets to the prejudice of its creditors and to preserve those assets for the benefit of the general body of creditors'.

9.8.3 Property

Section 127 avoids dispositions of the company's 'property'. In *Re Hirth* [1899] 1 QB 612, Rigby LJ said that 'the property of the company' in relation to a winding up is the property which ultimately turns out to be the property of the company when the time comes for the division of the company's assets. Thus if there is a dispute about the ownership of property which the company purports to dispose of after the presentation of a petition, the disposal will only be avoided if it is eventually determined that ownership of the property was vested in the company. Alternatively, on a sale of goods by the company, the disposition may be made at the time the contract was entered into (and which may be before the commencement of the winding up) rather than the later time when the goods are delivered by the company. See *Re Wiltshire Iron Co, ex p Pearson* (1868) LR 3 Ch App 443.

9.8.4 What amounts to a disposition?

Section 127 avoids 'dispositions' of the company's property. These are transactions involving an alienation of the company's property (*Mersey Steel and Iron Co Ltd v Naylor, Benzon and Co* (1884) 9 App Cas 434, Earl Selborne LC). Sales, exchanges and gifts of the company's property will therefore be dispositions, even if the price or other consideration received by the company is apparently substantial. The property involved may be the usual items traded by the company, or its capital assets, such as machinery or real property owned by the company, or even its entire business. The invalidity is limited to dispositions of property, so does not cover liabilities assumed by the company over the relevant period, such as for rates, utilities and the salaries of employees (*Coutts and Co v Stock* [2000] 1 WLR 906).

Bank accounts have generated a lot of case law over recent years. Banks, as a matter of prudence, usually do regular checks against the advertisements appearing in the *London Gazette* (see **9.5.3**) for winding-up petitions affecting their customers. It is fairly standard banking practice to close the accounts of customers subject to winding-up petitions, and only to allow further banking facilities against a newly opened account which must be kept continuously in credit and in respect of which a validating order under IA 1986, s 127, has been obtained. Where this does not happen, perhaps because the bank in error misses the advertisement, it used to be thought that the bank had a potential liability under s 127 for the full amount of all debits and credits from the account from the date of presentation of the petition (see *Re Gray's Inn Construction Co Ltd* [1980] 1 WLR 711). Liability on this wide basis is no longer the law. It is now clear that payments into a bank account which is at all times in credit are not dispositions within the meaning of the section (*Re Barn Crown Ltd* [1994] BCC 381). It is also clear that payments out of a bank account, whether the account is overdrawn or in credit, are also not dispositions as between the bank and the liquidator within the meaning of the section (*Hollicourt (Contracts) Ltd v Bank of Ireland* [2001] Ch 555). Where there are payments out of a bank account during the period between presentation and the making of a winding-up order, it is equally clear that these are dispositions as between the payees of the sums withdrawn from the account and the liquidator, the bank merely acting as the company's agent in making the payments on the cheques or other withdrawals from the account (*Hollicourt (Contracts) Ltd v Bank of Ireland* [2001] Ch 555).

Rather more difficult is whether payments into a bank account which is overdrawn during the period between presentation and the making of a winding-up order are dispositions as between a bank and the company. *Re Gray's Inn Construction Co Ltd* [1980] 1 WLR 711 was distinguished in *Hollicourt (Contracts) Ltd v Bank of Ireland* [2001] Ch 555 at [29] partly on the ground that the *Gray's Inn* case was dealing with payments into an overdrawn account. The better view is that the reasoning in the *Gray's Inn* case still applies in this situation, with the effect that payments into an overdrawn account are dispositions within the meaning of s 127, a view supported at first instance by *Re Tain Construction Ltd* [2003] 2 BCLC 374.

9.8.5 Consequence of avoidance

By its terms IA 1986, s 127, merely avoids dispositions. It says nothing about recovery of the property disposed of. Invalidation and recovery are two distinct matters, and recovery is not regulated by the statute, but by the general law. Further, simply because a disposition is 'void' does not mean that it never took place. Generally, however, unless a disposition caught by the section is validated by the court, the liquidator will be able to recover the property through the law governing restitutionary remedies. The invalidation of a disposition between a company and a payee does not affect the liability of a guarantor of the company's overdraft whose liability is increased by the bank honouring the payment (*Coutts and Co v Stock* [2000] 1 WLR 906).

Simply because a transaction is void under s 127 does not mean that the liquidator will have an effective claim against a director of the company to recover any money or property transferred under the void transaction (*Phillips v McGregor-Paterson* [2010] 1 BCLC 72). Some other cause of action has to be established against the director. This might be a restitutionary claim if the director was the actual recipient of the company's property, or it might be that the transfer involved a breach of the director's fiduciary duties (for which, see **Chapter 7**).

9.8.6 Nature of the validating power

In *Re Steane's (Bournemouth) Ltd* [1950] 1 All ER 21, in a passage approved by the Court of Appeal in *Re Clifton Place Garage Ltd* [1970] Ch 477, Vaisey J said:

> The legislature, by omitting to indicate any particular principles which should govern the exercise of the discretion vested in the court, must be deemed to have left it entirely at large, and controlled only by the general principles which apply to every kind of judicial discretion.

In exercising that discretion:

> . . . each case must be dealt with on its own facts and particular circumstances (special regard being had to the question of the good faith and honest intention of the persons concerned), . . . the court is free to act according to the judge's opinion of what would be just and fair in each case.

There is an inherent reluctance to make validating orders because they derogate from the principle of *pari passu* distribution of the company's assets. That reluctance may be overcome if there is evidence that there is no serious risk to creditors because the company is solvent, or where there is evidence that the company is likely to improve the position of its creditors by trading at a profit during the period before the hearing of the winding-up petition. However, the court always does its best to ensure the interests of the company's unsecured creditors are not prejudiced.

There is jurisdiction to exercise the power to validate limited to the extent of validating a third party's legal charge (*Re Dewrun Ltd* (2000) LTL 2/8/2000).

Applications to validate post-presentation dispositions fall into three categories:

(a) Applications intended to keep the company in business. The underlying thought may be that the petition will come to nothing, or it may be an intention to sell the business as a going concern. This is discussed at **9.8.7**.

(b) Applications to validate some specific transaction. These are considered at **9.8.8**.

(c) Applications to validate transactions involved in the operation of a bank account, discussed at **9.8.9**.

In each case the burden of proof is on the party seeking an order validating the disposition: *Re Webb Electrical Ltd* (1988) 4 BCC 230.

9.8.7 Salvage cases

In a frequently cited passage, Lord Cairns LJ in *Re Wiltshire Iron Co, ex p Pearson* (1868) LR 3 Ch App 443 said:

> . . . where a company actually trading, which it is the interest of everyone to preserve, and ultimately to sell, as a going concern, is made the object of a winding-up petition, which may fail or may succeed, if it were to be supposed that transactions in the ordinary course of its current trade, bona fide entered into and completed, would be avoided, and would not, in the discretion given to the court, be maintained, the result would be that the presentation of a petition, groundless or well-founded, would, *ipso facto*, paralyse the trade of the company, and great injury, without any counterbalance of advantage, would be done to those interested in the assets of the company.

The general approach was considered by Buckley LJ in *Re Gray's Inn Construction Co Ltd* [1980] 1 WLR 711. The desirability of the company being enabled to carry on its business is often speculative. It usually depends on whether a sale of the business as a going concern will probably be more beneficial than a break-up realisation of the company's assets. The court must carry out a balancing exercise weighing the likely benefits and dangers of the company continuing in business against the benefits and losses which may be the consequence of an immediate cessation of business.

In striking this balance the court acts on general commonsense lines. It will not demand a massive investigation into the consequences if the company is closed down: see Staughton LJ in *Re SA and D Wright Ltd* [1992] BCC 503.

These principles were applied in *Re Park Ward and Co Ltd* [1926] Ch 828. With full notice of the presentation of a winding-up petition, and in order to provide funds for the payment of the company's workmen to enable the company to be sold as a going concern, a

Mr Rowley advanced the company the sum of £1,200 secured by a debenture. The transaction was clearly for the benefit of the company, and was validated under the section.

9.8.8 Specific transactions

In applications to validate specific transactions the guiding principle is that the court seeks to preserve the value of the company's assets for the benefit of its creditors and contributories, while not unduly hampering the company in carrying out transactions which may be beneficial: *Re A.I. Levy (Holdings) Ltd* [1964] Ch 19.

A sale of an asset at its full market value after presentation of a petition involves no dissipation of the company's assets, and therefore cannot harm the company's creditors. Consequently, there is usually no reason why the court should not exercise its discretion to validate it. Even more so if the transaction preserves assets which would otherwise be lost (as in *Re Park Ward and Co Ltd* [1926] Ch 828), or where the value of the company's assets is increased by the transaction. See *Re Gray's Inn Construction Co Ltd* [1980] 1 WLR 711 and *Re Sugar Properties (Derisley Wood) Ltd* (1987) 3 BCC 88. Sometimes the benefit obtained by the company from a transaction will be susceptible of positive proof. However, there may be a dispute as to what is the true 'market value' of an asset. If there is evidence casting doubt on whether the proposed sale is at full market value, the court will almost certainly refuse to validate the transaction (*Re Rescupine Ltd* [2003] 1 BCLC 661). Also, if the application relates to the completion of a partially completed contract the question of prejudice to unsecured creditors may be more uncertain.

According to Staughton LJ in *Re SA and D. Wright Ltd* [1992] BCC 503, a judge is entitled to conclude that a transaction is at least *apt* to benefit the company's unsecured creditors and to validate the transaction even if there is no evidence to prove it will in fact do so. Contrast this with *Re Mountforest Ltd* [1993] BCC 565, where a s 127 order was refused. The company was in business running nursing homes. It was convicted of an offence connected with that business and under legislation introduced in 1990 was precluded from continuing running the homes. About the same time an unfair prejudice petition under what is now CA 2006, s 994, was presented. In those circumstances it was obvious that its business had to be sold. An application was made under s 127 seeking advance validation of a sale of the business to a company called Unicare plc. All the shares in Unicare were held by the majority shareholders in Mountforest, and both companies had three directors in common. Harman J held that although the court may validate a self-dealing transaction, it would not do so unless those proposing the transaction gave full and detailed particulars of the transaction. If full particulars are given, the court will also consider whether an intelligent and honest man could reasonably decide that the proposed transaction is necessary or expedient in the interest of the company.

9.8.9 Bank accounts

The question of whether payments in and out of a company's bank account are 'dispositions' within the meaning of the IA 1986, s 127, was considered at **9.8.4**. In relation to banking transactions that are caught by s 127, in *Re Gray's Inn Construction Co Ltd* [1980] 1 WLR 711 the Court of Appeal refused to penalise the bank further than was necessary to restore the fund of assets available for distribution in the liquidation. The total post-liquidation trading loss was found to be £5,000, and a validation order was made with the effect that only that sum had to be repaid to the liquidator.

Either the company or its bank may apply for a validation order before the petition is heard. A standard form of s 127 order is shown at Figure 9.2 (see PD 49B). Paragraph (1) validates payments into the company's accounts if they are 'in the ordinary course of the business of the company'. Although the company will know whether it is complying with this clause, it will be very expensive for banks to ensure it is complied with. The proviso to the order, which is in the form drafted by Mrs Jane Giret of Counsel and approved in *Re a Company (No 00687 of 1991)* [1991] BCC 210, removes this difficulty.

Figure 9.2 Standard form of s 127 order

IN THE HIGH COURT OF JUSTICE — No 1329 of 2014

CHANCERY DIVISION

COMPANIES COURT

IN THE MATTER of Woodcroft Kitchen Company Limited

AND IN THE MATTER of the Insolvency Act 1986

UPON THE APPLICATION of Woodcroft Kitchen Company Limited ('the Company') AND UPON HEARING counsel for the Applicant and counsel for the Petitioner named in the petition to wind up the Company presented to the court on the 24th of April 2014.

AND UPON READING the evidence.

ORDER that notwithstanding the presentation of the said Petition

(1) payments made into or out of the bank accounts of the Company in the ordinary course of the business of the Company and

(2) dispositions of the property of the Company made in the ordinary course of its business for proper value

between the date of presentation of the Petition and the date of judgment on the Petition or further order in the meantime shall not be void by virtue of the provisions of section 127 of the Insolvency Act 1986 in the event of an Order for the winding up of the Company being made on the said Petition provided that Regional Bank plc shall be under no obligation to verify for itself whether any transaction through the Company's bank accounts is in the ordinary course of business, or that it represents full market value for the relevant transaction.
DATED the 15th day of May 2014

9.8.10 Advance validation

It is a very common exercise of the discretion under s 127 for payments in the ordinary course of business to be sanctioned in advance of the making of the winding-up order. It is particularly important to seek advance validation when a proposed transaction is unusual, such as the sale of a business tenancy. Sometimes the courts take into account a failure to seek advance validation in considering whether to validate a disposition at a later stage.

9.8.11 Notice of the petition

As mentioned at **9.8.1**, time will certainly elapse between the presentation of a petition and persons dealing with the company receiving notice of it. Oliver J in *Re J. Leslie*

Engineers Co Ltd [1976] 1 WLR 292 regarded the absence of actual notice to the recipient of the company's property as being a very powerful factor in the exercise of the court's discretion, but not in itself conclusive. The court will not simply validate pre-advertisement transactions made before the party had notice of the petition as a matter of course (*Re Tain Construction Ltd* [2003] 2 BCLC 374).

A bona fide transaction in the ordinary course of the company's business at a time when the parties are unaware of the petition will, however, normally by validated (*Re Neath Harbour Smelting and Rolling Works* (1887) 56 LT 727).

9.8.12 Attempts to prefer

If the disposition is construed as an attempt to prefer a pre-presentation creditor, it will not be validated, even if the recipient was unaware of the petition and the company's intention to prefer (*Re J. Leslie Engineers Co Ltd* [1976] 1 WLR 292). Contrast the situation where it is in the interests of the creditors generally that the company's business should be carried on and this could only be achieved by paying for unpaid goods already supplied to the company when the petition was presented. In such a case the court might think fit to exercise its discretion to validate the payment (*Re Gray's Inn Construction Co Ltd* [1980] 1 WLR 711 per Buckley LJ).

9.8.13 Receivers

A similar approach to that adopted in *Re Gray's Inn Construction Co Ltd* [1980] 1 WLR 711 is taken when a receiver carries on the company's business after presentation of a winding-up petition (see *Re Clifton Place Garage Ltd* [1970] Ch 477).

9.8.14 Solvent companies

A winding-up petition may be presented by a contributory (eg a shareholder), and in such cases the company is likely to be solvent. In such cases:

(a) Payments in the ordinary course of the company's business will almost certainly be validated.

(b) Other transactions will also be validated if:

  (i) the directors consider that the transaction is within their powers and is necessary or expedient in the interests of the company; and

  (ii) their reasons for this opinion are such that an intelligent and honest person could reasonably hold.

See *Re Burton and Deakin Ltd* [1977] 1 All ER 631.

9.8.15 Contributory's petition

In PD 49B, para 2, it is stated that the prayer in a contributory's petition must state whether the petitioner consents to a s 127 order in the standard form. If the petitioner objects, or would consent to a modification of the standard form, a short statement of the reasons must be included in the written evidence in support of the petition (PD 49B, para 3).

9.8.16 Share transactions

Share transactions are specifically referred to in IA 1986, s 127. Different considerations apply than in respect of trading dispositions. Strong reasons are required before the court will exercise its discretion. In *Re Onward Building Society* [1891] 2 QB 463, Kay LJ said: 'before the court gives leave to register such a transfer, it ought to see that to do so would be of some benefit to the company or those interested in its assets, and . . . it would not so exercise its discretion unless for very strong reasons.'

9.8.17 Procedure

Urgent applications under s 127 before the hearing of the winding-up petition are made to the judge (and may be made without notice if the application is urgent). Applications after a winding-up order has been made are heard by the registrar. Detailed procedural requirements are laid down by the IPPD, paras 11.8.1–11.8.10.

Notice of the application in non-urgent cases should be given to:

(a) the petitioning creditor;

(b) any person entitled to receive a copy of the petition;

(c) any creditor who has given notice of intention to appear on the hearing of the petition pursuant to IR 1986, r. 4.16;

(d) any creditor who is substituted as petitioner under r. 4.19.

The application should be supported by evidence in the form of a witness statement. This should be given by a director or officer who is intimately connected with the company's affairs and financial circumstances, and should, if necessary, be supported by evidence from the company's accountant. A draft order should be attached to the application. If time permits, a skeleton argument should also be prepared for the hearing.

9.8.18 Costs

As always, costs are in the discretion of the court. However, if the application for validation is in respect of a transaction for the benefit of the company, the order will not be seen as simply an indulgence. Thus, in *Re Park Ward and Co Ltd* [1926] Ch 828 a debentureholder was entitled to add the costs of the application to its security.

9.9 Subsequent steps in the liquidation

9.9.1 On making the order

If a winding-up order is made, the court then notifies the official receiver (who becomes the liquidator of the company) and draws up the order. The official receiver serves a copy of the order on the company and on the Registrar of Companies. He also advertises it in the *Gazette* and another newspaper.

9.9.2 Early dissolution

If the official receiver considers:

- that the realisable assets of the company are insufficient to cover the expenses of the winding up; and
- that the affairs of the company do not require investigation,

he may apply to the Registrar of Companies for the early dissolution of the company. The official receiver first gives 28 days' notice to the company's creditors and contributories, then gives notice to the registrar. Dissolution takes effect three months later.

9.9.3 Liquidation

9.9.3.1 Powers and duties of liquidator

The official receiver will normally summon meetings of creditors and contributors, who choose a liquidator. The liquidator's main task is to take custody or control of all the company's property and things in action. Officers and employees of the company are required to give the liquidator information about the company's business and affairs. Various powers available to the liquidator are set out in IA 1986, Sch 4. These include powers to make compromises with creditors, to hold meetings of creditors, and even to carry on the company's business (provided this is necessary for the beneficial winding up of the company, eg to sell it as a going concern).

9.9.3.2 Priorities

When all the assets have been realised, the funds are applied to pay:

- the expenses of the liquidation;
- preferential debts (such as four months' pay for employees);
- unsecured creditors;
- shareholders.

Detailed rules on the order of priority of the expenses of the liquidation are set out in IR 1986, r 4.218. Expenses are essentially items of expenditure in the liquidation, normally being expenditure incurred by or on behalf of the liquidator (by analogy with *Re Nortel GmbH* [2013] 3 WLR 504, a case on administration). Members within each category rank *pari passu*. If there are insufficient funds to pay a category, the liquidator pays a dividend.

9.9.3.3 Proof of debt (unsecured creditors)

Where a company is being wound up by the court, a person claiming to be a creditor and wishing to recover that debt in the liquidation is required to submit a written claim to the liquidator in the form of a proof of debt (IR 1986, r 4.73). The required contents of the proof of debt are set out in r 4.75(1), and any documents substantiating the debt should be attached to the proof (r 4.75(2)). A proof may be admitted for dividend either in full or part (r 4.82(1)), but if rejected, written reasons must be provided by the liquidator (r 4.82(2)). A creditor who is dissatisfied with the liquidator's decision may apply to the court under r 4.83 for that decision to be reversed or varied.

In cases of doubt, IR 1986, r 13.12, provides a definition of 'debt':

> *(1) 'Debt', in relation to the winding up of a company, means (subject to the next paragraph) any of the following—*
>
> *(a) any debt or liability to which the company is subject—*
>
> *(i) in the case of a winding up which was not immediately preceded by an administration, at the date on which the company went into liquidation;*
>
> *(ii) in the case of a winding up which was immediately preceded by an administration, at the date on which the company entered administration;*
>
> *(b) any debt or liability to which the company may become subject after that date by reason of any obligation incurred before that date; and*
>
> *(c) any interest provable as mentioned in Rule 4.93(1).*
>
> *(2) For the purposes of any provision of the Act or the Rules about winding up, any liability in tort is a debt provable in the winding up, if either—*
>
> *(a) the cause of action has accrued—*
>
> *(i) in the case of a winding up which was not immediately preceded by an administration, at the date on which the company went into liquidation;*
>
> *(ii) in the case of a winding up which was immediately preceded by an administration, at the date on which the company entered administration; or*
>
> *(b) all the elements necessary to establish the cause of action exist at that date except for actionable damage.*
>
> *(3) For the purposes of references in any provision of the Act or the Rules about winding up to a debt or liability, it is immaterial whether the debt or liability is present or future, whether it is certain or contingent, or whether its amount is fixed or liquidated, or is capable of being ascertained by fixed rules or as a matter of opinion; and references in any such provision to owing a debt are to be read accordingly.*
>
> *(4) In any provision of the Act or the Rules about winding up, except in so far as the context otherwise requires, 'liability' means (subject to paragraph (3) above) a liability to pay money or money's worth, including any liability under an enactment, any liability for breach of trust, any liability in contract, tort or bailment, and any liability arising out of an obligation to make restitution.*

This rule provides an extended meaning of 'debt' which covers not only straightforward claims for sums due under contracts for the supply of goods and services, but also liabilities in tort without actionable damage. An 'obligation incurred' for the purpose of r 13.12(1)(b) means a legal rule applying before the date when the company goes into liquidation which might, contingently on some future event, give rise to a 'debt or liability' after the company goes into liquidation (*Re Nortel GmbH* [2013] 3 WLR 504). Typically this will arise where the company entered into a contract before the commencement of the winding up, but it also covers non-contractual obligations.

9.9.3.4 Liquidator's report

When the winding up is complete, the liquidator prepares a report, which is placed before a final meeting of creditors. The creditors receive the report and, if it is in order, release the liquidator. The liquidator then notifies the court and files his return with the Registrar of Companies. Three months later the company is dissolved.

9.9.4 Dissolution

On dissolution, the company's corporate existence ends, and the name of the company will be removed from the register at Companies House. This is subject to an application being made for the restoration of the company to the register under CA 2006, s 1029.

Figure 9.3 Usual order for the compulsory winding up of a company

IN THE HIGH COURT OF JUSTICE No 1329 of 2014

CHANCERY DIVISION

COMPANIES COURT

Mr Registrar Jenkins

Wednesday the 25th day of June 2014

IN THE MATTER of Woodcroft Kitchen Company Limited, Registered No: 9884321

AND IN THE MATTER of the Insolvency Act 1986

UPON THE PETITION of a creditor of the company presented to this court on 24th day of April 2014.

AND UPON HEARING counsel for the Petitioner and no one appearing for and on behalf of the said Respondent company.

AND UPON READING the evidence.

IT IS ORDERED that Woodcroft Kitchen Company Limited be wound up by this court under the provisions of the Insolvency Act 1986.

IT IS DECLARED that these proceedings are main proceedings under Council Regulation (EC) No 1346/2000.

AND IT IS ORDERED that the costs of Rosewall Electricals Limited of the said petition be paid out of the assets of the company.

DATED the 25th day of June 2014.

NOTE

One of the official receivers attached to the court is by virtue of this order liquidator of the company.

10 Advocacy in Companies Court proceedings

10.1 Introduction

This chapter will consider how to prepare for and how to present winding-up petitions before the Companies Court Registrar and applications before the judges of the Chancery Division.

High Court winding-up petitions proceeding in London are heard in one of the main court rooms in the Royal Courts of Justice on Wednesdays. Large numbers of petitions, often 40 or more every half hour, are heard throughout the morning and sometimes into the afternoon. Each petition is allocated, in effect, less than a minute of court time. All the papers will have been considered in advance both by the court and the parties. Opposed petitions are dealt with separately, so the Wednesday lists are intended for unopposed petitions. Essentially, the task of the Companies Court Registrar is to either make the winding-up order, stand it over if the formalities have not been completed or to dismiss the petition (if the creditor does not attend, or has been paid, or if the registrar takes the view the petition is not being proceeded with). Counsel's task is to assist with this process, and to present the key factors to the court in an efficient and accurate manner.

Judge's applications are made in open court. If the proceedings are in the High Court in London, the matter will be heard in one of the main court rooms in the Rolls Building, near Fetter Lane in London. Companies Court applications, like general Chancery Division applications, can be listed for any day of the week (*Practice Statement: Companies Judge* [2000] BCC 256).

10.2 Winding-up petitions

10.2.1 Background

A petition for the compulsory winding up of a company incorporated by registration under the Companies Acts may be presented by the company, or its directors, or by any creditor or creditors (including any contingent or prospective creditor or creditors), or by a contributory (ie shareholder) or contributories, a liquidator within the meaning of the EC Regulation (EC) No 2157/2001 on the Statute for a European Company, or various officials, or by all or any of those parties, separately or together (IA 1986, s 124(1)). The one met most frequently in practice is a creditor's petition on the ground that the company is unable to pay its debts. An inexperienced advocate should beware of believing that such petitions present no difficulties simply because they are very numerous and usually undisputed. Before appearing on the hearing of such a petition, the advocate should study carefully the relevant provisions of the IA 1986 and the IR 1986, SI 1986/1925 as amended. References to forms, by number, are references to the forms prescribed by the IR 1986. The IR 1986 prescribe the form which a petition should take (see Sch 4, Form 4.2 and Figure 9.1). Generally the High Court and county courts have concurrent jurisdiction and a petitioner may choose in which court to proceed. The procedure laid down by the IR 1986 is described at **9.5**.

10.2.2 The court

Winding-up petitions are listed for hearing before the Registrar of the Companies Court sitting in open court on Wednesday mornings at 10.30 am. Petitions are listed in 30-minute batches, so that a number of matters will be found in the list marked 'not before 11.00' and so on. The registrar is addressed as 'Sir'; counsel and solicitors must appear in robes.

10.2.3 Disputed petitions

While petitions may be presented by a variety of parties as mentioned previously, the most common category of petitioners are creditors. Some creditors may be described as 'trade' creditors (meaning that their debts have been incurred in the course of the company's business). Others may be 'judgment' creditors where the company has failed to satisfy a judgment or order made against it. If the company disputes the *locus standi* of the petitioner as a creditor, on the ground that the debt upon which a petition is to be or has been presented is disputed, the company may apply for an injunction restraining presentation in court or advertisement of the petition (see **9.6**). Such application will be made to the Applications Judge. If the company fails to take such preventive steps, it may still dispute the petitioner's entitlement to a winding-up order on the ground that the debt is disputed by giving notice to the solicitors for the petitioner. Because of the danger of spurious disputes being used to defeat creditors, the Chancery Division judges have introduced a practice of requiring the company in doubtful cases to make a payment into court of (or otherwise securing the amount of) the debt, pending an application for summary judgment by the petitioner.

10.2.4 Before the hearing

The following is a checklist of the matters which must have been attended to by the instructing solicitors before the hearing. Counsel should ensure that he or she has copies of these documents in preparing the case for the hearing and that any defects which are found in them, for example inconsistent dates or sums owed, erroneous title of company in the advertisement etc are discussed with the solicitor before the hearing. If there has been non-compliance with the rules, remedial action will be required, as indicated after each point.

10.2.4.1 Petition and verifying statement of truth

Counsel should have a copy of both of these documents.

10.2.4.2 Certificate of service

Service must be proved by a certificate of service in the form set out in CPR Form N215 (see *A Practical Approach to Civil Procedure,* 16th edn (OUP, 2013), Figure 6.6). The certificate of service should state the date on which the petition was served. It is a strict requirement that it must also specify the method of service used. Service of the petition and statement of truth verifying the petition must generally be effected at the company's registered office: IR 1986, r 4.8(2). Permissible methods of service are set out in r 4.8(3), for which, see **9.5.2**.

The certificate of service must contain sufficient details to identify the petition, and any order for substituted service must be attached to the certificate: r 4.9A. It is important to double-check that these requirements have been satisfied, as defects in service and proving service are among the most common problems encountered in winding-up petitions.

10.2.4.3 Remedies

If the certificate of service is defective the court will have to be asked for an adjournment of the petition either:

- to file a replacement certificate of service, if the petition was properly served but the certificate does not correctly state the facts or has failed to specify the manner of service; or
- to effect re-service, if the petition has not been properly served.

If the company appears on the hearing, it may seek dismissal of the petition on the ground that it has been advertised after a defective service. If the company has been properly served and appears, a defect in the certificate of service will cease to be relevant.

10.2.4.4 Advertisement

Unless the court directs otherwise, each petition must be advertised once in the *Gazette* and contain certain required information as set out in rr 4.11, 12A.33 and 12A.34. There is a prescribed form of advertisement, Form 4.6.

A copy of the advertisement should be included in the brief for counsel for the petitioner. Unless it is the company's own petition, the advertisement must have appeared not less than seven business days after service of the petition, nor less than seven business days (which do not include Saturdays, Sundays or bank holidays) before the hearing date (see r 4.11(4)). This is a most important requirement, as it enables the company to prevent the highly damaging consequences of advertisement by applying for an injunction if the petitioner's debt is disputed. It is also designed to ensure that the class remedy of winding up by the court is made available to all creditors, and is not used as a means of putting pressure on the company to pay the petitioner's debt. Failure to comply with the rule, without good reason, may lead to the summary dismissal of the petition on the return date (see IPPD, para 11.5.1). Counsel should check that the advertisement complied with r 4.11, that the time requirements have been met and that there are no typographical errors in the advertisement.

10.2.4.5 Remedies

If the advertisement rules have not been complied with, the court may dismiss the petition. In the case of premature publication, if the publication is a day early, for example because of an innocent failure to count a bank holiday, the court may waive the defect.

Counsel should point out the premature advertisement, state the reason shortly and ask that the defect be waived. There is always a serious risk that the petition will be dismissed on this ground.

If a court orders that a petition be re-served due to defective service, counsel should ask whether a second advertisement will also be required. If this is required, counsel may request that the required time periods be abated although this is at the discretion of the court.

If the court, in its discretion, grants an adjournment after a failure to advertise, this will be on the condition that the petition is advertised in due time for the adjourned hearing. No further adjournment for the purpose of advertisement will normally be granted (IPPD, para 11.5.1).

10.2.4.6 Certificate of compliance

Under IR 1986, r 4.14, the petitioner or its solicitor must, at least five business days before the hearing of the petition, file with the court a certificate of due compliance showing the dates of presentation, service, advertisement and hearing (Form 4.7), together with a copy of the advertisement. Applications to file the certificate any later will only be allowed 'if some good reason is shown for the delay'. The present practice is for the court office to refuse to accept a certificate brought to the court after the deadline. The registrar will normally mention this matter as soon as the petition is called on.

10.2.4.7 Remedy

If counsel has a certificate of compliance which has been filed out of time and has no instructions as to the explanation, or which has not been filed, counsel may ask that the court take the matter second time around for instructions to be obtained or for filing the certificate. On giving an explanation counsel can request that the defect be waived. However, counsel should be aware that, particularly in London, the court is likely to refuse to allow the matter to be taken second time around, and will simply stand over (adjourn) the application for, for example, 14 days to allow for filing within the time requirements. In these cases, counsel should ask for the petition to be stood over for 14 days for filing of the certificate of compliance.

10.2.4.8 List of appearances

Every person, including creditors or the company itself, intending to appear on the hearing to support or oppose the making of a winding-up order must give notice to the solicitors for the petitioner not later than 16.00 hours (4 pm) on the business day before the hearing (IR 1986, r 4.16). If the company intends to oppose the petition, its witness statement in opposition must be filed in court not less than five business days before the hearing (IR 1986, r 4.18). It is the duty of the petitioner's solicitors to prepare a list of the persons who have given such notice (Form 4.10, known formally as the 'list of appearances', informally in court as 'the list' and colloquially from its colour as 'the blue form'). The list must be handed in before the hearing (IR 1986, r 4.17(3)). If it is not handed in, the registrar will usually simply say when the petition is called on, 'There is no list', and decline to proceed further.

10.2.4.9 Remedy

The only help for this is to make sure that the solicitors' representative is seen well before the time for which the petition is listed, and told to hand in the list when the current half-hour's petitions are over. If the list has not been handed in, ask the registrar to 'take this matter second time round'.

10.2.4.10 Substitution

If the original petition is not proceeded with (because the petitioner withdraws), or is not advertised, or in other similar circumstances (see IR 1986, r 4.19(1)), the court may, on such terms as it thinks just, substitute as petitioner any creditor or contributory who in the court's opinion would have a right to present a petition, and who is desirous of prosecuting it. The 'new' petitioner asks for a substitution order (see **10.4.1**, 'The hearing', Counsel C).

10.3 Noting the back sheet

It is helpful to compile the relevant information and the dates on which the required steps were taken for use as a quick guide during the hearing to avoid having to search through your papers during the presentation. One example would be as follows:

Re: [name of company]
Trade creditor's petition based on a statutory demand in the sum of £ ____
List: [enter any creditors, contributories or others supporting/opposing the petition and the nature of their interest]
Co: [note whether the company will make an appearance]

Relevant dates:

Presented:	[eg, 27/2/2014]
Verified:	[24/2/2014]
Served:	[5/3/2014]
Cert.Service:	[5/3/2014]
Advert:	[2/4/2014]
Cert.Comp:	[20/4/2014]

UCO (Asking for the usual compulsory order.)

10.4 The hearing

10.4.1 Examples

The following applications may be heard in unopposed petition situations:

(1) Associate: 'Petition number 546, Tyro Advisers Limited.'

Counsel A (for petitioner): 'This is a trade creditor's petition based on a statutory demand for the sum of £3,459 odd. The company is not represented, and the list is clear (or 'negative'). I ask for the usual compulsory order, main proceedings.'

Registrar: 'Usual compulsory order, main proceedings.'

(2) Associate: 'Petition number 547, D-I-Y Services Limited.'

Counsel B: 'This is a petition based on a statutory demand for unpaid solicitors' fees.'

Registrar: 'This petition was advertised only five business days after service, and r 4.11 has not been complied with.'

Counsel B: 'Sir, I am instructed that my instructing solicitors unfortunately overlooked the fact that seven business days must elapse between service and advertisement, and therefore did not omit from their calculation of the time two days for the weekend and a bank holiday. In those circumstances, I ask that the defect be waived.'

Registrar: 'No. These errors are capable of causing severe damage to a company which may wish to dispute the debt. There has been no effort in this case by the solicitors to cure the error, or to communicate with the court office in lieu of complying with r 4.11. In the circumstances I propose to dismiss the petition.'

Counsel C: 'I appear for Suppliers Limited, a supporting creditor which has not given notice to the petitioner's solicitors prior to this hearing. My client has a trade debt amounting to £78,968 odd, and my application is for permission to be added to the list out of time and for an order substituting my client as petitioner.'

Registrar: 'I will give you permission to be added to the list out of time on the usual terms. I will also make an order substituting Miss C's client as the petitioner, and adjourn the matter for 28 days for amendment of the petition, re-service and re-advertisement.'

10.4.2 Notes on the hearing

(a) It is usual to describe the basis of the petition and to show what is alleged to prove the inability of the company to pay its debts (in this case failure to comply with a statutory demand, but other evidence may also be adduced).

(b) The court is told whether the company is represented. Directors of the company may address the court if the company complies with CPR, r 39.6 and PD 39A, paras 5.2–5.4.

(c) The court should be informed whether there are any supporting or opposing creditors or contributories on the list of appearances, and if so, how many of each and whether any of them have in fact appeared at the hearing. If there are none, the court is told that the list is clear or 'negative'.

(d) The usual compulsory order is set out in Form 4.11. (See Figure 9.3.) The references to 'main proceedings' are to Regulation 1346/2000, see **8.1.3**.

(e) The 'usual terms' on which a creditor is added to the list of appearances out of time are that the applicant's solicitor undertakes not to seek any costs of giving notice or of the application to be added to the list in the event of a compulsory winding up being made. (A substituted petitioner will normally obtain an order for the subsequent costs of amendment, re-service, re-advertisement and hearing.)

10.4.3 Opposed petitions

If it becomes apparent that the petition is opposed, the registrar will adjourn the petition for hearing before the judge of the Companies Court.

10.4.4 Adjournments

If an order is made, the winding up commences with the presentation of the petition (IA 1986, s 129(2)). Section 127 avoids dispositions of property of a company made after the commencement of the winding up, unless the court has otherwise ordered. For this reason, the court will not permit a petition to remain outstanding for more than a few months (except in the case of petitions by contributories, where a winding up is sought, the company is solvent and the judge has made appropriate orders under s 127). Even if the petitioner and the company have agreed that the company should have time to attempt to pay the petition debt, the court may refuse an adjournment if the petition has been current for a long period, and require the petitioner to seek a winding-up order or will dismiss the petition. Adjournments may also be necessary in disputed petitions in order to allow the company to prepare its evidence and for the petitioner to respond. If the need for the adjournment can be attributed to the fault of the company, stringent orders as to the costs of the adjournment may be imposed (*Re a Company (No 005448 of 1996)* [1998] 1 BCLC 98). There is an obligation on the petitioner to give notice of the adjourned hearing to the company and any supporting or opposing creditors (r 4.18A).

10.5 Function of judge's applications

Judge's applications in the Chancery Division usually seek interim relief, although orders may be made which dispose finally of some question in issue in the proceedings (eg rectification of the register of members). Although any interim application in the Chancery Division might in theory be made to a judge, para 5.2 of the *Chancery Guide* says that only applications which need to be heard by a judge (such as those for injunctions and committal proceedings) should be made to a judge. Procedural applications, such as for directions, should be made to a Registrar or Master unless there is some special reason for making it to a judge. Otherwise the application may be dismissed with costs. A special reason for applying to a judge may exist, for example where the applicant wants to apply to strike out and the respondent has already issued an application seeking an injunction.

10.6 Procedural aspects

Unless an application is to be made without notice, or the court gives permission to the contrary, the notice of application must be served at least three clear days before the day named in the application notice for the hearing (CPR, r 23.7(1)(b)). Where permission has been given to serve short notice, that fact must be stated in the notice. A judge of the Chancery Division sits to hear applications on every weekday (except the last day) of each sitting, and applications are listed for hearing by that judge at 10.30 am. The Chancery Listing Office is responsible for the listing of judge's applications. An application will only be listed if two copies of the claim form and the application notice (with a fee, currently £75.00), together with a Judge's Application Information Form, are lodged with the Clerk of the Lists, Chancery Listing Office, before 12 noon on the working day before the hearing date or on the preceding Friday if the date given for the hearing is a Monday (*Chancery Guide*, para 5.7). A draft order in Word format should be sent by email to the Chancery Listing Office before the hearing.

Applications are generally heard in open court and the procedure to be followed can be found in the *Chancery Guide*, para 5.14. Where it may be unjust for the application to be heard in public, the judge may exercise a discretion to sit otherwise than in open court; see CPR, r 39.2.

Bundles of documents for use in court will generally be required for all applications where more than 25 pages are involved (see the *Chancery Guide*, para 7.9). Also, the general rule is that skeleton arguments should be prepared for all judge's applications (*Chancery Guide*, para 7.18). The exceptions are where the application does not warrant a skeleton, or is so urgent that preparing a skeleton is impracticable. For substantial matters, skeletons should be lodged two clear days before the hearing (para 7.20), for applications without notice the skeleton should be lodged with the papers (para 7.21) and for all other interim applications the skeleton should be lodged no later than 10 am on the day preceding the hearing (para 7.22).

10.7 Conduct of judge's applications

10.7.1 General

Counsel briefed on a judge's application must robe and the application will be heard in open court. Where the circumstances of a case require a 'short notice' period, permission may be obtained on an application without notice, usually made after the midday adjournment.

The usual practice for normal applications is that the judge will ascertain at the sitting of the court which of the listed applications will be 'effective', that is, disputed, and if so, what counsel's estimate of length is, or 'ineffective', that is, disposed of by agreement. It is a matter of courtesy both to the court and to other counsel and litigants:

(a) to arrive in court at least ten minutes before the court sits, to assist the usher with the names of the advocates for the parties and any revised time estimate for the hearing. It is also necessary to allow time before the court sits to agree the terms of any order which is to be made by consent, if this has not already been done;

(b) to be present in court when the judge takes his seat;

(c) to be ready to say whether the application is 'effective' or 'ineffective';

(d) to have carefully considered the estimate of length (if the application is to be effective) and to have agreed that estimate with one's opponent;

(e) not to waste the time of the court when the judge is going through the list 'first time round' by explaining the substance of the application instead of simply indicating whether the application is effective or ineffective.

Although the judge has a discretion as to the order of hearing applications, he or she will normally deal with ineffective applications first, for example matters which are to be adjourned or have been settled. All other listed, unlisted and applications without notice will be heard in the order determined by the judge. Applications affecting the liberty of a subject (eg for release from committal to prison for contempt, or for *habeas corpus*) are always accorded priority.

Counsel with effective applications may be asked to wait, in case another judge becomes free to hear their application. The Applications Judge may transfer such of the day's applications as deemed appropriate, irrespective of priority. Counsel should not leave the precincts of the court unless released by the judge until a particular time. Counsel should also ensure that the court staff can easily locate them if a judge becomes free. Any application which at the end of the day is part heard (ie unfinished) will normally head the listed applications for the next court day.

10.7.2 Time estimates

Time estimates are critical. An application will only be listed before the Applications Judge if it is estimated to last less than two hours (*Chancery Guide*, para 5.11). The two hours includes the judge's pre-reading time, time in court and time for judgment. If the application is estimated to last longer, it must be stood over (ie, be adjourned) to come on as an 'application by order' (ie it is given a subsequently fixed date for the hearing, which is arranged by the solicitors or the clerks to counsel with the Clerk of the Lists). Counsel will be required to lodge with the Clerk a signed certificate stating the estimated length. An indication may be given that an application by order is to be treated as urgent. If it is apparent that the application will be likely to last more than two hours, the only proper course is to inform the court that it is ineffective, and 'second time round' to inform the judge, 'This application is likely to occupy the court for two days, and I therefore ask your Lordship to stand it over as an application by order. Subject to your Lordship's approval, the defendant is to give certain undertakings in the meantime'.

10.7.3 Unlisted applications and emergency applications

Frequently, counsel is instructed to apply to the court urgently without notice, so that the application has not been listed. It also happens that there are occasions when the instructing solicitors forget to lodge the papers for an application on notice in accordance with the directions mentioned previously. Counsel may in these circumstances ask the judge to hear an application although unlisted. The judge's clerk should be notified (usually through counsel's clerk) as early in the day as possible, that an application is to be made, and two copies of the claim form (showing the title of the claim), a completed Application Information Form and the draft of the order to be sought should be made available. If the proceedings have not yet been issued, every effort should be made to issue the originating process before the application is made (*Chancery Guide*, para 5.23). If this is not practical, the party making the application gives an undertaking to the court to issue the process forthwith. The usual practice is to rise in counsel's place after the judge has worked through the list for the first time, and to say, 'I have an unlisted application in the claim of Smith and Jones [giving the number]'. Such an application will only rarely be ineffective, and counsel should go on to indicate the time estimate. Unless the application affects the liberty of the subject or is of exceptional urgency and importance, listed applications will be given priority.

10.7.4 Ineffective applications

An application can only genuinely be described as 'ineffective' if there is *no point of disagreement between the parties which requires the decision of the judge*. Counsel must ensure that all such points have been dealt with, and not attempt to be heard first under the guise of an ineffective application. The degree of information which the judge will require to have on the substance of an application depends on the nature of the order which the court is to be asked to make. It is usual to indicate in very general terms the nature of the claim (eg 'This is an application for an injunction to restrain the defendant from dealing with certain land which is alleged to be subject to an option agreement'). Counsel will then usually inform the judge orally of the terms of the order which the judge is invited to make. If the order involves undertakings to the court or submission to an order (other than a purely procedural order) by one of the parties, the judge is likely to wish to know the exact terms of the undertakings. It is therefore not merely a formality to say 'The parties have agreed *subject to your Lordship's approval* that the application should stand over for 14 days on the defendant's undertaking not to dispose of the land known as [describing it]': the terms of the undertaking or an order in the same terms are subject to the approval of the judge.

If a party who is to consent to an order or give undertakings is neither present nor represented (either by counsel or a solicitor on the record), an order will only be made on production of a 'letter of consent' signed by or on behalf of the solicitors on the record for the party or a draft statement of agreed terms signed by the respondent's solicitors (see *Chancery Guide*, para 5.37). An acknowledgment of service by the respondent to an application is required and time is often wasted in court because the solicitors offering written consent (to avoid the cost of an attendance) have failed to return the acknowledgment. By filing an acknowledgment of service or a defence with their details as representing the respondent, the respondent's solicitors will go 'on the record', and there is no difficulty in the court approving the terms of the consent order provided those terms fall within the relief claimed in the application notice. Counsel for the claimant should always check in these circumstances whether the solicitors giving the consent are on the record. If they are not, the judge will sometimes make an order in the terms agreed, but direct that the order is not to be drawn up until the solicitors are on the record. It usually assists in obtaining that result if counsel has ascertained before the hearing that the solicitors are not yet on the record, and has explained that fact to the court. Alternatively, the court will usually accept as sufficient a written consent signed by the respondent's solicitors on their headed notepaper if the solicitors also certify in writing that they have fully explained the effect of the order to the respondent, and that the respondent appeared to have understood the explanation (para 5.39(2)).

10.7.5 Effective applications

The order in which effective, that is, disputed, listed applications are dealt with is in the discretion of the judge. Counsel will normally offer their colleagues the courtesy of allowing shorter applications to be made first. Naturally, this must not be abused by underestimating the time which an application will take. The procedure will then follow this outline:

- Counsel making the application will open by giving a short account of the facts giving rise to the application.
- Counsel then reads the evidence in support of the application.
- The opposing counsel will read (in the appropriate order) the evidence served by the other side.
- Counsel for the applicant then makes his or her submissions on the evidence as presented.
- Counsel for the respondent makes his or her submissions.
- Counsel for the applicant is entitled to reply on the submissions of the opposing party.

It will be noticed that the evidence is read aloud in court. When applications are made effectively for the first time, there has naturally been no opportunity for the judge to read any witness statements or affidavits, as these will not have been filed before the application is made. If the application has been stood over as an application by order, it is good practice to advise the instructing solicitors to prepare a paginated bundle of the evidence on the application and to lodge it in advance of the hearing. It may then be possible to follow the Commercial Court practice of hearing argument in open court only on those aspects of the evidence which are disputed. When making time estimates, therefore, counsel should bear in mind the probability that the evidence on an application will have to be read *in extenso* in court.

10.7.6 Agreed adjournments

If all parties agree, an application can be adjourned for not more than 14 days by counsel or solicitors attending the Chancery Listing Officer no later than 4 pm on the day before the listed hearing producing signed consents from the legal representatives for all parties. A litigant in person who is a party must attend before the Clerk as well as sign a written consent. Not more than three successive adjournments may be made and no adjournments are to be made to the last two application days of any sitting. See *Chancery Guide*, para 5.19. Undertakings previously given to the court may be continued unchanged over the duration of any adjournment. If an existing undertaking is to be varied or a new undertaking given, the adjournment must be dealt with by the judge.

An application may be adjourned to be heard as an application by order without attendance before the judge where the parties are agreed that the application will take two hours or more. The same procedure as noted previously is adopted, except that consents must include a timetable for filing evidence. See *Chancery Guide*, para 5.20.

10.7.7 Drafting of orders

10.7.7.1 Drawing up

In all but the most simple applications a draft order should be prepared and brought to the hearing (*Chancery Guide*, para 9.5). It is often helpful to provide the court with a copy as an attachment to an email (para 9.7), and this is obligatory in respect of interim applications (paras 5.29 and 9.8). If a digital storage device is provided to the court with the draft, it must be new and newly formatted, to reduce the risk of transferring a computer virus. Unless the court directs or permits a party to draw it up, or directs the parties to agree and sign a draft order, the court will draw up the order and send it out without reference to the parties, see para 9.10. An unusually complicated order may require that an initial draft be sent to the parties.

10.7.7.2 Tomlin order

Where the claim is to be stayed on agreed terms to be scheduled to the order, the minutes should contain a specially drafted clause. See *Chancery Guide*, para 9.16 and *A Practical Approach to ADR*, 2nd edn (OUP, 2012), Figure 23.7.

10.7.8 Use of information technology

PD 5B sets out the circumstances in which documents may be filed by email, and PD 5C on electronic working operates in designated specialist courts and also the Chancery Division (PD 5C, para 1.1(1)(b)). The *Chancery Guide*, para 14.2, says it must be remembered that a significant number of its cases involve litigants in person, and that not all solicitors have access to sophisticated IT facilities. Consequently, the use of IT has to ensure that no party will be unfairly prejudiced by its use, and that it should only be used where it will save time or money. In any case where the solicitors for one or more parties take the view that some form of IT will assist the presentation or management of a case, the solicitor should obtain, at an early stage, directions from the judge who is to try the case. Examples are using imaging techniques to deal with disclosure (see also PD 31B), or the provision of electronic bundles for hearings. Where no nomination of a specific judge has yet been made, solicitors who wish to use any form of IT should make an application by letter to the Chancellor (addressed to his clerk) to nominate a judge to hear the case including all interim matters (para 14.3).

Where the use of IT is contemplated, the solicitors for the parties should seek to establish a common protocol for the electronic exchange and management of information (para 14.4). The *Chancery Guide* suggests parties should adopt the Technology and Construction Solicitors' Association's protocol.

When draft orders, skeleton arguments or chronologies exist in electronic form, they are typically provided by email or on a digital storage device. Sometimes a judge will also request electronic versions of other documents, such as witness statements and experts' reports. Any digital storage device supplied to a judge should be new and newly formatted to minimise the risk of transferring a computer virus.

Where a party is entitled to a copy of a document which has been prepared by another party for use in court in electronic form, he or she may require that it also be provided to him or her in electronic form.

Telephone hearings for case management hearings etc are governed by the main rules in PD 23A, paras 6.1–6.13, as supplemented by the *Chancery Guide*, para 14.13. Video conferencing is permitted by CPR, r 32.3, with guidance being set out in PD 32, Annex 3 and the *Chancery Guide*, paras 14.14–14.17. An application for permission to use the court's video-conferencing facilities should be obtained as early as possible. Experience has shown that normally taking evidence by this means is comparatively straightforward, but its suitability may depend on the particular witness, and also the nature and volume of the documents that will need to be referred to in the course of the evidence.

11

Shareholder protection

11.1 Introduction

Control of the company rests with the members voting in general meeting or the directors to the extent that powers have been delegated to them. Members will have such control over the directors as the articles and statute give them, in particular they have the right to remove the directors or alter the articles and withdraw their powers (see **6.2**).

Members' decisions are usually by ordinary resolution (simple majority) of those who attend and vote at general meetings. All members will be bound by the resolutions properly passed at general meetings. In smaller private companies the directors may also be the majority shareholders with the result that minority shareholders have virtually no control over the company's activities.

Clearly where a shareholder objects to the manner in which a company is being conducted the most logical thing to do is to sell the shares and invest elsewhere. However, this is not always possible, as in small private companies there may be restrictions on the ability of shareholders to sell contained in the articles or in a practical sense in that no one will buy them. In addition, the mismanagement may be such that the aggrieved shareholder wishes to do something about it because the value of the shares has been affected or purely as a matter of principle. However, it is usually the case that shareholders who are aggrieved will simply sell their shares.

This chapter will consider a number of miscellaneous methods of affording some protection to a company's shareholders, and will then concentrate on the rule in *Foss v Harbottle*. Two very important statutory measures for protecting minority shareholders, namely, just and equitable winding up and petitions for relief against unfair prejudice, will be considered in **Chapters 12** and **13** respectively.

11.2 Breach of articles

If a member is dissatisfied with his or her treatment by the company, a claim may be brought against the company if the treatment amounts to an abuse of individual rights given by the articles (eg the right to a notice of meetings, or to vote): CA 2006, s 33; *Salmon v Quin and Axtens Ltd* [1909] AC 442. Such a claim may be a personal action to protect a personal right only or it may be a representative action to protect all those whose rights have been denied (eg for all shareholders not paid their dividend). Such a claim would be governed by CPR, r 19.6, and can only be brought if all parties have the same interest in the proceedings (see *Prudential Assurance Co Ltd v Newman Industries Ltd* [1981] Ch 229).

11.3 Statutory protection in running of a company

Statute gives some protection to the minority in the general running of the company by:

(a) Requiring a greater majority (eg special resolution) to pass resolutions to effect major changes in the company's constitution—for example, alter articles (CA 2006, s 21), name (CA 2006, s 77) or reduce capital (CA 2006, s 641).

(b) Providing that some things cannot be done without the consent of all members—for example, a member's liability cannot be increased without that member's written consent (CA 2006, s 25).

(c) Empowering members to require meetings to be called and/or information to be circulated to members (important as directors generally have the power to call meetings, set agendas and circulate information) (see **6.6.5**).

(d) Giving members the right to object to the court in some cases even though a resolution has been passed with the requisite majority—for example, alteration of class rights (CA 2006, s 633).

11.4 BIS investigation

Under CA 1985, s 431, the BIS may investigate the affairs of a company on the application of 200 shareholders or the holders of one-tenth of the share capital. Under CA 1985, s 432, the BIS may investigate the affairs of a company where the Secretary of State considers that they have been conducted, *inter alia*, in a manner unfairly prejudicial to some of its members, or proper information has not been given to its members. Inspectors are appointed with extensive powers to investigate and on receipt of their report the BIS may take a variety of actions including instituting civil proceedings on behalf of the company, petitioning for an order under CA 2006, s 996, for protection of members against unfair protection, or for winding up on grounds of public interest under IA 1986, s 124A.

11.5 The rule in *Foss v Harbottle*

11.5.1 The rule

In a company's affairs the maxim 'majority rules' prevails. This means that dissatisfied shareholders rarely have any remedy if they feel the company is badly managed to their detriment, for example if they feel they are getting a poor return on their investment through the incompetence of the directors. The rule is formulated to prevent a multiplicity of such actions. The case of *Foss v Harbottle* (1843) 2 Hare 461 clearly indicated that if a wrong is done to a company then the company is the proper claimant to right that wrong.

This rule stems from the court's reluctance to interfere in the management of a company (*Carlen v Drury* (1812) 1 Ves and B 154—'This court is not to be required on every occasion to take the management of every brewhouse and playhouse in the kingdom'). In *Foss v Harbottle* two shareholders brought proceedings against five directors alleging misappropriation of property by them. The court held that as the injury was to the company, the company was the proper claimant and the shareholders were not competent to bring the action. It did acknowledge that this rule could be departed from but only if there were reasons of a very urgent character.

In *Mozley v Alston* (1847) 1 Ph 790 two shareholders sought an injunction to restrain the board from acting until four of the directors who ought to have retired by rotation to allow four others to be elected did so. It expressly alleged that a majority of the shareholders supported the action and the court commented that if that was so there was obviously nothing to prevent the company from instituting a claim. Proceedings in the name of the company would be free from objection as the claimant would be the body vested with the cause of action. In *MacDougall v Gardiner* (1875) 1 ChD 13, the articles of the company provided for the taking of a poll at a general meeting if five shareholders demanded one. The chairman, in breach of the articles, refused to take a poll on the question of adjournment and MacDougall brought proceedings seeking a declaration and an injunction to restrain the directors from taking further action. The court emphasised that the rule in *Foss v Harbottle* must always be adhered to, that nothing connected with internal disputes can be made the subject of litigation by one shareholder on behalf of himself and others unless there was something illegal, oppressive or fraudulent. The nature of companies meant that there was nothing more likely than that there would be something more or less irregular done at company meetings and if every member had a right to bring proceedings everything would be litigated whereas if proceedings had to be taken in the name of the company then, unless the majority really wished for litigation, it would not go on. Thus there is no point in having litigation in respect of anything which in substance the majority of the company are entitled to do as the ultimate end is that a meeting is called and the majority gets its wish.

In *Edwards v Halliwell* [1950] 2 All ER 1064, where members of a trade union sought a declaration that an increase in union dues was invalid on the ground that a rule which required a two-thirds vote on a ballot had not been followed, the rule in *Foss v Harbottle* was analysed as having two aspects, first the proper claimant principle (the company as the wronged person is the proper claimant) and secondly the majority rule principle (where the transaction is one which a simple majority may resolve to do and bind the company, proceedings by an individual shareholder cannot be maintained). The reasons for and exceptions to the rules are the subject of much academic debate.

The decision to sue must therefore be made by the company and this means either a decision of the board or a decision of the members in general meeting. (It is open to debate whether the members may resolve to sue if the general management powers have been delegated to the board: see *Marshall's Valve Gear Co Ltd v Manning Wardle and Co Ltd* [1909] 1 Ch 267 and *John Shaw and Sons (Salford) Ltd v Shaw* [1935] 2 KB 113.) One view is that it is a shared power. The clear rule laid down in *Foss v Harbottle*

(1843) 2 Hare 461 is that a single shareholder, or indeed minority shareholders, may not sue.

Given the multitude of cases, complexity and differing views of the law, the following can be no more than a broad overview of the generally accepted exceptions to the rule. However, before setting out the exceptions the different types of proceedings which may be commenced by members of the company are described.

11.5.2 Types of claim

11.5.2.1 Personal claims

This is a claim by a member to enforce personal rights arising from the CA 2006, s 33, contract or under the general law. It is commenced by the member as claimant in the same way as any other claim to enforce a right, with the company and wrongdoer as defendants.

11.5.2.2 Representative proceedings

A claim by a member on behalf of a group of shareholders to enforce a common right. CPR, r 19.6, will apply to the proceedings which may be brought where:

(a) all members on whose behalf the claim is brought have a separate cause of action and the relief claimed would not confer a right of action where none previously existed; and

(b) all members of the class represented share an interest which is common to all of them; and

(c) the court is satisfied that it is for the benefit of the class that the claimant should be permitted to sue in such a representative claim (*Prudential Assurance Co Ltd v Newman Industries Ltd* [1981] Ch 229).

The nature of representative claims is considered in BCP, para 14.62.

Representative claims are used in a variety of circumstances, for example challenging administrative decisions and litigation by or against unincorporated associations as well as in the context of company law.

11.5.2.3 Derivative claims

A derivative claim is the term used for proceedings by a member of a company in respect of a cause of action vested in the company and seeking relief on behalf of the company (CA 2006, s 260(1)). Such proceedings were allowed under the common law where the court permitted a member to pursue such a claim by way of an exception to the rule in *Foss v Harbottle*. The CA 2006, Part 11, ss 260–264, puts the derivative claim on a statutory footing. The Explanatory Notes to the CA 2006 make it clear that Part 11 does not formulate a substantive rule to replace the rule in *Foss v Harbottle*, but introduces a 'new derivative procedure'. However, the changes make it easier for shareholders to bring a derivative claim in the name of the company.

A derivative claim must be brought by a member of the company. This includes a person who is not a member but to whom shares in the company have been transferred or transmitted by operation of law, for example on death or by bankruptcy. Such a person can bring proceedings on a cause of action which arose before or after he or she became a member of the company. The cause of action must be vested in the company and the relief must be sought on the company's behalf.

A derivative claim is usually brought against the company's directors. It may be brought against third parties, but only if the claim depends on the negligence, breach of duty or breach of trust of the company's directors (*Iesini v Westrip Holdings Ltd* [2011] 1 BCLC 498).

Section 260(2) makes it clear that a member can only bring a derivative claim in the name of the company in one of two ways:

(1) under ch 1 of Part 11 (the derivative claim); or

(2) where the court orders proceedings to be brought in the name of and on behalf of the company by a member pursuant to proceedings under CA 2006, s 994 (unfair prejudice).

Section 260(3) provides that a derivative claim can be brought against a director of the company or another person (or both) only in respect of a cause of action arising from an actual or proposed act or omission involving negligence, default, breach of duty or breach of trust. The Explanatory Notes to the CA 2006 make it clear that this enables a derivative claim to be brought for an alleged breach of one of the statutory duties of directors. The Explanatory Notes also make it clear that a derivative claim will only be permitted to be continued against third parties in very limited circumstances. Examples are claims for knowing receipt of the company's money or property transferred to the third party in breach of trust or for knowing assistance in breach of trust.

The procedure on derivative claims is set out in CPR, rr 19.9–19.9F and PD 19C, and is described in BCP, para 14.27. An applicant wishing to bring a derivative claim will have to go through a two-stage procedure:

(1) He or she will be required to make out a prima facie case for permission to continue the derivative claim (CA 2006, s 261(2)). The court will avoid holding a mini-trial, and will normally consider whether to grant permission to continue the claim on the basis of the applicant's evidence without submissions by the company. At this stage the court has to be satisfied that the claimant is able to establish a prima facie case that an act or omission by the directors involves negligence, breach of duty or breach of trust (*Iesini v Westrip Holdings Ltd* [2011] 1 BCLC 498). If the applicant does not establish a prima facie case, the claim will be dismissed (s 261), and the court can make any consequential order that it considers appropriate (eg costs).

(2) If the court does not dismiss the application at the first stage, then the court may require the defendant to put in evidence, or adjourn the case to enable evidence to be obtained, or give permission to continue the claim on such terms as the court determines. Permission may be granted up to a stated point in the litigation, such as the conclusion of disclosure, when a further application for permission would be required (*Stainer v Lee* [2011] 1 BCLC 537). Alternatively, the court may refuse permission and dismiss the claim.

By s 262, if the company has brought a claim and the cause of action on which it is based could be pursued as a derivative claim, a member can apply to the court to continue the claim as a derivative claim. Permission to continue as a derivative claim may be granted if:

(a) the manner in which the company commenced or continued the claim amounts to an abuse of the process of the court;

(b) the company has failed to prosecute the claim diligently; and

(c) it is appropriate for the member to continue the claim as a derivative claim.

In deciding whether to grant permission to the applicant to bring or continue a claim under s 261 or 262, the court must refuse permission (see s 263) if it is satisfied that:

(a) a person acting in accordance with the general duty to promote the success of the company under s 172 (see **7.3.4**) would not seek to continue the claim. This mandatory bar only operates if no director acting in accordance with s 172 would seek to continue the claim (*Franbar Holdings Ltd v Patel* [2009] 1 BCLC 1). Where a decision not to defend a claim was taken on the advice of eminent and specialist counsel, no person acting in accordance with s 172 would have sought to continue it, and permission to continue a derivative claim was accordingly refused in *Iesini v Westrip Holdings Ltd* [2011] 1 BCLC 498; or

(b) the act or omission giving rise to the cause of action has been authorised or ratified by the company (which is exactly the same position as at common law). Section 180(4) preserves the rule enabling the company to authorise anything done by directors which would otherwise be a breach of duty. Section 239 provides that ratification must be by resolution of the members disregarding the votes of the director(s) whose breach is under consideration and any member connected to him or her.

The court must also take into account the following factors (s 263(3), (4)):

(a) whether the member is acting in good faith in seeking to continue the claim;

(b) the importance that a person acting in accordance with the duty to promote the success of the company would attach to continuing the claim;

(c) where the cause of action results from an anticipated or actual act or omission, whether it could be, and in the circumstances would be likely to be, authorised or ratified by the company. The more likely it is that the conduct would be authorised or ratified, the less suitable it is to permit a derivative claim. Where such authorisation or ratification is regarded as improper, the appropriate route may be through unfair prejudice relief (see **Chapter 13**);

(d) whether the company has decided not to pursue the claim;

(e) whether the act or omission in respect of which the claim is brought gives rise to a cause of action that the member could pursue in his or her own right rather than on behalf of the company. This does not require exact identity of defendants. What is required is that the acts or omissions give rise to a cause of action available to the shareholder in his or her own right (*Franbar Holdings Ltd v Patel* [2009] 1 BCLC 1); and

(f) any evidence before the court as to the views of the members of the company who have no personal interest (direct or indirect) in the matter (s 263(4)). This will make it harder for a shareholder to bring a claim if the majority of the shareholders would not wish to do so.

The member bringing the claim runs the risk of having to pay both his or her own costs and the other parties' costs. The court can direct the company to indemnify the member for such costs, and a claimant seeking such an order must state this in the claim form (PD 19C, para 2(2)). It is likely that the court will only make an order if the claim stands a reasonable chance of success and would be for the benefit of the company. In *Smith v Croft* [1986] 1 WLR 580 an order was refused where the claim stood little chance of success and the majority of shareholders were against it.

A claimant was able to join a personal claim with a derivative claim with permission of the court, which was normally given under the old rules (*Cooke v Cooke* [1997] 2 BCLC 28). It is likely this will not change.

11.5.3 Exceptions to the rule

11.5.3.1 Illegal or *ultra vires* acts

A member may apply for an injunction to restrain the company from doing an illegal or *ultra vires* act (*Simpson v Westminster Palace Hotel Co* (1860) 8 HL Cas 712). This is preserved by CA 2006, s 40(4), see **7.2.2**. The injunction may be sought in a personal or a representative claim (*Prudential Assurance Co Ltd v Newman Industries Ltd (No 2)* [1982] Ch 204). In this respect it is not truly an exception to the rule. However, where the act complained of has been completed and the claim is brought to recover property disposed of by the transaction the proper claimant is the company. Where a minority claim is brought to recover property it must be a derivative one. At common law a company could not ratify an *ultra vires* act, but the CA 1985, s 35(3), allowed this by special resolution. Section 35(3) has been repealed and is not re-enacted by the CA 2006. A company seeking to validate an *ultra vires* act under the CA 2006 therefore needs to alter its articles by special resolution under CA 2006, s 21 (see **3.5.3**). However, a company may resolve not to pursue a claim for damages or restitution and this is binding on minority shareholders unless fraud on the minority can be shown (*Smith v Croft (No 2)* [1988] Ch 114).

11.5.3.2 Fraud on the minority

This is the true exception to the rule and a most difficult area to establish comprehensive principles from the numerous and varied cases. However, it is clear that there are two matters which must be proved: fraud and control. Exactly what amounts to fraud is unclear but the word does have a meaning wider than fraud at common law and includes an unconscionable abuse of majority power. It will include the appropriation of assets or advantages belonging to the company to the majority who then resolve in general meeting not to recover it (*Cook v Deeks* [1916] 1 AC 554, but note the contrast with *Regal (Hastings) Ltd v Gulliver* [1967] 2 AC 134 discussed in **7.5.1**). It will also include the compromising of litigation by a resolution of the majority to benefit themselves and disadvantage the company (*Estmanco (Kilner House) Ltd v Greater London Council* [1982] 1 WLR 2). In *Pavlides v Jensen* [1956] Ch 565 it was held that mere negligence on the part of directors who controlled the majority of the shares in the company was not sufficient. There was no allegation of fraud on the part of the directors nor of appropriation of company assets. The allegation was that company property had negligently been sold at an undervalue. Thus a resolution by the company that no action should be taken against the directors was binding on the shareholders and a minority claim was not allowed. However, this case was distinguished in *Daniels v Daniels* [1978] Ch 406 where three minority shareholders brought proceedings against the two directors and majority shareholders alleging that they had caused the company to sell property at a gross undervalue to a director who was one of the majority shareholders. No fraud was alleged as the minority shareholders did not really know what had happened, only that the sale had been at an undervalue and that the director who bought had made a substantial profit. The court said that it would be monstrous, particularly as fraud is so hard to plead and prove, to restrict the exceptions to the rule in *Foss v Harbottle* to such an extent as to allow directors to make a profit by their negligence. A minority claim was allowed on the basis that negligence may amount to fraud on the minority if it results in a benefit to the wrongdoers at the company's expense. What amounts to fraud on the minority is also often discussed in the context of the difference between a ratifiable and non-ratifiable breach.

It must be shown that the company is being prevented from bringing proceedings because of the control of the wrongdoer. Generally this will be shown by the fact that the wrongdoer has voting control. Thus there must be some attempt to persuade the company to sue before issuing a minority claim. It is not clear whether *de facto* control is sufficient. In *Prudential Assurance Co Ltd v Newman Industries Ltd (No 2)* [1982] Ch 204 the Court of Appeal appeared to prefer voting control but did comment that control embraced a broad spectrum from overall absolute majority of votes to a majority of votes made up of the delinquent directors and those voting with them as a result of influence or apathy. In *Smith v Croft (No 2)* [1988] Ch 114 the court said that it was appropriate to have regard to the views of the shareholders, independent of the wrongdoer, who made up the majority of the minority who did not wish to continue the proceedings.

11.5.3.3 Where justice requires

There has been some discussion of whether there is a fifth exception in that the rule will be relaxed where it is necessary in the interests of justice or whether this is the basis of all the exceptions noted previously (see *Edwards v Halliwell* [1950] 2 All ER 1064 and *Estmanco (Kilner House) Ltd v Greater London Council* [1982] 1 WLR 2). In *Prudential Assurance Co Ltd v Newman Industries Ltd (No 2)* [1982] Ch 204 the Court of Appeal commented that it was not convinced that this was a practical test.

11.5.4 Situations outside the rule in *Foss v Harbottle*

Two other types of claims which in the past have tended to be included in consideration of exceptions to the rule but which are in reality outside the rule are individual members claiming in respect of rights denied and where an activity requiring approval by a special majority has not been so approved.

11.5.4.1 Personal rights

A member may take action to protect his or her own personal rights under the articles, a separate shareholders' agreement or statute. This then is not really an exception to the rule in *Foss v Harbottle* because it is not an attempt to enforce the company's rights (it is frequently cited as an exception nevertheless). Thus a member may bring a personal claim to enforce payment of dividends which have been declared (*Wood v Odessa Waterworks Co* (1889) 42 ChD 636) or to have his or her vote recorded (*Pender v Lushington* (1877) 6 ChD 70 where a personal claim was combined with a representative one). However, the difficulty with the exception is determining what is a personal right which can be so enforced. Compare *Pender v Lushington* with *MacDougall v Gardiner* (1875) 1 ChD 13 (see **11.5.1**) where a right to demand a poll was not enforceable. Exactly what provisions in the articles will be enforced under the CA 2006, s 33, contract between the company and the member is a much debated question (see **3.6** and cases referred to there). It is clear, however, that a member cannot bring a personal claim for loss in value of shares which resulted from damage to the company (*Prudential Assurance Co Ltd v Newman Industries Ltd (No 2)* [1982] Ch 204). The proper remedy is for the company to take action against the person who caused the damage to recover the loss which in turn will restore the value of the shares. See also *Johnson v Gore Wood and Co* [2002] 2 AC 1.

11.5.4.2 Special majorities

Although it was said in *MacDougall v Gardiner* (1875) 1 ChD 13 that where a majority are entitled to do something there is no use in litigation as ultimately the majority can just resolve to do it in general meeting, this rule does not apply where, for example, a special resolution is required. In *Edwards v Halliwell* [1950] 2 All ER 1064, two trade union members who challenged an increase of dues which had been made without obtaining the required two-thirds majority consent were successful. In *Quin and Axtens Ltd v Salmon* [1909] AC 442 the articles of association gave the two managing directors a power of veto on certain transactions. On one transaction one of the directors dissented from the board resolution. The members in general meeting resolved to authorise the transaction. However, an injunction was granted restraining the company from acting on the resolutions as they were inconsistent with the articles and alteration of the articles requires a special resolution. This exception may be extended to cover other procedural irregularities, for example inadequate notice of meetings because insufficient information is given (*Baillie v Oriental Telephone and Electric Co Ltd* [1915] 1 Ch 503 and *Kaye v Croydon Tramways Co* [1898] 1 Ch 358). However, it is not clear how far this exception will extend.

12 Just and equitable winding up

12.1 Introduction

As we saw at **9.3.1**, one of the eight statutory grounds for the compulsory winding up of a company provided for by the IA 1986, s 122(1), is that 'the court is of the opinion that it is just and equitable that the company should be wound up'. After winding up on the ground that the company is unable to pay its debts, the 'just and equitable' ground is the most important of the grounds set out in s 122. In the past, seeking an order for the winding up of a company on this ground served the important function of providing a practical avenue through which a minority shareholder could seek redress for overbearing conduct on the part of those in control of the company. This was particularly important given the difficulties in bringing a derivative action or for seeking relief from oppression under the (now repealed) CA 1948, s 210.

Since 1980 this particular use of the just and equitable ground has been largely supplanted by the jurisdiction to provide relief for conduct which is unfairly prejudicial under CA 2006, s 994. Relief for unfair prejudice is considered in **Chapter 13**. It will be seen that if unfair prejudice is established, the court is given wide powers for granting flexible relief designed to remove that prejudice. One of the drawbacks with relief on the just and equitable ground is that there is only one remedy available if it is established, namely, the winding up of the company. Obviously, in many cases this can only be regarded as a rather drastic remedy.

This chapter will consider the various types of cases where the courts have considered it appropriate to make winding-up orders on this ground, and on the interrelation between the just and equitable ground and other available forms of relief. Before doing so a number of procedural matters will be considered.

12.2 *Locus standi*

The same categories of persons who can present ordinary winding-up petitions also have *locus standi* to present petitions on the just and equitable ground. The discussion at **9.4** therefore applies in full to these petitions. However, they are most commonly presented by shareholders. As discussed previously, to be a 'contributory' a shareholder must have held the shares for at least six out of the 18 months before presenting the petition, or must have been the original allottee of the shares, or they must have devolved on the petitioner through the death of a previous owner: IA 1986, s 124(2)(b). Further, the petitioner must have a financial interest in the winding up of the company. This will be satisfied either if the shares are partly paid (fairly rare in modern times) or if there is likely to be a surplus available for distribution to shareholders on a winding up of the company. The fact that the petitioner holds a small proportion of the issued shares is not a bar to presenting a petition if the company is likely to be solvent (see *Bryanston Finance Ltd v de Vries (No 2)* [1976] Ch 63, where the petitioner held 62 out of 7,500,000 issued shares, each share being worth just a few pence).

12.3 Procedure

12.3.1 General

The petition must specify the grounds on which it is presented. On presentation the petitioner must pay the court fee of £220 and make the usual £1,165 deposit. There are, however, a few differences. PD 49B, para 2, provides that contributories' petitions (as just and equitable winding-up petitions commonly are) must state whether the petitioner consents or objects to a standard-form order validating transactions during the period between presentation and determination of the petition, pursuant to the IA 1986, s 127. As was seen at **9.8**, this is of great importance as a safeguard to persons dealing with the company and for the company itself, particularly as these petitions are rarely resolved quickly.

When a contributory's petition is presented, instead of the court appointing a return date for the final resolution of the petition (which is what happens in typical creditors' petitions), the court will fix a return date on which the Companies Court Registrar will consider the case and give directions in relation to the procedure on the petition (IR 1986, r 4.22(2)). At the directions hearing the registrar will consider:

(a) Giving directions for service of the petition on additional persons.

(b) Whether particulars of claim and defence should be delivered.

(c) General procedural matters, such as disclosure of documents.

(d) Whether, and by what means, the petition should be advertised (creditors' petitions have to be advertised in the *London Gazette*: as advertisement can cause serious harm to a company's business, it is not uncommon for the registrar to make an order that the petition is not to be advertised).

(e) The manner in which evidence is to be adduced at the hearing. Matters to be considered include whether the evidence can be given by witness statement or orally, whether deponents should attend for cross-examination and whether restrictions should be imposed on the issues to be dealt with in evidence.

(f) Other matters affecting the petition and its disposal. Such a matter is the mode and place of trial.

Notice of intention to appear needs to be given by 4 pm on the day before the hearing by supporting and opposing creditors, and the petitioner must compile a list of appearances.

12.3.2 Role of the company

Although the company will suffer the ignominy of being wound up if the petition is successful, the reality is that the company itself is little more than a formal party to the proceedings, which typically take the form of disputes between rival groups of shareholders. Company money must not, therefore, be used to pay the legal costs of one of the sides in the dispute (*Re A and BC Chewing Gum Ltd* [1975] 1 WLR 579), and an injunction may be sought if this is attempted by one side to the litigation (*Re Milgate Developments Ltd* [1993] BCLC 291).

12.4 Principles

At one time it was thought that the 'just and equitable' ground for winding up should be construed *eiusdem generis* with the other grounds set out in what is now the IA 1986, s 122(1), with the effect that a petition on this ground could only be successful if the circumstances were similar to those set out in the other grounds in the section. Since the end of the nineteenth century this idea has slowly been put to rest, and it is fair to say that today it no longer plays any part in the principles informing the courts when dealing with just and equitable winding-up petitions.

In *Ebrahimi v Westbourne Galleries Ltd* [1973] AC 360 the House of Lords took the view (particularly Lord Wilberforce at 374–375) that the just and equitable ground should be applied flexibly and was a concept that could be adapted in suitable cases, and criticised previous attempts to categorise the situations in which relief under the section could be granted. Despite this, it is helpful for the purposes of exposition to attempt a classification of the circumstances where winding-up orders on the just and equitable ground have been made in the past, and this will be attempted at **12.6**. It should simply be borne in mind that these categories are not set in stone, and that the court can approach individual cases in a flexible manner. The categories should perhaps be seen more as examples or illustrations of situations where winding up on this ground may be appropriate.

In a helpful general statement of principle, Lord Shaw of Dunfermline in *Loch v John Blackwood Ltd* [1924] AC 783 said:

> It is undoubtedly true that at the foundation of applications for winding up, on the 'just and equitable' rule, there must lie a justifiable lack of confidence in the conduct and management of the company's affairs. But this lack of confidence must be grounded on conduct of the directors, not in regard to their private life or affairs, but in regard to the company's business. Furthermore the lack of confidence must spring not from dissatisfaction at being outvoted on the business affairs or on what is called the domestic policy of the company. On the other hand, wherever the lack of confidence is rested on a lack of probity in the conduct of the company's affairs, then the former is justified by the latter, and it is under the statute just and equitable that the company be wound up.

As was mentioned in **12.1**, winding up on the just and equitable ground suffers from the drawback that only one form of relief can be granted if the petition is successful. There is judicial reluctance to winding up successful companies, which is reflected in stronger cases being required where the company is successful than if it were struggling. As Nicholls LJ said in *Re Walter L. Jacob and Co Ltd* [1989] BCLC 345, the compulsory winding up of an active company is a serious step, and a petitioner asking the court to do this must put forward and establish reasons which have a weight justifying this remedy being granted.

12.5 Quasi-partnership

In addition to the success (or otherwise) of the company, another factor that clearly influences the courts when considering just and equitable petitions is whether the company can be described as a 'quasi-partnership'. These are businesses which are, as said by Lord Cozens-Hardy MR in *Re Yenidje Tobacco Co Ltd* [1916] 2 Ch 426, in substance partnerships but existing in the form of limited companies. They will typically be private companies with small numbers of members and formed on the basis of personal relationships between the members involving mutual confidence and on the understanding that the shareholders will participate in managing the business by being directors. The courts find it far easier to, or will only, grant relief on the basis of deadlock, loss of substratum and exclusion from management if the company is a quasi-partnership.

The leading case on this concept is *Ebrahimi v Westbourne Galleries Ltd* [1973] AC 360. When the company was formed it took over a business previously carried on in partnership between a Mr Ebrahimi and a Mr Nazar, who were allotted all the shares in the new company and were its first directors. Later, Mr Nazar's son was brought into the company as a director, at which stage the Nazars held 60 per cent of the shares and Mr Ebrahimi the other 40 per cent. No dividends were ever declared in favour of the shareholders, with profits being distributed in the form of directors' remuneration. Nine years after the company was formed the Nazars used their voting power to remove Mr Ebrahimi from his post as a director under what is now the CA 2006, s 168 (see **6.10**). From a strict legal point of view the Nazars were acting within their rights in exercising their votes in this way. Mr Ebrahimi petitioned for the winding up of the company on the just and equitable ground, basing his petition on his removal from the management of the company and his loss of a share in the company's profits as he was no longer being paid as a director.

Lord Wilberforce said the jurisdiction to wind up on the just and equitable ground is:

> a recognition of the fact that a limited company is more than a mere legal entity, with a personality in law of its own: that there is room in company law for recognition of the fact that behind it, or amongst it, there are individuals, with rights, expectations and obligations *inter se* which are not necessarily submerged in the company structure. That structure is defined by the Companies Act and by the articles of association by which shareholders agree to be bound. In most companies and in most contexts, this definition is sufficient and exhaustive, equally so whether the company is large or small. The 'just and equitable' provision does not, as the respondents suggest, entitle one party to disregard the obligation he assumes by entering a company, nor the court to dispense him from it. It does, as equity always does, enable the court to subject the exercise of legal rights to equitable considerations; considerations, that is, of a personal character arising between one individual and another, which may make it unjust, or inequitable, to insist on legal rights, or to exercise them in a particular way.
>
> It would be impossible, and wholly undesirable, to define the circumstances in which these considerations may arise. Certainly the fact that a company is a small one, or a private company, is not enough. There are very many of these where the association is a purely commercial one, of

> which it can safely be said that the basis of association is adequately and exhaustively laid down in the articles. The superimposition of equitable considerations requires something more, which typically may include one, or probably more, of the following elements: (i) an association formed or continued on the basis of a personal relationship, involving mutual confidence—this element will often be found where a pre-existing partnership has been converted into a limited company; (ii) an agreement, or understanding, that all, or some (for there may be 'sleeping' members), of the shareholders shall participate in the conduct of the business; (iii) restriction upon the transfer of the members' interest in the company—so that if confidence is lost, or one member is removed from management, he cannot take out his stake and go elsewhere.
>
> It is these, and analogous, factors which may bring into play the just and equitable clause.

Although Lord Wilberforce in the second of the paragraphs quoted said a quasi-partnership would typically have one or more of the three elements he then described, subsequent cases, such as *O'Neill v Phillips* [1999] 1 WLR 1092, HL, have tended to look for all three elements before deciding whether a company can be categorised as a quasi-partnership. The following matters may be relevant when considering whether a company can be described as a quasi-partnership:

(a) Restrictions in share transfers may be by way of express provision in the articles of association or a shareholders' agreement, but can also be established if there is no practical market for the petitioners' shares (as is often the case with minority share interests in small private companies).

(b) The number of shareholders is important, but not determinative. Generally, the smaller the number of shareholders, the more likely the company is to be a quasi-partnership. If the other factors are strong enough, the fact a company may have eight, ten or 12 members will not necessarily prevent it from being a quasi-partnership.

(c) There may be indications one way or the other in the articles or shareholders' agreement. For example, provisions aimed at ensuring named founders remain in post as directors points towards a quasi-partnership. A provision stating a members' agreement is not to be construed as creating a partnership tends the other way, but again is not determinative (*Re a Company (No 003028 of 1987)* [1988] BCLC 282).

(d) Changes in the membership or ethos of a company may change its status (or may mean that some members remain as quasi-partners, while others are not). For example, the acceptance of service contracts by the petitioning shareholders after a change in shareholders (which resulted in the emergence of a new majority shareholder) terminated the company's status as a quasi-partnership in *Third v North East Ice and Cold Storage Co Ltd* [1998] BCC 242.

(e) A member who was not a quasi-partner when he or she first acquired shares in the company may become a quasi-partner at a later stage. For example, the member may have received shares in an existing company as a gift or by inheritance, so that initially they were not a quasi-partner. Over time, their relationship with the other members may change, by, for example, participation in management, making personal investments in the business or charging their home to secure the company's overdraft and there may come a point where they will be regarded as a quasi-partner (*O'Neill v Phillips* [1999] 1 WLR 1092, HL).

(f) Equal shareholdings point towards a quasi-partnership. Again this is not determinative one way or the other.

(g) The fact that all the members are individuals and all are to play a part in management points towards a quasi-partnership. However, it is possible for shareholders who are themselves limited companies to be quasi-partners.

12.6 Grounds

12.6.1 Exclusion from management of a quasi-partnership

Directors cannot always expect that they will be directors for life. In general they are subject to removal by the shareholders under CA 2006, s 168, and may be subject to retirement by rotation (see Model Articles for Public Companies SI 2008/3229, reg 21 and 1985 Table A, regs 73 and 74). However, there are cases where shareholders will have legitimate expectations (which may never have been expressed in writing whether in the articles of association or elsewhere) that they will be actively involved in managing the company's affairs. In *Ebrahimi v Westbourne Galleries Ltd* [1973] AC 360 Lord Wilberforce said:

> The just and equitable provision nevertheless comes to [the petitioner's] assistance if he can point to, and prove, some special underlying obligation of his fellow members in good faith, or confidence, that so long as the business continues he shall be entitled to management participation, an obligation so basic that, if broken, the conclusion must be that the association must be dissolved.

Typically, cases where winding-up orders are made on this basis will involve quasi-partnership companies where little or nothing has been paid to shareholders by way of dividends, and where the shareholders have also been the directors and making their livings from their salaries as directors. Often the articles or a shareholders' agreement will name the people who are to serve as directors, and will provide that they are all to use their votes to ensure that each of them will remain in post. In such cases it is very unfair if minority shareholders are later excluded from management, with the result that their investments are retained in the company, but they are deprived of day-to-day control and of any meaningful return on their investment. Nowadays such cases are usually resolved under the unfair prejudice jurisdiction in CA 2006, s 994.

12.6.2 Irretrievable breakdown of business relationship

What is required to justify winding up is a situation (which is unlikely to be retrieved) in which it is impossible for the members to place necessary business confidence in each other, the situation not having been caused by the person seeking to take advantage of it. The leading case on this is *Re Yenidje Tobacco Co Ltd* [1916] 2 Ch 426. There were two shareholders, each with equal numbers of shares (a very common situation, and one which very often leads to conflict at some stage in the life of the company). The company was very successful, making large profits, which apparently increased after the shareholders fell out with each other. They refused to speak to each other. A dispute concerning the dismissal of an employee was referred to arbitration at great cost, and the loser refused to accept the decision of the arbitrator. There were further disputes about most aspects of the running of the company, ranging from the fundamental to the extremely trivial. Board and shareholders' meetings were deadlocked as neither party had a casting vote. The Court of Appeal affirmed the decision to wind up the company, holding that similar principles as apply when considering whether to decree a dissolution of a true partnership (for which see the Partnership Act 1890, s 35(d)) should apply in relation to the breakdown of the business relationship between quasi-partners in a limited company. In *Re Worldhams Park Golf Course Ltd* [1998] 1 BCLC 554 one of the directors had misappropriated company money. In the absence of any condonation of this misconduct by the co-director and other shareholder, it was held that the relationship between the two shareholders had irretrievably broken down, and the misconduct of itself justified the making of a winding-up order.

12.6.3 Failure of substratum

Where a company was formed for specific purposes which are completed or become impossible to achieve, it is likely to be just and equitable for the company to be wound up. The simple justification is that the shareholders will have invested their money with a view to achieving those purposes, and should not have their money locked into a company that will not, or will no longer, be seeking to achieve those purposes. The money should be released so the shareholders can invest elsewhere.

In these cases it is first necessary to determine what the substratum of the company is. For pre-CA 2006 companies this is done primarily by considering the objects clause in the memorandum of association of the company. Companies incorporated under the CA 2006 are unlikely to have objects clauses (see **3.10** for further details). For these companies there is little scope for saying there has been a failure of substratum, unless a common understanding about what business a quasi-partnership company would engage in can be proved by other means. Companies incorporated before the CA 2006 but after 1989 will typically say simply that the company is to carry on business as a general commercial company (as allowed under CA 1985, s 3A, see **3.10.3**). Older companies tend to have very detailed objects clauses. The approach in these cases is to find what the main objects of the company are. As it was put by Salmon J in *Anglo-Overseas Agencies Ltd v Green* [1961] 1 QB 1, the court will usually take the first, or the first two or three, sub-paragraphs of the objects clause as the main object of the company, and will treat the other sub-paragraphs (often there will be 15 or 20 more) as merely ancillary to this main object. Other companies are formed with a specific project or particular business in mind. In these cases finding the substratum of the company is reasonably straightforward.

Examples of cases where there might be a failure of substratum include:

(a) A company formed to run a particular mine, but was unable to acquire the mine: *Re Haven Gold Mining Co* (1882) 20 ChD 151.

(b) A company formed to build a theatre on a particular site, which proved to be too small: *Re Varieties Ltd* [1893] 2 Ch 235.

(c) A company formed to provide facilities connected with Queen Victoria's jubilee in 1897, once the celebrations were over: *Re Amalgamated Syndicate* [1897] 2 Ch 600.

(d) A quasi-partnership company's business was running a nightclub. Its objects clause was not limited to any particular club, but allowed the company to engage in just about any activity in the leisure industry. It was alleged there was an understanding at the time it was formed that the company would not involve itself in any business other than the particular nightclub. After running the nightclub for some time the business was sold. It was regarded as arguable that the company's substratum had gone: *Virdi v Abbey Leisure Ltd* [1990] BCLC 342.

12.6.4 Lack of probity on the part of the directors

Irretrievable breakdown in business relations cases (**12.6.2**) can arise through a clash of personalities rather than through any misconduct on the part of the other side. The breakdown in business relations cases are restricted to quasi-partnership companies. Winding-up petitions based on a lack of probity by the directors do not depend on the company being a quasi-partnership. In *Baird v Lees* 1924 SC 83, Lord President Clyde made the point that shareholders invest in companies, among other things, on the basis that the business of the company will be conducted in accordance with established principles of commercial administration. These are mainly defined by the Companies Act and well-known principles of good faith and honesty, and are intended to provide some guarantee of probity and efficiency. Lord Clyde went on to say:

> If shareholders find that these conditions or some of them are deliberately and consistently violated and set aside by the action of a member and official of the company who wields an overwhelming voting power, and if the result of that, for the extrication of their rights as shareholders, they are deprived of the ordinary facilities which compliance with the Companies Acts would provide them with, then there does arise, in my opinion, a situation in which it may be just and equitable for the court to wind up the company.

12.7 Clean hands

In *Ebrahimi v Westbourne Galleries Ltd* [1973] AC 360, Lord Wilberforce said:

> A petitioner who relies on the 'just and equitable' clause must come to court with clean hands, and if the breakdown in confidence between him and the other parties to the dispute appears to have been due to his misconduct he cannot insist on the company being wound up if they wish it to continue.

Causation is important. Thus, in *Re Yenidje Tobacco Co Ltd* [1916] 2 Ch 426 it was clear that both shareholders had participated in the breakdown of relations, but winding up was ordered as it could not be said that the breakdown was created by the petitioner. The way it was put by Plowman J in *Re Lundie Brothers Ltd* [1965] 1 WLR 1051 was that the petitioner's misconduct could be a bar to relief if it is shown that the breakdown in business relations was caused exclusively by the person seeking to take advantage of it.

12.8 Alternative remedy

12.8.1 Statutory restriction on just and equitable winding up

The IA 1986, s 125(2), provides:

> *If the petition is presented by members of the company as contributories on the ground that it is just and equitable that the company should be wound up, the court, if it is of the opinion—*
>
> *(a) that the petitioners are entitled to relief either by winding up the company or by some other means, and*
>
> *(b) that in the absence of any other remedy it would be just and equitable that the company should be wound up,*

shall make a winding-up order; but this does not apply if the court is also of the opinion both that some other remedy is available to the petitioners and that they are acting unreasonably in seeking to have the company wound up instead of pursuing that other remedy.

The proper approach under this subsection in cases where the judge is of the opinion that the petitioner is entitled to some form of relief, was considered by Vinelott J in *Re a Company (No 002567 of 1982)* [1983] 1 WLR 927. The first stage is for the judge to ignore the possibility of other forms of relief, and to decide whether it is just and equitable for the company to be wound up. Secondly, if the judge concludes that in the absence of any other remedy the company should be wound up on the just and equitable ground, such an order must be made unless the petitioner is acting unreasonably in seeking to wind up instead of pursuing some other remedy.

12.8.2 Alternative remedies

Alternative remedies typically are:

(a) Seeking relief for unfair prejudice.

(b) Seeking a voluntary winding up of the company.

(c) Seeking relief by way of derivative proceedings or otherwise in respect of any breach of fiduciary or other duty by the directors.

(d) Using a specific procedure laid down in the articles of association of the company dealing with the situation that has arisen (such as what should happen if any of the shareholders are excluded from management).

(e) One side (usually the petitioner) selling its shares to the other, either pursuant to machinery contained in the articles or a shareholders' agreement, or pursuant to an open offer to buy or sell.

Unfair prejudice petitions are considered in **Chapter 13**. The jurisdiction under CA 2006, s 994, covers many of the situations formerly dealt with by winding-up petitions on the just and equitable ground, and as a result just and equitable petitions are not as common as they once were.

In practical terms, voluntary winding up can usually only be achieved on securing a 75 per cent majority vote in a shareholders' meeting (IA 1986, s 84). Voluntary winding up will only be a realistic alternative remedy if the controlling shareholders will vote for such a resolution, so this possibility will rarely be a bar to relief to petitions which are brought in order to protect the interests of minority shareholders. However, voluntary liquidation is the obvious solution in cases of failure of a company's substratum.

As discussed in **Chapter 11**, claims for breach of fiduciary duty can only be brought if a majority in the company want this to happen, and there are significant difficulties in bringing derivative claims. For a case on articles providing a procedure to remedy the situation complained about in the petition, see *Re a Company (No 004377 of 1986)* [1987] 1 WLR 102.

12.8.3 Offer to buy shares

To be effective as an alternative remedy an offer to buy the petitioners' shares must be on reasonable terms. Whether the offer is based on a provision in the articles or a shareholders' agreement, or on a letter written before or after proceedings are commenced, the following points should be kept in mind:

(a) The method of valuation must be realistic. Any unusual financial circumstances of the company must be dealt with in a manner fair to both sides.

(b) The valuer should be independent of the opposing parties.

(c) If there has been any impropriety in the affairs of the company, the price must reflect the value the shares would have had if the improper conduct had not occurred.

(d) Generally, the value of minority shares should not be reduced by what is called the 'minority interest discount', as the offer is to buy the shares more or less on a forced sale basis.

If a reasonable offer to buy the petitioners' shares is refused, the respondents may, in a plain and obvious case, apply to strike out a just and equitable winding-up petition, or may seek an order for a stay, instead of waiting until the final determination of the petition before raising the point under IA 1986, s 125(2).

13 Unfair prejudice

13.1 Introduction

Since 1948 it has been recognised that minority shareholders need protection going above and beyond their rights under the constitution of the company and the established principles of company law. There are always risks that majority shareholders will make use of their dominant position so as to vote themselves and their nominees on to the board of directors, vote themselves large remuneration packages and prevent the company from distributing much to the shareholders in the form of dividends on the shares. In this way the majority can ensure that most or all of the spare cash in the company goes to themselves, and that the minority shareholders see little or none of it. Where the minority shareholders own up to 49 per cent of the issued shares, this can appear very unfair, particularly as in many private companies there are restrictions on share transfers. These can often be found in the articles of such companies, and, in any event, there are always limited numbers of investors who will be prepared to pay more than nominal sums for minority shareholdings in private companies. The effect was that the minority shareholders had their capital tied into the company, with little hope of getting it back so they could invest elsewhere, and with little hope of getting a meaningful return on their investment. (The same problem does not arise in respect of shareholders in publicly quoted companies. If they do not like the way in which the company is being run they can simply sell their shares on the Stock Exchange and invest elsewhere.)

There are severe restrictions on the ability of a shareholder who is complaining about the conduct of the directors and those in control of a limited liability company in bringing an action in the courts by reason of the rule in *Foss v Harbottle* (see **11.5**). Prior to 1948 the most direct route open to minority shareholders in seeking relief from conduct such as that described in the previous paragraph was to petition for the just and equitable winding up of the company, a topic discussed in **Chapter 12**. The great drawback in the just and equitable jurisdiction is that there is only one form of relief available, namely the winding up of the company. While this does provide relief for the minority shareholders in that they will be able to get back their investments once the liquidation is complete, the obvious problem is that this is a very drastic remedy to impose upon the company. The company may be very profitable, but there may be fears that much of its value will be lost if it is liquidated. Unless the business is sold on as a going concern, there will also be fears that granting a winding-up order will result in the employees losing their jobs.

The CA 1948, s 210, was enacted to enable minority shareholders to obtain relief without winding up the company. It provided that a member could complain where the affairs of the company were being conducted in a manner 'oppressive' to some part of the membership of the company, including the petitioner. If the case was made out, the section enabled the court to make such order as it thought fit with a view to bringing an end to the matters complained of, including orders regulating the future affairs of the company or for the purchase of the shares of any of the members of the company. The word 'oppressive' was construed in a very restrictive way. Relief could only be granted if the conduct was continuing, and it was necessary to show that the facts would justify the making of a winding-up order on the just and equitable ground. It was also established that where the petitioner was in reality complaining about being removed from the board of directors, relief would be refused on the ground that the petitioner had not suffered oppression 'qua member'. The result was that very few cases succeeded.

A fresh start was made with the enactment (originally in CA 1980, s 75) of what became CA 1985, s 459. Section 994 of the CA 2006 effectively restates s 459 and provides the court with jurisdiction to grant relief for unfairly prejudicial conduct. Courts dealing with unfair prejudice petitions have not regarded themselves as bound by the restrictions imposed under the now repealed CA 1948, s 210. If a petition under s 994 is successful, the court is given by s 996 wide powers to act as it thinks fit for granting relief against the matters complained of. The most common form of relief is to provide for the purchase of the shares of the minority shareholders by the majority at a fair valuation.

13.2 Jurisdiction

The key provisions are to be found in the CA 2006, s 994(1) and (2), which, in their current form, provide as follows:

> (1) *A member of a company may apply to the court by petition for an order under this Part on the ground—*
>
> (a) *that the company's affairs are being or have been conducted in a manner that is unfairly prejudicial to the interests of members generally or of some part of its members (including at least himself), or*
>
> (b) *that an actual or proposed act or omission of the company (including an act or omission on its behalf) is or would be so prejudicial.*
>
> (2) *The provisions of this Part apply to a person who is not a member of a company but to whom shares in the company have been transferred or transmitted by operation of law as they apply to a member of a company.*

Section 994(1A) provides that removal of the company's auditor from office on the ground of divergence of opinions on accounting treatments or audit procedures or any other improper grounds is treated as being unfairly prejudicial to the interests of some part of the members. Section 995 empowers the Secretary of State to apply where, having received a report, it appears to him or her that there is unfair prejudice.

An application under s 994 may be made by a member, or by a person to whom shares have been transferred or transmitted even though that person's name does not yet appear on the register. However, a mere agreement to transfer will not suffice (*Re a*

Company (No 003160 of 1986) [1986] BCLC 391). The question of standing should be settled first.

A petition under s 994 must allege that a company's affairs are being, or have been, conducted in a manner unfairly prejudicial to the interests of its members generally or some part of its members (including the petitioner). It is possible to petition on the basis of conduct before the petitioner obtained shares in the company (*Lloyd v Casey* [2002] 1 BCLC 454).

The wording of s 994(1)(b) makes it clear that it is no longer necessary to show a course of conduct. Isolated acts may suffice to found a petition. The court also need no longer consider whether the facts would justify a winding up on the just and equitable ground.

13.3 Procedure

13.3.1 Bringing unfair prejudice proceedings

Special provision is made for the procedure on unfair prejudice applications by the Companies (Unfair Prejudice Applications) Proceedings Rules 2009, SI 2009/2469. Except so far as inconsistent with the CA 2006 and the 2009 Rules, the CPR 1998 apply to unfair prejudice applications with any necessary modifications (r 2(2)).

The application is made by petition, and a form is set out in the schedule to the Rules. A precedent can be found in Figure 13.1. On presentation of the petition, details of the return day are endorsed on the reverse of the form. The company and any other respondents must be served with sealed copies of the petition at least 14 days before the return day.

On the return day the registrar gives directions on all matters affecting the procedure of the petition, but will give particular consideration to:

(a) Service of the petition on further persons.

(b) Whether points of claim and defence are to be delivered.

(c) Whether and how the petition is to be advertised. Until the court has given directions concerning advertising it will be a breach of the spirit of the rules, and a prima facie abuse of the process of the court, for any party to bring the fact that a petition has been presented to the attention of anyone who is not a party to the petition (*Re a Company (No 002015 of 1996)* [1997] 2 BCLC 1). If a party disregards this and informs someone else about the petition, the court has a discretion to make such order as might be fair and reasonable in the circumstances. If the conduct is regarded as sufficiently serious, the petition might be dismissed.

(d) The manner of adducing evidence of trial. The registrar will consider whether evidence will be given orally or taken in whole or part by witness statement, whether witnesses should be cross-examined and the matters which may be dealt with in evidence.

(e) Any other matter affecting the procedure on the petition.

(f) Whether a stay should be imposed for mediation or the use of other ADR procedures.

When unfair prejudice petitions come before the registrar for directions, consideration should be given to making directions for the parties to meet with a view to narrowing the issues in order to reduce costs (*Re Rotadata Ltd* [2000] BCC 686), and for the appointment of a joint expert or an assessor on the question of determining a fair price for the petitioner's shares (*North Holdings Ltd v Southern Tropics Ltd* [1999] 2 BCLC 625).

13.3.2 Company not to pay costs of parties

The company is a necessary formal party to the proceedings. In most cases it will not have any direct interest in the result. Although it will therefore be named in the petition as one of the respondents, the real dispute is between the petitioners and the individuals (usually the current directors and majority shareholders) named in the petition. Company money should not usually be used by the respondents for funding the defence to the proceedings (*Re Kenyon Swansea Ltd* (1987) 3 BCC 259 and *Re Crossmore Electrical and Civil Engineering Ltd* (1989) 5 BCC 37).

Interim injunctions have been granted to prevent the company from financing resistance to CA 2006, s 994 petitions where it does not have an interest in the outcome of a dispute which in essence is a dispute between competing shareholders (see *Re Milgate Developments Ltd* [1991] BCC 24 and *Re a Company (No 004502 of 1988), ex p Johnson* [1991] BCC 234). In the two cases cited for this proposition, once the judges found they had jurisdiction to make the order they immediately went on to do so with little additional reasoning, apart from a brief reference to *American Cyanamid Co v Ethicon Ltd* [1975] AC 396, because there was no real defence to the application for the injunctions.

13.3.3 Joining just and equitable winding up

At one time it used to be common to add prayers for the just and equitable winding up of the company as an alternative to the relief sought for unfair prejudice. This is regarded as undesirable, and PD 49B, para 1, provides that an alternative prayer for winding up should be included in a petition under s 994 only if that is the relief which the petitioner prefers or if it is considered that it may be the only relief to which the petitioner may be entitled. In *Re a Company (No 004415 of 1996)* [1997] 1 BCLC 479 there were three petitions relating to three connected companies in which minority shareholders alleged that they had been unfairly prejudiced by policies of declaring low dividends while the companies paid excessive remuneration to the majority shareholders, who were the directors of the companies. The petitions asked for winding-up orders on the just and equitable ground in the alternative. The companies had substantial accumulated assets, so there would be substantial distributions to the minority shareholders if the companies were to be wound up. Scott V-C pointed out that winding up in these circumstances was a remedy of last resort, and would only have allowed the alternative relief to remain if there was a real possibility of the trial court making winding-up orders. As share purchase orders were the most likely form of relief, the winding-up prayers were struck out. On the other hand, an alternative prayer for winding up was allowed to remain in *Re Copeland and Craddock Ltd* [1997] BCC 294, CA, where there were allegations that the respondents had by secret transactions sold company property for cash without recording the receipts in the company's books. The court felt there was a chance the petitioner might obtain an order that the majority should sell their shares to him, and that it was therefore not unreasonable to seek a winding up in the alternative.

Figure 13.1 Unfair prejudice petition under CA 2006

IN THE HIGH COURT OF JUSTICE — No 004499 of 2014

CHANCERY DIVISION

IN THE MATTER of R. W. Mitchell and Co Limited

AND IN THE MATTER of the Companies Act 2006

BETWEEN

MR ERIC PETER LYON — Petitioner

and

(1) MR RONALD WILLIAM MITCHELL
(2) MR NIGEL JOHN MITCHELL
(3) MRS JUDITH MARGARET DICKSON
(4) R.W. MITCHELL and CO LIMITED — Respondents

TO Her Majesty's High Court of Justice
The petition of Eric Peter Lyon of 89 York Road, Bradford, BD7 6TR

1. R. W. Mitchell and Co Limited ('the Company') was incorporated on 18th March 1979 under the Companies Act 1948.
2. The registered office of the Company is at 24 High Street, Bradford BD1 4AZ.
3. The nominal capital of the Company is £20,000 divided into 20,000 shares of £1 each. The amount of the capital paid up or credited as paid up is £15,000. The petitioner is the holder of 2,000 shares of £1 each and at the date of this petition those shares are registered in the name of the petitioner.
4. The principal business which is carried on by the Company is that of building and civil engineering contracting.
5. The respondents Ronald William Mitchell and his son Nigel John Mitchell were the original directors of the Company. On incorporation the Company had a nominal capital of £100 divided into 100 shares of £1 each, the respondent Ronald William Mitchell being at that time the holder of 99 shares and the respondent Nigel John Mitchell being the holder of 1 share.
6. From time to time the nominal capital of the Company was increased by resolutions passed by the Company in general meeting, and further shares were allotted by the directors.
7. By a written contract of employment dated 14th October 1991 (hereinafter 'the employment contract') the petitioner was employed by the Company as a civil engineer. At that time the Company had 10 employees.
8. Subsequently the business of the Company expanded at a considerable rate, and by August 2003 the Company employed 50 staff and in the year ending 31st May 2003 had a turnover of £4,529,528 and pretax profits of £48,327.
9. The success of the Company was largely due to the hard work and technical skill of the petitioner. In recognition of this, the petitioner was appointed a director of the Company at the annual general meeting of the Company held on 3rd August 2003. The other directors of the company at that time were the respondents Ronald William Mitchell, Nigel John Mitchell and Judith Margaret Dickson, the daughter of the respondent Ronald William Mitchell.

10. At a meeting of the board of directors also held on 3rd August 2003 the petitioner was allotted 2,000 shares of £1 each in the Company. Immediately before the said allotment to the petitioner there were 6,500 issued shares of the Company. These were held as to 4,500 thereof by the respondent Ronald William Mitchell, as to 1,000 thereof by the respondent Nigel John Mitchell, and as to 1,000 thereof by the respondent Judith Margaret Dickson.
11. By a letter to the Company dated 20th April 2011 the petitioner resigned his employment with the Company with effect from 31st October 2011 pursuant to the terms of the employment contract.
12. At the annual general meeting of the Company held on 14th August 2011 the petitioner was removed from his directorship of the Company on a show of hands by 3 votes to 1.
13. During the period 2002 to 2010 inclusive, dividends of 15p per share were declared each year at annual general meetings of the Company.
14. The profits of the Company in the year ending 31st May 2011 available for distribution were at least £62,000, in the year ending 31st May 2012 at least £78,000, and in the year ending 31st May 2013 at least £37,000. Notwithstanding such profits being available for distribution, the Company has not declared any dividends after 2010.
15. The respondent Ronald William Mitchell's remuneration from the Company in the year ending 31st May 2011 was £39,000, in the year ending 31st May 2012 it was £43,000, and in the year ending 31st May 2013 it was £50,000. The respondent Nigel John Mitchell's remuneration from the Company in the year ending 31st May 2011 was £22,000, in the year ending 31st May 2012 it was £27,000, and in the year ending 31st May 2013 it was £36,000. The respondent Judith Margaret Dickson's remuneration from the company was £6,000 in each of the years ending 31st May 2011 to 31st May 2013.
16. The Company's accounts for the year ending 31st May 2013 were made available to the petitioner on 3rd February 2014. These accounts showed that during the year ending 31st May 2013 a further 4,500 shares had been allotted to the respondent Ronald William Mitchell at par, a further 1,000 shares had been allotted to the respondent Nigel John Mitchell at par, and a further 1,000 shares had been allotted to the respondent Judith Margaret Dickson at par. No further shares at that time were or subsequently have been offered to the petitioner.
17. In the circumstances the conduct of the respondents Ronald William Mitchell, Nigel John Mitchell and Judith Margaret Dickson as directors of the Company have been deliberately designed to damage the petitioner's interest in his shares in the Company by ensuring no dividends are paid while the respondents are able to draw remuneration as directors and by diluting the petitioner's shareholding in the Company from 23.5 per cent to 13.3 per cent of the issued share capital.
18. In these circumstances the petitioner submits that the affairs of the Company are being conducted in a manner which is unfairly prejudicial to the interests of some part of the members including your petitioner.

THE PETITIONER therefore prays as follows:

(1) that the respondents and each of them may be ordered to purchase the petitioner's shares at a fair value to be determined by the court;

(2) that the Company may be ordered to pay a dividend for the year ending 31st May 2013 if profits are available for that purpose;

(3) that there be an inquiry ordered as to what dividends ought to have been declared by the Company in the years ending 31st May 2011, 31st May 2012 and 31st May 2013;

(4) and that such other order may be made as the court thinks fit.

NOTE
It is intended to serve this petition on:

(1) Ronald William Mitchell of 18 Fairmile, Bradford, BD8 3LR

(2) Nigel John Mitchell of 92 Ellesmere Road, Bradford, BD8 2DA

(3) Judith Margaret Dickson of 41 Landhope Close, Mold, Clwyd, CH7 6RJ

(4) R.W. Mitchell and Co Limited of 24 High Street, Bradford, BDI 4AZ.

ENDORSEMENT TO BE COMPLETED BY THE COURT

This petition having been presented to the court on 19th March 2014 all parties should attend before the Registrar on:
Date: 4th June 2014
Time: 3 p.m.
Place: Rolls Building, near Fetter Lane, London, EC4A 1NL
for directions to be given.
The solicitors for the petitioner are:
Name: Messrs Dixon and Comyn
Address: 83 High Street, Bradford, BDI 4BD
Tel. No.: 01274 793692
Reference: ALC/LYON

13.4 Interim relief

13.4.1 Interim payments

It was held in *Re a Company (No 004175 of 1986)* (1987) 3 BCC 41 that there is no power to grant an interim payment in an unfair prejudice petition prior to the hearing. This is because it is only after judgment that the statutory criterion for granting relief under CA 2006, s 996 (namely, that the court is satisfied that the petition is well founded) can be established. However, an interim payment can be ordered after judgment if the judgment is under appeal (*Ferguson v Maclennan* [1990] BCC 702, Court of Session).

13.4.2 Interim injunctions

Interim injunctions to restrain a director of the company from continuing unfairly prejudicial conduct pending the hearing of the petition were granted in *Re a Company (No 003061 of 1993), Safinia v Comet Enterprises Ltd* [1994] BCC 883. It was alleged that certain agency agreements were being diverted from the company. Applying *American Cyanamid* principles, interim injunctions were granted so as to preserve commission payments alleged to be due to the company, and to prevent active diversion of assets which appeared to belong to the company. In *Re a Company (No 00330 of 1991), ex p Holden* [1991] BCC 241, an interim injunction was granted to prevent majority shareholders from buying out the petitioner's shares pursuant to a provision in the company's articles. In the absence of a derivative claim it is not possible to grant a freezing injunction against directors of the company, because CA 2006, s 994, takes the form of granting relief for mismanagement, and does not create a substantive cause of action (*Re Premier Electronics (GB) Ltd* [2002] 2 BCLC 634).

13.4.3 Security for costs

It has been held that a petitioner in an unfair prejudice petition brings proceedings as a claimant for the purpose of enabling the court to make an order for security for costs (*Re Unisoft Group Ltd (No 1)* [1993] BCLC 1292).

13.5 Principles

13.5.1 General concepts

There is no statutory definition of the term 'unfair prejudice', which has been left by the legislature as a deliberately wide concept which can be applied by the courts so as to give relief where it is just to do so. In an influential passage from an unreported decision (*Re Bovey Hotel Ventures Ltd*, 31 July 1981), which is quoted in full in *Re RA Noble and Sons (Clothing) Ltd* [1983] BCLC 273 at 290–291, Slade J said:

> Broadly, and without prejudice to the generality of the wording of the section, which may cover many other situations, a member of a company will be able to bring himself within the section if he can show that the value of his shareholding in the company had been seriously diminished or at least seriously jeopardised by reason of a course of conduct on the part of those persons who have had de facto control of the company, which has been unfair to the member concerned. The test of unfairness must, I think, be an objective, not a subjective one. In other words it is not necessary for the Petitioner to show that the persons who have had de facto control of the company have acted as they did in the conscious knowledge that this was unfair to the Petitioner or that they acted in bad faith; the test, I think, is whether a reasonable bystander observing the consequences of their conduct, would regard it as having unfairly prejudiced the Petitioner's interests.

The central idea behind the section is that the court may intervene where the conduct of the respondents has seriously diminished the value of the petitioner's shares, or at least put the value of those shares at serious risk. In most of the cases brought to court this has been fairly self-evident from the facts, with the main areas of dispute being whether the conduct of the respondents was unfairly prejudicial; whether the petitioner was damaged as a shareholder or in some other capacity; or whether the petitioner should be refused relief because of the petitioner's own misconduct or through failing to accept a reasonable offer for the purchase of the petitioner's shares. However, it is important to establish substantial harm or potential harm to the value of the petitioner's interest in the company, or the petition will fail on this ground alone. Thus, in *Re Blackwood Hodge plc* [1997] 2 BCLC 650 the directors failed to give a proposal to merge two pension schemes the consideration it deserved, and failed to declare their interest to the board contrary to the CA 2006, s 177. On the face of it the transaction appeared to involve giving away a substantial funding surplus under the company's pension scheme to the merged scheme and receiving nothing in return. On analysis of the evidence, however, the judge found (after a four-week trial) that the transaction was neutral, so the company lost nothing in the merger. That finding meant, despite the failures of the directors, that the petition had to be dismissed.

The references in the passage previously quoted from *Re Bovey Hotel Ventures Ltd* to 'a course of conduct' and 'to the member concerned' must be regarded as being more restrictive than the present law: the former phrase is too restrictive because subsequent decisions have made it plain that isolated incidents may be unfairly prejudicial, and the latter phrase is also too restrictive because of the change of wording in the section in 1989. Nevertheless, six basic propositions can be derived from this decision and that in *Re DR Chemicals Ltd* (1989) 5 BCC 39:

- The test of unfair prejudice is objective.
- It is not necessary for the petitioner to show bad faith.
- It is not necessary for the petitioner to show a conscious intention to cause prejudice.
- The test is one of unfairness, not unlawfulness.
- The alleged conduct must affect the petitioner as a shareholder.
- Laches (ie delay) may bar relief under s 994.

13.5.2 Unfairness

In *Re Saul D. Harrison and Sons plc* [1994] BCC 475, CA, Hoffmann LJ pointed out that it is important to bear in mind that the word 'unfairness' in the section has to be applied in the context of a commercial relationship. Conduct may be technically unlawful without being unfair, and it may be unfair without being unlawful. For example, a technical breach of the statutory requirements regarding issuing shares might not amount to unfairly prejudicial conduct (*Re DR Chemicals Ltd* (1989) 5 BCC 39). Nevertheless, Hoffmann LJ said the starting point in a s 994 case is to consider whether the conduct complained about was in accordance with the articles of association of the company. Even if the letter of the articles has been complied with by the majority, their conduct may be unfairly prejudicial if either:

- the majority have failed to use their fiduciary powers as directors for the benefit of the company as a whole; or
- the petitioner can show that some legitimate expectation not formally expressed in the constitution of the company has been infringed (see **13.5.5**).

In *O'Neill v Phillips* [1999] 1 WLR 1092, Lord Hoffmann said that the concept of fairness had to be applied in the context of the case in hand. Conduct which might be perfectly fair between competing businessmen might not be fair between members of a family. The court has to apply two principles. One is that the articles and other express terms on which the shareholders have become associated must be respected. The other is that equity will intervene where the respondents have not acted in good faith. It is for this reason that successful unfair prejudice petitions are those based either on breach of the terms on which the parties became associated, or where those terms are used in a manner which equity would regard as contrary to good faith. A petition was dismissed in *Re Benfield Greig Group plc* [2001] BCC 92 where shares had been valued by an outside valuer in accordance with the company's articles at what the petitioners alleged was an unfairly low value, because there was nothing unfairly prejudicial about parties being bound by the articles.

13.5.3 Past and continuing conduct

A successful petition will have to be based either on continuing unfairly prejudicial conduct, or on past conduct which has a continuing unfairly prejudicial effect. Where past unfairly prejudicial conduct has been remedied, or could be remedied because the petitioners have control of the company, the petition should be dismissed (*Re Legal Costs Negotiators Ltd* [1999] 2 BCLC 171).

13.5.4 Conduct of the company

Section 994(1) applies to unfairly prejudicial conduct arising from any 'act or omission of the company' (see **13.2**). In *Re Phoneer Ltd* [2002] 2 BCLC 241 there were two shareholders, one of whom contributed skill and effort, and the other contributed capital. It was alleged by the shareholder who had contributed the capital that he was unfairly prejudiced because the other shareholder had stopped working for the company and was attempting to renegotiate his remuneration. In response it was alleged that these acts were not those of 'the company' itself, and so fell outside s 994. It was held that they were nevertheless breaches of the terms on which the parties had agreed the company's affairs would be conducted, which entitled the petitioner to relief under s 996.

An expectation that another shareholder will not sell his shares without the consent of some or all of the other shareholders was held in *Re Leeds United Holdings plc* [1996] 2 BCLC 545 not to relate to the conduct of the company's affairs, and was not capable of being protected under s 994.

13.5.5 Legitimate expectations

In most cases the basis on which the parties became associated will be adequately and exhaustively laid down by the articles of association (see Lord Wilberforce in *Ebrahimi v Westbourne Galleries Ltd* [1973] AC 360). The superimposition of equitable considerations requires 'something more', or 'some special circumstances' (see *Re Posgate and Denby (Agencies) Ltd* (1986) 2 BCC 99, 352). Although it is just about possible for parties to have legitimate expectations going beyond the terms of the articles in a public company, such cases will be rare (*Re Leeds United Holdings plc* [1996] 2 BCLC 545). In *O'Neill v Phillips* [1999] 1 WLR 1092, Lord Hoffmann said the concept of 'legitimate expectations' is a consequence, not a cause, of the equitable restraint of unconscionable conduct, and the concept should not be given an unrestrained life of its own. In practical terms the concept is restricted to smaller, quasi-partnership, companies. To be recognised by the court the alleged legitimate expectation has to relate to the conduct of the company's affairs. The most obvious and common example is an expectation of being able to participate in decisions relating to the conduct of the company's affairs.

Although the courts will act to protect the shareholders' legitimate expectations, it is established that the court is not able to rewrite the terms and understandings on which the members became associated (*Re Posgate and Denby (Agencies) Ltd* (1986) 2 BCC 99, 352). Where the parties have spelt out their arrangements in detailed documentation (such as in a full shareholders' agreement and/or by detailed provisions in the articles tailored to their particular company), there may be limited scope, if any, for suggesting that the shareholders might have some legitimate expectations over and above what they have agreed in writing. However, there have been cases, such as *Re Elgindata Ltd*

[1991] BCLC 959 and *Re a Company (No 002015 of 1996)* [1997] 2 BCLC 1, where the possibility of finding the necessary 'something more' was not ruled out despite voluminous documentation between the parties.

In *O'Neill v Phillips* [1999] 1 WLR 1092 the petitioner had worked his way up in the company. There came a point when the majority shareholder handed over the running of the company to the petitioner and agreed in principle, and subject to certain business objectives being satisfied and the execution of formal documents, to increase the petitioner's share holding to 50 per cent. However, the fact there was no formal agreement to do so was held to be fatal to a petition based on what was alleged to be a legitimate expectation that his share holding would be increased. Similarly, in the same case it was held that the petitioner did not have an enforceable 'legitimate expectation' that the share in the company's profits that he had been receiving when he was running the company would not be reduced when the majority shareholder resumed running the company at a later date.

13.5.6 Clean hands

Although the jurisdiction under CA 2006, s 994, is equitable in character, the fact that the petitioner may not come to the court with clean hands will not always of itself bar relief (*Re Abbington Hotel Ltd* [2012] 1 BCLC 410, where there were cross-petitions for unfair prejudice, and both succeeded). However, where the act complained of as being unfairly prejudicial resulted from the petitioner's wrongdoing, there is unlikely to be any unfairness (*Mears v R. Mears and Co (Holdings) Ltd* [2002] 2 BCLC 1). Misconduct by the petitioner may also have an effect on the remedy that the court may grant (*Re London School of Electronics Ltd* [1986] Ch 211).

13.5.7 Interests as a member

As mentioned in **13.1**, under the old CA 1948, s 210, a petitioner had to show that the oppression complained about had been suffered in the petitioner's capacity as a shareholder. Being removed from office as a director was regarded as conduct affecting the petitioner as a director, not as a shareholder. An early unfair prejudice case, *Re a Company (No 004475 of 1982)* [1983] Ch 178, applied the same principle to unfair prejudice petitions. However, later cases applied the concept of petitioning as a shareholder in a more flexible way. In *Re a Company (No 00477 of 1986)* [1986] BCLC 376 Hoffmann J said the exclusion from management of a managing director of a large public limited company who happens to hold a few shares (perhaps as a share qualification for being a director) would not be able to petition for relief under s 994 in the event of being removed from his office as a director. On the other hand, the same is not true of small private companies in which two or three members have invested their capital on the footing that dividends were unlikely to be declared, but that each would earn a living by working for the company and drawing remuneration as a director. In such cases, if it can be said that the members had a legitimate expectation of continued employment as a director by the company, dismissal from office may constitute unfairly prejudicial conduct.

Exclusion from management resulting in loss of control over capital invested in a company by a person connected with the excluded director may, in appropriate circumstances, affect the excluded director as a shareholder. Thus, in *R and H Electric Ltd v Haden Bill Electrical Ltd* [1995] 2 BCLC 280 a company effectively controlled by the petitioner had made a loan of £200,000 in order to provide working capital for a quasi-partnership in which the petitioner held 25 per cent of the shares and was the chairman. Later, problems arose between the petitioner and the other directors, who then summarily dismissed him without consultation and without any discussion about the future of the loan capital. It was held that the petitioner had a legitimate expectation of being able to participate in the management of the quasi-partnership company for at least as long as the lending company and the petitioner were closely associated with it. Accordingly, even though the petitioner's conduct was open to criticism his removal was held to be unfairly prejudicial to his interests as a member. See also *Gamlestaden Fastigheter AB v Baltic Partners Ltd* [2008] 1 BCLC 468, PC.

Other forms of conduct complained about by petitioners may also fall outside CA 2006, s 994, on the basis that they do not affect the petitioner as a shareholder. An example is *Re J.E. Cade and Sons Ltd* [1991] BCC 360, where the minority shareholder had granted a licence to the company over a farm. In his petition he claimed the business relationship between the members had irretrievably broken down, that he had been unfairly prejudiced, and as part of the relief sought he asked for an order that the company should give up possession of the farm. It was held that this head of relief had to be struck out, because the petitioner's interests as the freeholder were in fact adverse to his interests as a shareholder in the company.

13.5.8 Matters amounting to unfair prejudice

13.5.8.1 Exclusion from management

This has already been discussed in **13.5.7**. This is one of the most common forms of complaint in unfair prejudice petitions. As discussed previously, it is most likely to be successful if the company is a small, quasi-partnership company (a concept discussed at **12.5**). However, there must be an exclusion from management, not merely an alteration in the capacity in which the petitioner is managing (see *O'Neill v Phillips* [1999] 1 WLR 1092, where the petitioner failed despite being reduced from running the company to being a director). The exclusion must be without cause. In *Mears v R Mears and Co (Holdings) Ltd* [2002] 2 BCLC 1 a director was removed from his post as a result of serious misconduct (forgery, deception, bribery and wrongful retention of company money), and it was held that the exclusion from management was not unfair.

13.5.8.2 Payment of inadequate dividends

This is commonly combined with exclusion from management and/or with allegations that the directors have paid themselves excessive remuneration. In *Re a Company, ex p Glossop* [1988] BCLC 570, Harman J said that directors must remember that the members are the owners of the company, that the profits belong to the members and that, subject to the proper needs of the company, the trading profits ought to be distributed by way of dividends. In *Re Sam Weller and Sons Ltd* [1990] Ch 682 the ground said to amount to unfair prejudice was that the company had paid 'the same derisory dividend' of 14p per share for the past 37 years, and that the most recent accounts showed that net profits had covered the dividend declared by 14 times. On an application to strike out the petition as disclosing no reasonable grounds for bringing a claim it was held that the allegation could amount to unfair prejudice. *Re*

McCarthy Surfacing Ltd [2009] BCC 465 distinguished between a bona fide decision not to declare dividends in the best interests of the company and a consistent failure to consider whether or not to declare dividends which amounted to a breach of duty and was unfairly prejudicial.

13.5.8.3 Payment of excessive remuneration

Payment of inadequate dividends is often combined with the majority being accused of voting for themselves excessive remuneration. The question is whether the level of remuneration can be justified by objective commercial criteria (*Re a Company (No 004415 of 1996)* [1997] 1 BCLC 479). A high level of remuneration may be justified if the company operates in a very special field where high remuneration is usual (*Smith v Croft (No 2)* [1988] Ch 114).

13.5.8.4 Failure to file or provide information

A failure to file accounts and other information at Companies House can be unfairly prejudicial if it prevents members from understanding the true position of the company (*Re a Company (No 00789 of 1987), ex p Shooter* [1990] BCLC 384). Where filing is merely late, it is unlikely to be unfairly prejudicial (*Re a Company (No 005685 of 1988), ex p Schwarcz (No 2)* [1989] BCLC 427). Treating a quasi-partner who had resigned as an employee as also having resigned as a director, and consequently refusing him access to financial information for the purpose of valuing his shares, was not unfairly prejudicial in *Re Phoenix Office Supplies Ltd, Phoenix Office Supplies Ltd v Larvin* [2003] 1 BCLC 76, where the real complaint was that the other shareholders would not offer him the price that he wanted for his shares.

13.5.8.5 Improper allotments of shares

Re DR Chemicals Ltd (1989) 5 BCC 39 was regarded as a blatant case of unfairly prejudicial conduct. This was a company with two shareholders, one holding 60 shares and the other 40 shares. The shareholders split up, with the majority shareholder continuing the business. The majority shareholder then used his position as director and majority shareholder to allot himself a further 900 shares at par without informing the petitioner of what he was doing. It was found that he did this for the wholly improper purpose of diluting the shareholding of the petitioner (reducing his interest to 4 per cent).

13.5.8.6 Discriminatory rights issue

A rights issue operates by the company offering to sell new shares to the existing shareholders in proportion to the number of shares they hold at the time of the offer. If any shareholders do not take up the offer, it is commonly provided that the company can sell the shares that have not been bought by the original offerees to the other shareholders. Normally there is nothing wrong in making a rights issue. Occasionally, however, this can operate unfairly. In *Re a Company (No 007623 of 1986)* [1986] BCLC 362, Hoffmann J said:

> If the majority know that the petitioner does not have the money to take up his rights and the offer is made at par when the shares are plainly worth a great deal more than par as part of a majority holding (but very little as a minority holding), it seems to me arguable that carrying through the transaction in that form could, viewed objectively, constitute unfairly prejudicial conduct.

A large rights issue which the majority shareholder was able to take up by offsetting sums which the court found were not due to him, and which was motivated to increase pressure on the minority shareholders to sell their now diluted shareholdings at a discount, was held to be unfairly prejudicial in *Re Regional Airports Ltd* [1999] 2 BCLC 30. In *Re Sunrise Radio Ltd* [2010] 1 BCLC 367 it was held that a rights issue must be priced at a level which was fair to all which would depend on the particular circumstances of the case.

13.5.8.7 Diverting business opportunities

Breach of fiduciary duty on the part of the directors can amount to unfairly prejudicial conduct even in the absence of any breach of the terms of the articles of association. One of the most common complaints is that directors in control of one company have diverted business opportunities away from a company in which the petitioner holds a minority interest to another company where the directors (or those appointing the directors) hold all the shares. Where this can be proved it will clearly amount to unfair prejudice (*Re London School of Electronics Ltd* [1986] Ch 211). In *Wilkinson v West Coast Capital* [2005] All ER (D) 346, ChD, it was held that diversion of a corporate opportunity by the directors in circumstances where the company was unable to take advantage of it would not amount to unfair prejudice, although it would amount to a breach of fiduciary duty.

13.5.8.8 Preventing the company recovering its property

An example of this is *Whyte, Petitioner* (1984) 1 BCC 99, 044, Court of Session. The petitioner held 49 per cent of the shares in the company, the other 51 per cent being held by the subsidiaries of R Ltd. The company had six directors, who resolved at a board meeting to bring proceedings against R Ltd. The majority shareholders then requisitioned a meeting (see **6.6.5.1**) for the purpose of removing two of the existing directors and appointing a further nominee director, which would have the result of nominee directors forming the majority on the board of the company. The nominee directors would then be able to stop the litigation against R Ltd. It was held that this amounted to unfair prejudice of the petitioner, and an injunction was granted.

13.5.8.9 Mismanagement

Allegations of mismanagement on the part of those in control of a company will not, on their own, generally amount to unfair prejudice. The reason, as stated by Roger Kaye QC in *Re a Company (No 002015 of 1996)* [1997] 2 BCLC 1, is that managerial decisions are just as they imply, decisions by management. The courts are ill-equipped to resolve disputes about whether given management decisions were or were not proper, let alone to characterise them as amounting to unfair prejudice. Nevertheless, in suitable cases allegations of this nature will be allowed to remain in unfair prejudice petitions as forming part of the context of the case, and perhaps lending weight to other, more obvious, allegations of unfairly prejudicial conduct. Further, serious mismanagement can constitute unfair prejudice (*Re Elgindata Ltd (No 2)* [1992] 1 WLR 1207). See also *Oak Investments Partners v Boughtwood* [2010] 2 BCLC 459.

13.5.8.10 Unfair share valuation

In *Re Benfield Greig Group plc, Nugent v Benfield Greig Group plc* [2002] 1 BCLC 65, the articles of the company provided that on the death of a member, the deceased's shares would be sold to persons connected with the company at market value to be determined by the auditors. The auditors were not independent, because they had previously argued with the Inland Revenue for a low share valuation for the company's shares, and it was held that a petition based on a low valuation of the deceased's shares had a real prospect of success.

13.5.8.11 Breach undermining trust and confidence

In *Re Abbington Hotel Ltd* [2012] 1 BCLC 410 two married couples were equal shareholders in a company incorporated to buy and run a hotel as a going concern. In breach of that agreement, one of the couples negotiated a sale of the hotel, and produced false board minutes purporting to authorise the sale. Although the attempted sale was blocked before it went through, the attempt was held to be wholly contrary to the agreement between the shareholders when the company was incorporated, and the resulting loss of trust and confidence was unfairly prejudicial conduct within s 994.

13.5.8.12 Totality of conduct

In some cases a number of complaints, none of them in themselves sufficient to amount to unfairly prejudicial conduct, may, when taken together, be held to satisfy the test in CA 2006, s 994. An example is *Re a Company (No 00314 of 1989)* [1990] BCC 221, where the respondents had made proposals for removing the petitioner as a director, proposed the appointment of new directors, proposed altering the memorandum and articles of association, and had offered to purchase her shares without providing her with information relevant to ascertaining their value, in total constituted unfairly prejudicial conduct.

13.6 Remedies

If the court is satisfied that the petitioner's interests have been unfairly prejudiced by the conduct of the company's affairs, it has wide powers for granting relief under s 996. Subsections (1) and (2) provide:

> *(1) If the court is satisfied that a petition under this Part is well founded, it may make such order as it thinks fit for giving relief in respect of the matters complained of.*
>
> *(2) Without prejudice to the generality of subsection (1), the court's order may—*
>
> *(a) regulate the conduct of the company's affairs in the future;*
>
> *(b) require the company—*
>
> *(i) to refrain from doing or continuing an act complained of, or*
>
> *(ii) to do an act that the petitioner has complained it has omitted to do;*
>
> *(c) authorise civil proceedings to be brought in the name and on behalf of the company by such person or persons and on such terms as the court may direct;*
>
> *(d) require the company not to make any, or any specified, alterations in its articles without the leave of the court;*
>
> *(e) provide for the purchase of the shares of any members of the company by other members or by the company itself and, in the case of a purchase by the company itself, the reduction of the company's capital accordingly.*

The court has the same powers where the respondent concedes for the purposes of the petition that the petitioner's interests have been unfairly prejudiced (*Re Scitec Group Ltd* [2011] 1 BCLC 277).

13.6.1 Share purchase orders

By far the most common order made on a successful s 994 petition will be an order for the purchase of the shares of one side by the other. Most unfair prejudice cases are brought by shareholders in small private companies. Often there will be express restrictions on share transfers set out in the articles of association, or major practical difficulties in selling shares at realistic prices. If an unfair prejudice case is made out, the probability is that the shareholders are no longer able to continue doing business with each other, and the best solution is that the company should be left in the hands of one side or the other, with the outgoing party having their capital returned to them so they can invest elsewhere.

13.6.1.1 Who goes?

Although s 996 provides that either party may be ordered to buy the other side out, usually it is clear that it will be the majority who will be ordered to buy out the minority. Often it will be the majority who will have been running the business in the period leading up to the final disposal of the proceedings (so there will be continuity of management), and generally they will find it easier to buy out the smaller number of shares owned by the minority rather than the other way around. However, the usual position can be displaced by other factors, with each case turning on its own facts. Factors can include who founded the business, the respective roles of the parties in building up the company's business, any special qualifications needed for running the business successfully and any dishonesty or breach of fiduciary duty established against either side. The purpose behind s 996 is to grant relief in respect of the matters complained about in the petition (*Re a Company (No 00836 of 1995)* [1996] BCC 432). Its purpose is not to expropriate the shares of the majority. In cases where there are majority shareholders in control of the business it will therefore be very rare for the court to order them to sell their shares to the minority. The most difficult cases are those where both sides hold an equal number of shares, an example being *Re a Company (No 003096 of 1987)* (1988) 4 BCC 80.

13.6.1.2 Who buys?

Usually this simply follows from the previous paragraph. In exceptional cases, however, someone who is not a shareholder and not a director may be joined as a party and ordered to buy out the petitioner's shares; see *Supreme Travels Ltd v Little Olympian Each-Ways Ltd* [1994] BCC 947.

13.6.1.3 Share valuation

The general principle is that the shares must be valued at a price that is fair on the facts of the particular case (*Re London School of Electronics Ltd* [1986] Ch 211). Outside the area of unfair prejudice it is clear that a fair valuation of shares representing a minority interest in a private company will have to take into account the fact that such a holding does not carry with it control of the company and that the minority shareholder is therefore subject to the whims of the majority regarding dividend policy and management decisions. There will therefore be a substantial minority interest discount when determining the value of minority shares (*Howie v Crawford* [1990] BCC 330).

In *Re Bird Precision Bellows Ltd* [1986] Ch 658, the Court of Appeal, approving the judgment of Nourse J at first instance (reported at [1984] Ch 419), said a different approach was required where a minority shareholder's shares were ordered to be bought after a finding of unfair prejudice, because the minority shareholders could not be regarded as voluntary sellers. Instead, the general rules are:

(a) The shares held by a quasi-partner should not be discounted for minority interest, but should be valued on a pro-rata basis according to the value of the shares as a whole.

(b) If the minority shareholder had acted so as to deserve his exclusion from the company, the price should be appropriately discounted to reflect that fact.

(c) In cases where delinquent majority shareholders in a quasi-partnership company are ordered to sell their shares to the minority the price should not generally include a premium to reflect the fact their shares carry majority control.

(d) Where shares in a quasi-partnership company were acquired by the petitioner as an investment at a price which was discounted because they represented a minority holding, any sale order would most probably be at a price incorporating a minority interest discount.

There is no universal rule that non-quasi-partners always have their shares bought at a discounted price (*Re Sunrise Radio Ltd* [2010] 1 BCLC 367). The court has a wide discretion to do what is fair and equitable in the circumstances of the case. In *Elliott v Planet Organic Ltd* [2000] BCC 610 the company had ordinary shares which were owned by quasi-partners, and a number of preferred shares. It was held that the preferred shareholders, who were ordered to sell their shares to the majority ordinary shareholder, were in effect voluntary sellers and their shares were valued by the court subject to a 30 per cent discount. The ordinary shares were valued on a going-concern basis using the figure for maintainable profits multiplied by a price-earnings ratio of 11.5 based on figures published by *Acquisitions Monthly* and the BDO Index (reflecting the optimistic future of the business), and adding the cash in the business.

The price-earnings ratio used will depend on the expert evidence in each case. The general theory is that it is possible to find from published sources the price-earnings ratios for different categories of the 600 or so quoted UK companies, choose the correct category for the company in question and then apply a differential based on figures such as those published in *Acquisitions Monthly* to reflect factors such as the relative lack of marketability of private companies. The theory can break down when there is no suitable comparator category of listed companies, and has to be modified to take into account the circumstances of the company in question. See *Re Phoenix Office Supplies Ltd* [2002] 2 BCLC 556 (reversed on appeal on a different point) at [106]–[120], where a ratio of 8.1 was applied. A lower factor of 3.5 was applied in *Parkinson v Eurofinance Group Ltd* [2001] 1 BCLC 720 where there was a risk of future departure of key personnel.

13.6.1.4 Date of valuation

Usually the shares should be valued as at the date of the order for the purchase. Sometimes it will be necessary to find some other date in order to ensure the valuation is fair. This might be the case where the unfairly prejudicial conduct has had an effect on the value of the assets of the company. In such a case a date for the valuation might be a date just before the unfairly prejudicial conduct started (*Re O.C. (Transport) Services Ltd* [1984] BCLC 251). Another alternative is the company's usual year-end immediately preceding the date of the trial, a solution adopted in *Quinlan v Essex Hinge Co Ltd* [1997] BCC 53. Where a date prior to judgment is taken as the reference date for valuation purposes, there is no right to interest for the period between that date and judgment, because until the sale the petitioner remains the owner of the shares (*Elliott v Planet Organic Ltd* [2000] BCC 610). However, in *Profinance Trust SA v Gladstone* [2002] 1 BCLC 141, the Court of Appeal said s 996 was wide enough to enable the court to make an order equivalent to interest, but on the facts did not do so because it valued the shares in accordance with the usual rule by taking the value as at the date of the order.

13.6.2 Loans

In *Re Nuneaton Borough AFC Ltd (No 2)* [1991] BCC 44 it was held that s 996 was wide enough for the court to make an order for the transfer of shares to be made conditional on the party buying the other side out repaying loans made by the outgoing shareholders to the company. On the facts it was held that it would have been unjust to allow the company to retain the loans after the outgoing shareholder had been bought out. See also *R and H Electric Ltd v Haden Bill Electrical Ltd* [1995] 2 BCLC 280 and *Gamlestaden Fastigheter AB v Baltic Partners Ltd* [2008] 1 BCLC 448, PC.

13.6.3 Civil proceedings

The power contained in s 996(2)(c) to authorise civil proceedings to be brought in the name and on behalf of the company by such persons as the court may direct is a way of getting around the problems caused by the rule in *Foss v Harbottle* (see **11.5**). It is not always necessary to go through a two-stage process on this, with the unfair prejudice petition being the first stage, granting as relief the authorisation of the second stage, namely, proceedings brought on behalf of the company. Where the alleged unfairly prejudicial conduct involves the diversion of company funds it has been held (*Re Fahey Developments Ltd* [1996] BCC 325) that the petitioner is entitled to seek an order under s 996 for payment to the company from the members, former members and directors allegedly involved in the diversion of assets and also from third parties who may be proved to have knowingly received or improperly assisted in the wrongful diversion.

13.6.4 No appropriate relief

In *Antoniades v Wong* [1997] 2 BCLC 419, CA, the petition succeeded, and investigations were made into ascertaining the net assets of the company for the purpose of a share sale order, taking into account all the wrongs done to the company. This proved so complicated that the judge described it as an impossible task. The Court of Appeal approved the judge's finding that there was no practical relief that he could grant under s 996, and approved the judge's offer to the petitioner of amending the petition so as to provide for the winding up of the company on the just and equitable ground.

13.7 Striking out

Striking out is discussed in some detail in BCP, chapter 33. It is very much a live issue in unfair prejudice proceedings. Striking-out applications in this context broadly fall into two categories. One is where it is argued by respondents that the proceedings (or parts of them) or the relief sought falls outside the scope of ss 994 and 996, and hence should be struck out as disclosing no reasonable grounds for bringing the claim. Like general striking-out cases, s 994 petitions will only be struck out if they are plainly and obviously unsustainable. Applications in the first category are based on the principles described in the previous sections, and do not call for further comment here.

In the second category are cases where it is argued that the petition is an abuse of process on the ground that the petitioner should have sought the remedy prayed for in the petition by adopting a remedy readily available under the articles of association, or should have accepted an open offer made by the respondents giving the petitioner all the relief that could realistically be obtained on the petition. In *Re a Company (No 004377 of 1986)* [1987] 1 WLR 102 Hoffmann J pointed out that for small companies the legal costs and the loss of management time incurred in defending unfair prejudice claims can be overwhelming. His lordship therefore stated the view that a member seeking a share sale order should not present a petition until after an attempt has been made to sell the shares under the provisions in the articles of association of the company (which often have provisions dealing with proposed sales of shares by members). His lordship also pointed out that the common form of wording of such provisions in articles of association that the auditors of the company should fix the price at a 'fair value' gives the auditors the same function as the court has to perform under s 996. This procedure for first seeking an agreed sale under the articles was recognised as being inappropriate where either:

- the respondents have been guilty of bad faith or plain impropriety; or
- if the articles provide for some arbitrary or artificial method of valuation.

Hoffmann J went further in *Re a Company (No 006834 of 1988)* [1989] BCLC 365, where he said that where it is plain that the court would make a share sale order on a petition under s 994 and the articles provide machinery for determining the fair price for the petitioner's shares, an unfair prejudice petition would ordinarily be struck out as an abuse of process unless an attempt to sell under the terms of the articles had been made. This was so even if there was no guarantee that the valuer would not apply a minority interest discount on a valuation under the articles even though no such discount would be applied by the court (following the reasoning in *Re Bird Precision Bellows Ltd* [1984] Ch 419, see **13.6.1.3**). Striking out is probably inappropriate on this ground in cases where the parties are equal shareholders. In such cases it may be far from obvious that a share purchase order over the petitioner's shares would be the result of the petition, and striking out for refusal of a reasonable offer to buy-out is not intended to permit the respondent with merely an equal shareholding to seize control of the company by forcing the other out (*Harborne Road Nominees Ltd v Karvaski* [2012] 2 BCLC 420).

Some doubt about whether the *Re a Company (No 004377 of 1986)* line of cases should continue to apply was caused by the decision in *Virdi v Abbey Leisure Ltd* [1990] BCLC 342, CA. This was a petition for winding up on the just and equitable ground. The company had sold its business, and its only asset was cash. It was held that the petitioner was not obliged to use the machinery in the articles before presenting the petition because the valuer might have applied a minority interest discount and also might have reduced the valuation by too much to reflect certain disputed claims. The *Abbey Leisure* decision was applied at first instance in the unfair prejudice case of *Re a Company (No 00330 of 1991), ex p Holden* [1991] BCC 241, where the facts were very similar to *Abbey Leisure*. Although the *Abbey Leisure* approach applies to cases where the company has ceased trading (where the petitioner has real grounds for expecting the valuation to be proportionate to the net assets of the company as on a winding up), the better view is that it does not apply to cases where the company is still a going concern. Where the business is still in operation, the petitioner should still, in general, seek a remedy first under the articles, and only if that is unsuccessful should a petition be presented (*Re J.E. Cade and Sons Ltd* [1991] BCC 360). Further, in *CVC/Opportunity Equity Partners Ltd v Demarco Almeida* [2002] 2 BCLC 108 (a Privy Council case on just and equitable winding up) it was held that the petition would not be struck out where the petitioner had refused an offer to buy his shares on a break up valuation of the business. In the circumstances he was entitled to be bought out on a share valuation based on the company as a going concern.

If a striking-out application is to be made on the basis that an open offer has been made after proceedings were commenced which has been unreasonably refused, great care has to be taken in formulating the offer to ensure that it gives the petitioner all the relief that could reasonably be expected if the matter had been dealt with by the court.

The following principles were laid down by Lord Hoffmann in *O'Neill v Phillips* [1999] 1 WLR 1092 where an offer to buy is relied upon in a striking-out application:

(a) The offer must be to purchase the shares at a fair value. This will ordinarily be a value representing an equivalent proportion of the total issued share capital, without a discount for the shares being a minority holding. Although there may be special circumstances justifying applying a discount, it will seldom be possible to say that a discounted offer is plainly reasonable for the purposes of striking out.

(b) The value, if not agreed, should be determined by a competent expert. Appointing an expert to be agreed by the parties, or, in default of agreement, an expert nominated by the president of the Institute of Chartered Accountants (or some similar mechanism) would suffice.

(c) The offer should be to have the value determined by the expert as an expert (expert determination, see *A Practical Approach to ADR*, 2nd edn (OUP, 2012), chapter 24), in order to promote speed and economy.

(d) Both parties should be treated equally, such as by having equal access to information about the company having a bearing on the value of the shares, and both having the right to make written or oral submissions to the expert.

(e) It may be necessary for the offer to include payment of the petitioner's costs. Whether this is necessary depends on the circumstances. There would be no need to offer to pay the petitioner's costs if the petition was presented before the respondents had a reasonable time to formulate an offer. If the offer is made some years into proceedings, an effective offer will almost certainly need to include payment of the petitioner's costs.

There will be some cases where even if these above guidelines are followed, an unfair prejudice petition will still not be struck out. One example is *North Holdings Ltd v Southern Tropics Ltd* [1999] 2 BCLC 625, where there were grounds for believing that the respondents had diverted business opportunities to another company, so valuing the petitioner's shares involved mixed questions of fact and law which were better resolved by a court than an expert valuer. It may also be inappropriate to strike out a petition where shares have been valued using the internal valuation procedure, if none of the other shareholders is willing to buy the shares at that price (*Re Rotadata Ltd* [2000] BCC 686).

13.8 Stay for arbitration

Stays are orders preventing further steps being taken in legal proceedings, and are discussed in some detail in BCP, chapter 56. One ground on which a stay may be sought is where court proceedings are brought in breach of an agreement to refer disputes to arbitration (Arbitration Act 1996, s 9, and see *A Practical Approach to ADR*, 2nd edn (OUP, 2012), para 31.07). There is no public policy reason to prevent unfair prejudice disputes being resolved through arbitration. Consequently, where there is an arbitration agreement, a stay will be imposed on any court proceedings brought in breach of the agreement unless the court is satisfied that the arbitration agreement is null and void, inoperative or incapable of being performed (Arbitration Act 1996, s 9(4) and *Fulham Football Club (1987) Ltd v Richards* [2012] Ch 333).

14 Worked example

14.1 Introduction

The papers in this chapter were the formal assessment for the Company Law Module a number of years ago. The case *Beadnell Bay Petroleum Limited*, is set in the context of a company engaged in the exploration of oil in the North Sea. Counsel has been asked to advise the company on the merits of a possible claim against its former managing director, Mr Gallagher, and to settle proceedings. No knowledge of oil exploration law is required beyond the information given in the papers. The Instructions to Counsel have an express statement that there is no need for an application for a freezing injunction (which would otherwise have been something that ought to have been considered), thereby allowing Counsel to concentrate on the company law issues raised.

The background is that the company had incurred expense in conducting various geological investigations in the North Sea, and had identified a location that had some promise as the site of a possible oilfield. Instead of applying for a Department of Energy and Climate Change production licence in the name of the company it appears Mr Gallagher applied for and was granted a production licence for the relevant site in his own name. Oil was subsequently confirmed at the site, which is now being exploited by a rival company. It is thought that Mr Gallagher is making substantial sums in the form of royalties from oil produced from the site.

The Instructions to Counsel are set out at **14.2**. The extracts from the articles of association of the company at the end of the papers are based loosely on the 1948 Act version of Table A. Regulation 94 is the same as reg 80 of the 1948 Table A, and regs 99 and 100 correspond to reg 84(1) and (2).

The assessment criteria for the Opinion and Particulars of Claim are set out at **14.3**. Similar (though not always identical) formulations for assessment criteria have always been used for Company Law assessments. At **14.4** and **14.5** are the suggested Opinion and Particulars of Claim. Some brief comments appear at **14.6**.

14.2 *Re Beadnell Bay Petroleum Limited:* Instructions to Counsel

Re: BEADNELL BAY PETROLEUM LIMITED

INSTRUCTIONS TO COUNSEL TO
ADVISE AND SETTLE PARTICULARS
OF CLAIM

Counsel will find herewith:

1. Draft statement of Mr Keith Symons;
2. Draft statement of Mr William Knight;
3. Extracts from Exploration Licence;
4. Extracts from Production Licence;
5. Extracts from Board Minutes;
6. Correspondence;
7. Extracts from Articles of Association.

Counsel is instructed on behalf of Beadnell Bay Petroleum Limited ('the Company') following a board resolution on 13th January 2014 to seek legal redress against its former Managing Director, Mr Michael Gallagher. In essence, it is alleged that Mr Gallagher has dishonestly taken the Production Licence (enclosure 4) in his own name instead of the name of the Company, and is pocketing the extremely large royalties derived from it.

The Company is in the business of oil and petroleum exploration and production. Throughout its existence it has been principally engaged in the North Sea area. An Exploration Licence (enclosure 3) was granted in its favour in 2007. Over the next two years it conducted various geological investigations of the seabed in an area about 60 miles off the Northumberland coast. In 2009 certain financial problems were encountered by the Company, as set out in the draft statement of Mr Symons (enclosure 1). About the same time applications were invited by the Department of Energy and Climate Change for Production Licences in respect of a number of blocks of the seabed, including part of the area surveyed by the Company. One particular block was felt by the Board of the Company to have real promise as a potential oil field.

At that time Mr Gallagher was the Company's Managing Director, but was not employed by the Company. Instead of applying for a Production Licence in the name of the Company, he lodged an application in his own name. As Counsel will see, the Production Licence granted in relation to block 79452 on 18th September 2009 is in Mr Gallagher's name.

In October 2010 substantial petroleum reserves were discovered in block 79452. This is now known as the Olen Horst field. Instructing Solicitors are aware that in February 2011 the Secretary of State gave written consent to the assignment of the Production Licence from Mr Gallagher to Earlsferry Oil and Gas Public Limited Company ('Earlsferry'), a large and established oil production company. Commercial production of the Olen Horst field commenced in March 2012. Although the Company is not privy to the terms of

Mr Gallagher's arrangement with Earlsferry, nor of the production figures for the field, the published estimate is that there are reserves of 100 million barrels in the field. It is anticipated that Mr Gallagher will be paid very large sums by Earlsferry over a period of some years.

Counsel is asked to advise on the merits of a claim against Mr Gallagher, to advise in outline on remedies, and to settle Particulars of Claim.

DRAFT STATEMENT OF KEITH HARVEY SYMONS

I am Keith Harvey Symons of Watermill House, Billings Lane, North Kyme, Lincolnshire.

I am the Chairman of the Board of Directors of Beadnell Bay Petroleum Limited ('the Company'), and have been since 2008. I graduated from Aston University in 1989 with a degree in Business Studies and Financial Management and have spent my entire working life in management roles in the Theobald group.

At present the Company has two directors in addition to myself: Mr William Knight, who is the present Managing Director, and who became a director of the Company for the first time in May 2009; and Mr Trevor Alan Walsh, who was appointed in 2005. Mr Walsh has expertise in interpreting seismic readings in connection with oil exploration. He has attended no more than two or three Board meetings since I was appointed.

The Company was incorporated on 9th July 2003. It was originally a £100 company, but its nominal capital was increased to 10,000 £1 ordinary shares in 2008. Of these shares 3,000 have been issued to North Sea Shelf Drilling Limited ('Shelf Drilling') and 2,900 have been issued to Howdenbury (UK) Limited ('Howdenbury'), the remainder being unissued. Shelf Drilling is a company controlled by Theobald International Holdings PLC, the principal holding company of the Theobald family. I have been a director of Shelf Drilling for the last 10 years.

Howdenbury has always been almost wholly owned by Mr Michael Gallagher. Before 2008 the Company was almost wholly owned by Howdenbury. Mr Gallagher is a geologist and has been involved in oil exploration for all his working life. He is 52. In its early years the Company was funded by an American oil company. It had obtained an Exploration Licence from the government, and had been conducting geological surveys of the area off the Northumberland coast. In about August 2008 Mr Gallagher approached Mr Theobald with a proposal for participation in the Company's activities in the North Sea. At that time Mr Theobald had no interests in the North Sea, but was attracted to the prospect of moving into oil. I have since that time discovered that the American finance was about to be withdrawn. The end result of quite intensive negotiations was that in December 2008 the Theobald group made a substantial investment of capital in the Company, was allocated additional shares, and I was appointed Chairman of the Board of Directors. Mr Gallagher continued as Managing Director.

I have fairly substantial commitments elsewhere in the Theobald group, and the only member of the Board engaged full time in running the day-to-day affairs of the Company was Mr Gallagher. My position as Chairman and Mr Gallagher's as Managing Director were confirmed at the Company's AGM in January 2009.

The arrangements made between the Company, Shelf Drilling and Howdenbury in December 2008 were as follows:

(a) The Company would complete the programme of testing and investigation of the strata under the seafloor it had commenced in 2007 as set out in documents (including estimates for costs) provided by Mr Gallagher at that time.

(b) The costs of the programme, which were estimated at £34 million, would be met by Shelf Drilling.

(c) In the event that commercially exploitable oil reserves were discovered by the Company:

   (i) Shelf Drilling would have first call on profits made for reimbursement of its costs of the exploration programme;

   (ii) After paying costs, further distributions of profits would be 70 per cent to Shelf Drilling and 30 per cent to Howdenbury.

(d) To give effect to the agreement a further 3,883 ordinary shares would be issued to Shelf Drilling at that time at par.

Board meetings were held monthly. Mr Gallagher would always report on the progress of operations in the North Sea. From April or May 2009 he indicated that one particular area off the Northumberland coast was showing every sign of containing a reasonably sized oil deposit. This area was subsequently incorporated in block 79452 as designated by the Department of Energy and Climate Change. In June 2009 the Department of Energy and Climate Change advertised inviting applications for Production Licences for a number of blocks or areas in the North Sea, including block 79452.

Payments totalling £27.24 million were made by Shelf Drilling to the Company in the period from December 2008 to July 2009 for drilling, etc operations. This sum, together with compound interest at 2 per cent above Barclays Bank base rate, at present stands in the Company's books as a debt owed to Shelf Drilling.

In the second week of July 2009 the Theobald group suffered a wholly unconnected serious cash flow problem following the collapse of its restaurant division in Canada. From July 2009 I was fully engaged trying to shore up the financial crisis facing the group. Mr Gallagher was informed of the group's difficulties at about that time. In any event they were widely reported in the financial press. As there was no money available I told Mr Gallagher not to allow the Company to incur any further expense until further notice.

I am aware that on 6th August 2009 there was a meeting between Mr Theobald and Mr Gallagher concerning their future operations in the North Sea. My understanding is that they discussed the possibility of a new company being formed to make an application for a Production Licence in respect of block 79452, but so far as I am aware nothing concrete was agreed.

Mr Gallagher orally tendered his resignation as a director and as Managing Director of the Company at the Board meeting on 3rd September 2009 to take effect immediately. Although I was reluctant to accept he was adamant he wanted to go, and as he was not an employee I could not insist on any notice being given to the Company.

I was never told by Mr Gallagher that he intended to apply for a Production Licence in respect of block 79452. I was not invited to the so-called Board meeting on 6th August 2009. Questions relating to the Production Licence have never been raised or voted upon at meetings of the shareholders of the Company. The Company has been dormant since the summer of 2009.

It is a matter of record that substantial oil reserves were confirmed to exist in block 79452 in October 2010. This deposit is now known as the Olen Horst oilfield.

Signed:

Dated: 12th March 2014

DRAFT STATEMENT OF WILLIAM KNIGHT

I am William Knight of 35 Beresford Road, Wallsend, Newcastle upon Tyne.

I have been the Managing Director of Beadnell Bay Petroleum Limited ('the Company') since September 2009. I graduated from the University of Portsmouth in 1993 with a Master's Degree in Mining Engineering, where I wrote a dissertation on the problems in extracting oil shale. I have spent my entire working life in the mining industry, originally with the National Coal Board, but since 2000 with drilling operations in the North Sea.

Persons intending to prospect for oil in the North Sea have to apply for licences from what is now the Secretary of State for Energy and Climate Change. This the Company did in 2006. A small fee (£1,000) is payable. An Exploration Licence was granted to the Company in February 2007. Various exploratory operations were then conducted by the Company under an arrangement with an American oil company.

I have a good relationship with the present Managing Director of Earlsferry Oil and Gas PLC ('Earlsferry'), and have made a number of inquiries as to what happened in relation to the granting of the Production Licence relating to block 79452. The application was made by Mr Gallagher in his own name on 27th July 2009. Apparently the application fee of £10,200 was paid by Mr Gallagher himself. There was some correspondence between Mr Gallagher and the Department of Energy and Climate Change, and I have been given a copy of one letter from Mr Gallagher dated 17th August 2009.

In February 2011 the Secretary of State gave written consent to the assignment of the Production Licence to Earlsferry. My understanding is that Earlsferry are paying Mr Gallagher royalties on the price of sales of oil related products from the Olen Horst field at a rate of 1 per cent.

Signed:

Dated: 12th March 2014

EXPLORATION LICENCE

This exploration licence is made this 8th day of February 2007 between the Secretary of State for Energy and Climate Change of Thames House South, 1 Palace Street, London SW1 of the one part and Beadnell Bay Petroleum Limited whose registered office is situate at 62 Westgate Road, Newcastle upon Tyne, NE1 4YG of the other part.

Interpretation

1. (1) In the following clauses the following expressions have the meanings hereby respectively assigned to them, that is to say:
'the Act of 1934' means the Petroleum (Production) Act 1934;
'the Act of 1964' means the Continental Shelf Act 1964;
'the exploration area' means the area for the time being in which the Licensee may exercise the rights granted by this licence;
'the Licensee' means the person or persons to whom this licence is granted, his personal representatives and any person or persons to whom the rights conferred by this licence may lawfully have been assigned;
'the Minister' means the Secretary of State for Energy and Climate Change;
'petroleum' includes any mineral oil or relative hydrocarbon and natural gas existing in its natural condition in strata, but does not include coal or bituminous shales or other stratified deposits from which oil can be extracted by destructive distillation;
'well' includes borehole....

Right to search for petroleum

2. In consideration of the payments hereinafter provided and the performance and observance by the Licensee of all the terms and conditions hereof, the Minister, in exercise of the powers conferred upon him by the Act of 1934 and the Act of 1964, hereby grants to the Licensee LICENCE AND LIBERTY in common with all other persons to whom the like right may have been granted or may hereafter be granted during the continuance of this licence and subject to the provisions hereof to search for petroleum in the strata in the islands and in the seabed and subsoil:

(a) comprised in the seaward areas defined by Regulation 3(1) of the Petroleum (Production) (Seaward Areas) Regulations 1988; and
(b) where the lines drawn in accordance with Schedule 1 to the said Regulations dividing landward areas from seaward areas are not the low-water line, in the areas between that line and the said dividing lines:

Provided that no rights conferred by this licence shall be exercisable in any area in respect of which a licence (not being a methane drainage licence) is for the time being in force, entitling the grantee thereof to search and bore for and get petroleum, except with the agreement of the holder of that licence to the exercise in any such area of any such rights.

Prospecting methods

3. The right to search for petroleum conferred by this licence shall include prospecting and carrying out geological surveys by physical or chemical means and drilling for

the purpose of obtaining geological information about strata in the exploration area but shall not include any right to get petroleum or any right to drill wells for production of petroleum or any other well of a depth exceeding three hundred and fifty metres below the surface of the seabed or such greater depth as the Minister may from time to time approve either generally or in relation to a particular well or in relation to a class of wells to which that well belongs.

Term of licence

4. This licence unless sooner determined under any of the provisions hereof shall be and continue in force for the term of three years from 8th February 2007 but may, if the Minister sees fit and the Licensee has at least three months before the expiry of the said term made a written request for its extension, be continued for a further period of three years....

Payment of consideration for licence

6. (1) The Licensee shall pay to the Minister during the term of this licence the consideration for the grant of this licence specified in Schedule 1 to this licence at the times and in the manner so specified....

Avoidance of harmful methods of working

9. (1) The Licensee shall maintain all apparatus and appliances and all wells which have not been abandoned and plugged as provided by clause 7 of this licence in good repair and condition and shall execute all operations in or in connection with the exploration area in a proper and workmanlike manner in accordance with methods and practice of exploration customarily used in good oilfield practice and without prejudice to the generality of the foregoing provision the Licensee shall take all steps practicable in order

(a) to prevent the escape or waste of petroleum discovered in the exploration area;

(b) to conserve the exploration area for productive operations;

(c) to prevent damage to petroleum bearing strata;

(d) to prevent the entrance of water through wells to petroleum bearing strata; and

(e) to prevent the escape of petroleum into any waters in or in the vicinity of the exploration area....

Returns

13. (1) The Licensee shall furnish to the Minister on or before the fifteenth day of each month in which this licence is in force a return in a form from time to time approved by the Minister of the progress of his operations in the exploration area. Such return shall contain

(a) a statement of the areas in which any geological work, including surveys by any physical or chemical means, has been carried out;

(b) the number assigned to each well, and in the case of any well the drilling of which was begun or the number of which was changed in that month, the site thereof;

(c) a statement of the depth drilled in each well; and

(d) a statement of any petroleum, water, mines or workable seams of coal encountered in the course of the said operations.

Power to execute works

18. If the Licensee shall at any time fail to perform the obligations arising under the terms and conditions of any of clauses 7, 9 and 11 of this licence then and in any such case the Minister shall be entitled, after giving to the Licensee reasonable notice in writing of such his intention, to execute any works and to provide and install any equipment which in the opinion of the Minister may be necessary to secure the performance of the said obligations or any of them and to recover the costs and expenses of so doing from the Licensee....

Schedule 1

1. The Licensee shall pay to the Minister yearly in advance during the first three years of the term of this Licence the sum of TWENTY THOUSAND POUNDS payable on the 8th day of February in every year.

2. If the period of this Licence is extended in accordance with clause 4 hereof, the Licensee shall pay to the Minister yearly in advance during the term of such extension the sum of THIRTY THOUSAND POUNDS payable on the 8th day of February in every year commencing on 8th February 2010.

IN WITNESS

where of etc.

PRODUCTION LICENCE

This production licence is made this 19th day of September 2009 between the Secretary of State for Energy and Climate Change of Thames House South, 1 Palace Street, London SW1 of the one part and Michael Ryan Gallagher of Marigold House, Lower Wynd, Aylesbury, Buckinghamshire, HP20 6DN of the other part.

Interpretation

1. (1) In the following clauses, the following expressions have the meanings hereby respectively assigned to them, that is to say
'the Act of 1934' means the Petroleum (Production) Act 1934;
'the Act of 1964' means the Continental Shelf Act 1964;
'appropriate percentage' has the meaning assigned thereto by clause 10;
'block' means an area comprised in this licence which is delineated on the reference map deposited at the principal office of the Department of Energy and Climate Change and to which a reference number was assigned at the date of this licence;
'chargeable period' has the meaning assigned thereto by clause 10;
'development scheme' has the meaning assigned thereto by clause 28;
'half year' means the period from 1st January to 30th June in any year and the period from 1st July to 31st December in any year;
'initial term' has the meaning assigned thereto by clause 3 and 'second term' has the meaning assigned thereto by clause 4(4);
'the licensed area' means the area for the time being in which the Licensee may exercise the rights granted by this licence;
'the Licensee' means the person or persons to whom this licence is granted, his personal representatives and any person or persons to whom the rights conferred by this licence may lawfully have been assigned;
'the Minister' means the Secretary of State for Energy and Climate Change;
'oilfield' has the meaning assigned thereto by clause 28;
'petroleum' includes any mineral oil or relative hydrocarbon and natural gas existing in its natural condition in strata but does not include coal or bituminous shales or other stratified deposits from which oil can be extracted by destructive distillation;
'section' means a part of a block comprising an area bounded by minute lines of latitude and longitude one minute apart respectively;
'well' includes borehole. . . .

2. In consideration of the payments and royalties hereinafter provided and the performance and observance by the Licensee of all the terms and conditions hereof, the Minister, in exercise of the powers conferred upon him by the Act of 1934 hereby grants to the Licensee EXCLUSIVE LICENCE AND LIBERTY during the continuance of this licence and subject to the provisions hereof to search and bore for, and get, petroleum in the seabed and subsoil under the seaward area comprising an area of 20 square kilometers more particularly described in Schedule 1 to this Licence being the area comprising block No 79452 on the reference map deposited at the principal office of the Department of Energy and Climate Change:

Provided that nothing in this licence shall affect the right of the Minister to grant a methane drainage licence in respect of the whole or any part of the licensed area or affect the exercise of any rights so granted.

Term of licence

3. This licence unless sooner determined under any of the provisions hereof shall be and continue in force for the term of six years next after 1st October 2009 (hereinafter called 'the initial term'); but if the terms and conditions of this licence are duly performed and observed and, in particular, if the work programme described in Schedule 4 to this licence has been duly performed, it may be continued for a further term of twelve years as provided by clause 4 of this licence and, if the terms and conditions of this licence continue to be duly performed and observed, thereafter as provided by clause 5 (and subject to the provisions of clause 6) of this licence for a further maximum period of eighteen years....

Payment of consideration for licence

9. (1) The Licensee shall make to the Minister as consideration for the grant of this licence

(a) payments of royalty in accordance with clauses 10 to 12 of this licence;

(b) deliveries of petroleum in accordance with clause 13 of this licence; and

(c) payments in accordance with Schedule 2 to this licence.

(2) The Licensee shall not by reason of determination of the licence or surrender of any part of the licensed area be entitled to be repaid or allowed any sum payable to the Minister pursuant to this licence before the date of determination or surrender.

Royalty payments

10. (1) Subject to paragraph (2) of this clause the Licensee shall pay to the Minister, in respect of each half year in which this licence is in force (hereafter in this clause and in clauses 11 and 12 of this licence referred to as a 'chargeable period'), a royalty of an amount equal to the percentage specified in Schedule 3 to this licence (hereinafter referred to as 'the appropriate percentage') of the value of the petroleum relating to that period....

Working obligations

16. (1) The Licensee shall before the expiry of the initial term of this licence carry out such scheme of prospecting including any geological survey by any physical or chemical means and such programme of test drilling (hereinafter collectively referred to as a 'work programme') as may be set out in Schedule 4 to this licence.

(2) If at any time the Minister serves a notice in writing on the Licensee requiring him to submit to the Minister, before a date specified in the notice, an appropriate programme for exploring for petroleum in the licensed area during a period so specified, the Licensee shall comply with the notice; and for the purposes of this paragraph an appropriate programme is one which any person who, if he

(a) were entitled to exploit rights granted by the licence; and

(b) had the competence and resources needed to exploit those rights to the best commercial advantage; and

(c) were seeking to exploit those rights to the best commercial advantage:

could reasonably be expected to carry out during the period specified in the notice, and that period must be within the term of this licence.

(5) The Licensee shall carry out any programme submitted by him in pursuance of this clause as to which either

(a) the Minister serves notice in writing on the Licensee stating that the Minister approves the programme; or

(b) it is determined in consequence of any reference to arbitration in pursuance of this licence that the programme satisfies the relevant requirements;

and any programme approved by the Minister in pursuance of this paragraph shall be deemed for the purposes of this licence to satisfy the relevant requirements....

Avoidance of harmful methods of working

23. (1) The Licensee shall maintain all apparatus and appliances and all wells in the licensed area which have not been abandoned and plugged as provided by clause 19 of this licence in good repair and condition and shall execute all operations in or in connection with the licensed area in a proper and workmanlike manner in accordance with methods and practice customarily used in good oilfield practice and without prejudice to the generality of the foregoing provision the Licensee shall take all steps practicable in order

(a) to control the flow and to prevent the escape or waste of petroleum discovered in or obtained from the licensed area;

(b) to conserve the licensed area for productive operations;

(c) to prevent damage to adjoining petroleum bearing strata;

(d) to prevent the entrance of water through wells to petroleum bearing strata except for the purposes of secondary recovery; and

(e) to prevent the escape of petroleum into any waters in or in the vicinity of the licensed area....

Restrictions on assignment, etc

41. (1) The Licensee shall not, except with the consent in writing of the Minister and in accordance with the conditions (if any) of the consent do anything whatsoever whereby, under the law (including the rules of equity) of any part of the United Kingdom or of any other place, any right granted by this licence or derived from a right so granted becomes exercisable by or for the benefit of or in accordance with the directions of another person.

(2) An agreement permitting the carrying out of geological surveys by physical or chemical means in the licensed area otherwise than by drilling is not prohibited by paragraph (1) of this clause if the person by whom such surveys are to be carried out is

(a) the holder of a licence granted by the Minister of the right, in common with all other persons to whom the like right may have been granted, to search for petroleum in respect of an area which would include the licensed area, but for a proviso therein excluding the exercise of such rights in the licensed area without the consent of the Licensee; or

(b) the holder of a licence granted by the Minister to search and bore for, and get, petroleum in an area adjacent to the licensed area.

Schedule 1

[Technical description of block No 79452]

Schedule 2

1. The Licensee shall pay to the Minister the sum of SIXTY THOUSAND POUNDS as an initial payment on the grant of this licence, such sum to be paid on or before 24th September 2009.

2. The Licensee shall pay to the Minister yearly in advance during the first six years of the term of this licence the sum of NINETY THOUSAND POUNDS payable on the 1st day of October in every year.

3. If the period of this licence is extended in accordance with clause 4 hereof, the Licensee shall pay to the Minister yearly in advance during the term of such extension the sum of ONE HUNDRED THOUSAND POUNDS payable on the 1st day of October in every year commencing on 1st October 2015.

Schedule 3

The appropriate percentage shall be eight per cent.

Schedule 4

[Detailed working obligations undertaken by the Licensee]

IN WITNESS whereof etc

BEADNELL BAY PETROLEUM LIMITED
Extracts from Board Minutes
(Each meeting was recorded on a separate page)

9.4.2009
Present: KHS; MG
3. MG reported latest seismic surveys were being analysed. Promising geological structure about 60 miles E of Seahouses being given particular attention.

7.5.2009
Present: KHS; MG
2. MG reported area E of Seahouses had all the right characteristics for oil deposit. Further test bore justified.
Agreed: Estimate to be prepared by MG of costs of further bore. To proceed on signature of KHS.

2.7.2009
Present: KHS; MG
2. It will not be possible for further bore at site off Seahouses to be undertaken before August as drilling vessel otherwise engaged until then. Confirmed go ahead when ready.
3. MG reported Department of Energy and Climate Change advertised for production licences for a number of areas including the Seahouses site. Discussion as to whether an application should be lodged.
4. Discussion as to the probabilities that commercial deposits exist at Seahouses site.
Agreed: MG to provide KHS with more precise assessment by 16.7.2009.

16.7.2009
Present: KHS; MG
2. MG reported no present offshore activities in progress. No firm commitments for drilling operations.
3. Discussion of Theobald group difficulties.
Agreed: No additional expenditure to be incurred until further notice. Economies to be made where possible.

6.8.2009
Present: MG; TAW
2. Discussion of Theobald group difficulties and Seahouses site (now known as Department of Energy and Climate Change block 79452).
Agreed: MG to apply for production licence in own name.

3.9.2009
Present: KHS; MG
1. MG tendered his resignation as director and MD. After discussion MG's resignation accepted by KHS.

Marigold House
Lower Wynd
Aylesbury
Buckinghamshire
HP20 4RK

Mrs F Creaney
Department of Energy and Climate Change
Thames House South
1 Palace Street
London SW1

17th August 2009

Dear Madam,

Re: Block 79452

Further to our letter of 10th inst., I can confirm that I have been actively employed in the oil exploration industry since 1993. I have experience with offshore oil operations both in the North Sea and in the Gulf of Mexico. Since 2003 I have been the Managing Director of Beadnell Bay Petroleum Limited, which as you will know holds an Exploration Licence issued by your department on 8th February 2007 in respect of the seaward areas of the North Sea. Beadnell Bay Petroleum Limited has extensive knowledge and expertise within the oil industry, and I attach a copy of the programme of works undertaken by the company since February 2007.

Should you need to discuss further matters with me, please contact me so that a meeting can be arranged.

Yours faithfully,

Michael Gallagher

DANIELS AND AWFORD
Solicitors

73 Granger Street
Newcastle upon Tyne
NE1 3SL
Tel: 0191 201 8376
Fax: 0191 201 8272
Our Ref: 94/DGY
Your Ref:

Date: 20th January 2014

Mr M Gallagher
Marigold House
Lower Wynd
Aylesbury
Buckinghamshire
HP20 4RK

Dear Mr Gallagher,

BEADNELL BAY PETROLEUM LIMITED

We are instructed by the Board of the above-named company in relation to the granting to you of a North Sea Oil Production Licence over block 79452 on 19th September 2009.

At all material times you were a director and Managing Director of the above-named company. In that capacity you owed it various fiduciary duties which prohibited you from making a personal profit at the expense of the company. Accordingly it was your duty to apply for the above-mentioned Production Licence in the name of the company rather than in your own name.

We understand that as the Licensee of block 79452 you were able to enter into an arrangement with Earlsferry Oil and Gas PLC relating to the exploitation of the oil reserves found in the Olen Horst oilfield in the North Sea. We also understand that under that arrangement you are and will continue to be in receipt of considerable royalties in respect of oil produced by that oilfield. In the circumstances you are liable to account to our client for those royalties. Please confirm that you are holding all sums received from Earlsferry Oil and Gas PLC to the account of our client Company, and will provide full facilities for the inspection of your books for the purpose of verifying the amount due to our client.

Enclosed with this letter is a schedule of the documents on which our client relies in support of its claim, and a list of the documents that we seek from you.

Please confirm receipt of this letter in the next 14 days, and provide us with a full reply within 3 months of receipt of this letter confirming whether liability is accepted or denied. If liability is denied, you should give a full explanation of your reasons. A copy of the Practice Direction on Pre-action conduct is enclosed.

This is an important letter. It may be in your interests to consult a solicitor before replying.

Yours faithfully,

Daniels and Awford

Marigold House
Lower Wynd
Aylesbury
Buckinghamshire
HP20 4RK

8th February 2014

Messrs Daniels and Awford
73 Granger Street
Newcastle upon Tyne
NE1 3SL

Dear Sirs,

BEADNELL BAY PETROLEUM LIMITED

I was disappointed to receive your letter of 20th January and to read the allegations made in it on behalf of your clients. There is absolutely no truth in what you say about misconduct on my part.

As you will be aware, Beadnell Bay Petroleum Limited as originally formed eleven years ago was wholly owned by one of my other companies, Howdenbury (UK) Limited. It is now controlled by the employers of the present chairman. In the years up to 2009 it was actively engaged in the North Sea. After my resignation in 2009 it has achieved absolutely nothing.

Exploration for and recovery of offshore oil requires a sustained commitment. What happened was that in the summer of 2009 your real clients ran out of money and reneged on the 2008 investment contract between Howdenbury (UK) Limited and North Sea Shelf Drilling Limited at a very delicate time, jeopardising several years of investment by my companies.

As your clients are aware, licensees are required to enter into a large number of expensive obligations when they take production licences. After July 2009 your clients were in no position to comply with those obligations. On instructions from his employer, Mr Theobald, Beadnell Bay's chairman, Mr Symons, laid down a directive in July 2009 that no further expenditure was to be incurred by the company. It was clear at that time that there was no prospect of Beadnell Bay obtaining a production licence in its own right.

Being unable to finance a licence of its own, it was agreed that I could apply for a production licence myself. This was at my own risk and, if it proved that there was oil in the area concerned, for my own personal benefit. This was expressly agreed to at a meeting between myself and Mr Theobald at that time, and was approved by the directors of Beadnell Bay Petroleum Limited at a meeting on 6th August 2009.

I made the position clear to the Department of Energy and Climate Change in November 2009. The Department was fully aware of the financial problems of the Theobald group and Beadnell Bay's inability to finance the proper development of the licensed area. I made it clear that I would honour the terms of the licence from my own resources or finance that I would seek elsewhere.

Considerable expenditure (well into seven figures) was in fact incurred over the next year in test drilling, all of which came from my personal resources.

There is a great deal of being wise after the event in all this on the part of your clients. Back in 2008 I was the only person confident that there was oil at Olen Horst, and I met no end of scepticism from Mr Symons. In the light of all this I trust that you will confirm that your clients will not be taking these allegations any further.

Yours faithfully,

Michael Gallagher

Extracts from the Articles of Association of BEADNELL BAY PETROLEUM LIMITED

Director's appointments

82. The company may by ordinary resolution appoint a person who is willing to act to be a director either to fill a vacancy or as an additional director. In addition, by ordinary resolutions one person so appointed may be appointed chairman of the board of directors and a second person may be appointed as managing director of the company.

Proceedings of directors

86. The directors may meet together for the dispatch of business, adjourn, and otherwise regulate their meetings, as they think fit. A director may at any time summon a meeting of the directors. It shall not be necessary to give notice of a meeting of directors to any director for the time being outside the United Kingdom. Questions arising at any meeting shall be decided by a majority of votes. In case of an equality of votes, the chairman shall have a second or casting vote.

87. The quorum necessary for the transaction of the business of the directors may be fixed by the directors, and unless so fixed shall be two.

91. All acts done by any meeting of the directors shall, notwithstanding that it be afterwards discovered that there was some defect in the appointment of any such director or that they or any of them were disqualified, be as valid as if every such person had been duly appointed and was qualified to be a director.

Powers of directors

94. The business of the company shall be managed by the directors, who may pay all expenses incurred in promoting and registering the company, and may exercise all powers of the company as are not by the Companies Act 1985 or by these regulations, required to be exercised by the company in general meeting, subject, nevertheless, to any of these regulations, to the provisions of the Companies Act 1985 and to such regulations, being not inconsistent with the aforesaid regulations or provisions, as may be prescribed by the company in general meeting; but no regulation made by the company in general meeting shall invalidate any prior act of the directors which would have been valid if that regulation had not been made.

Duties of directors

99. A director who is in any way, whether directly or indirectly, interested in a contract or proposed contract with the company shall declare the nature of his interest at a meeting of the directors in accordance with section 317 of the Companies Act 1985.

100. A director shall not vote in respect of any contract or arrangement in which he is interested, and if he shall do so his vote shall not be counted, nor shall he be counted in the quorum present at the meeting.

103. The directors shall cause minutes to be recorded:

(a) of all appointments of officers made by the company;

(b) of the names of directors present at each meeting of the directors; and

(c) of all resolutions and the proceedings at all meetings of the company, and of the directors;

and every director present at any meeting of directors shall sign his name on the minutes of the preceding meeting.

14.3 Assessment criteria

A OPINION WRITING

In order to be graded competent or above your opinion must satisfy these criteria:

(1) LANGUAGE (20%)

(a) is written in clear, grammatical English, correctly spelt and appropriately punctuated;

(b) is written in language and in a style appropriate to an opinion.

(2) STRUCTURE (20%)

Has a clear and appropriate structure in that:

(a) it is properly and neatly laid out;

(b) it is divided into an appropriate number of paragraphs;

(c) it makes appropriate use of subheadings;

(d) it deals with each issue in a logical order;

(e) it gives each issue its due weight and significance;

(f) it sets your conclusions out clearly and prominently;

(g) it is of a suitable length overall.

(3) CONTENT (20%)

Write an opinion that:

(a) identifies and addresses the material facts and issues;

(b) does not address immaterial facts and issues;

(c) is based on a sound understanding and application of the relevant law.

(4) CONCLUSIONS (20%):

(a) Express sound and justifiable conclusions.

(b) Expresses a definite conclusion where appropriate, but not where inappropriate.

(c) Answer all the questions expressly or implicitly asked in the instructions.

(5) PRACTICALITY (20%):

Write an opinion that:

(a) is based on a sound understanding and practical analysis of the law, facts and issues;

(b) is justified by sound reasoning;

(c) explains where appropriate why you cannot express a definite conclusion;

(d) identifies and asks for relevant further information;

(e) indicates any practical and procedural steps to be taken;

(f) addresses the needs and objectives of the clients.

B PARTICULARS OF CLAIM

In order to perform the exercise satisfactorily you must show your ability to draft Particulars of Claim which meet the following criteria:

(1) LANGUAGE (10%)

Is written in clear grammatical English, correctly spelt and appropriately punctuated.

(2) STRUCTURE (20%)

(a) is properly headed and laid out;

(b) is neat on the page;

(c) deals with the material issues in an appropriate order and in an appropriate number of paragraphs;

(d) tells a clear story.

(3) LAW AND CONTENT (30%)

Draft a statement of case that:

(a) is based on a sound understanding and application of the relevant law;

(b) sets out the material facts;

(c) identifies or helps to identify the material issues;

(d) accurately states the client's case and any remedy sought;

(e) omits all immaterial matters.

(4) EFFECTIVENESS (10%)

Draft a statement of case that serves its purpose in that it:

(a) sets out a sustainable claim; and

(b) goes as far as it reasonably can in helping the client to achieve his/her objectives.

(5) DRAFTING SKILL (30%)

Draft a statement of case that:

(a) is written in language and in a style appropriate for a statement of case;

(b) is precise and unambiguous;

(c) is concise;

(d) does not rely excessively on precedents or follow inappropriate precedents.

Note that not only Opinion Writing Skills but also Legal Research Skills and Fact Management Skills are required in order to satisfy these criteria.

14.4 Suggested opinion

Re: BEADNELL BAY PETROLEUM LIMITED

OPINION

1. I am instructed on behalf of Beadnell Bay Petroleum Limited ('the Company') to advise on the merits of a claim against Mr Michael Gallagher for breach of fiduciary duty, and to advise in outline on remedies. I am also asked to settle particulars of claim.

2. The Company was formed to search for and extract petroleum, and has been engaged principally in the North Sea. Mr Gallagher was a director and the managing director of the Company from its incorporation in 2003 until his resignation on 3 September 2009.

3. Substantial investment was made by the Company in the period up to July 2009 in exploration operations under an Exploration Licence granted to it by the Secretary of State on 8 February 2007. These identified one area, block 79452 (the 'Olen Horst field'), as the potential site of an oilfield. A Production Licence from the Department of Energy and Climate Change is required for extraction of petroleum from the North Sea. Financial difficulties were encountered by the Company in July 2009, and Mr Gallagher applied for and obtained on 19 September 2009 a Production Licence in respect of the Olen Horst field in his own name. Substantial petroleum reserves were found in the Olen Horst field in October 2010, and Mr Gallagher entered into an arrangement with Earlsferry Oil and Gas PLC ('Earlsferry') in February 2011 under which he appears to be in receipt of substantial royalties.

Summary of Advice

4. As a director, Mr Gallagher owed a duty to the Company to avoid conflicts of interest with the Company, without due authorisation from the directors of the Company. The duty to avoid conflicts of interest extends to the exploitation of property, information or opportunities (Companies Act 2006, s 175(2)), which in this case will cover Mr Gallagher's application for and securing the Production Licence for the Olen Horst field. It does not matter that the Company was probably unable to take advantage of this opportunity for itself. He could not avoid that duty by resigning just before taking the Production Licence in his own name.

5. The real question in this case is whether there was proper authorisation from the directors to Mr Gallagher taking the Production Licence in his own name. At present the evidence on this is not absolutely clear, but there is a prima facie case of breach of duty against Mr Gallagher. If it is established that Mr Gallagher breached his fiduciary duty to the Company he will hold the profits he appears to be making under the assignment of the Production Licence as a constructive trustee for the Company, and will be bound to account to it for the royalties he has and will receive. Given the blanket denial in the letter of response, the next steps should be to consider ADR, failing which it will be necessary to commence proceedings.

Duty to avoid Conflicts of Interest

6. As a director of the Company, Mr Gallagher was under a duty to avoid situations in which he had, or could have had, a direct or indirect interest that conflicted, or possibly may have been in conflict, with the interests of the Company (Companies Act 2006, s 175(1)). This duty was owed to the Company (s 170(1)). Although the duty extends to situations where there is a mere 'possibility' of a conflict of interest, this case seems to me to be one where there has been an actual conflict of interest in relation to Mr Gallagher obtaining the Production Licence for the Olen Horst field. One aspect of this duty is that a director is not permitted to use the Company's property, information or opportunities or information for his own benefit without due authorisation (s 175(2)). In interpreting and applying the general duties imposed on directors under these provisions, the court is required to have regard to the corresponding common law rules and equitable principles (s 170(4)).

7. A strict approach is taken by the Courts. As Lord Wright said in *Regal (Hastings) Ltd v Gulliver* [1967] 2 AC 134, 154, ... 'if a person in a fiduciary relationship makes a secret profit out of the relationship, the court will not inquire whether the other person is damnified or has lost a profit which otherwise he would have got. The fact is in itself a fundamental breach of the fiduciary relationship. Nor can the court adequately investigate the matter in most cases.' In this case liability rests on two conditions being satisfied:

(a) whether the obtaining of the Production Licence was so related to the affairs of the Company that it can properly be said to have been done in the course of Mr Gallagher's management of the Company and in utilisation of his opportunities and special knowledge as a director; and

(b) whether obtaining the Production Licence in his own name resulted in a profit to himself.

Use of Corporate Opportunity

8. In the period leading up to Mr Gallagher's application for the Production Licence the Company had expended considerable sums in conducting geological investigations in the area including the Olen Horst field. Obviously this expenditure was incurred for the purpose of putting the Company in a position to apply for a Production Licence or Licences which it could then exploit. Mr Gallagher is a geologist and, in his capacity as Managing Director of the Company, was privy to the findings of the Company's survey work. This is clear enough from the Board minutes for April to July 2009 and Mr Gallagher's letter of 8 February 2014 in response to the letter before claim.

9. When the opportunity arose in the summer of 2009 to apply for a Production Licence over the Olen Horst field it was, given the knowledge I assume the Company's directors had about the prospects for the site, the duty of the directors to apply for such a licence on behalf of the Company. Making the application in his own name was, therefore, on the face of it a breach of Mr Gallagher's fiduciary duty to the Company. The detailed documentation in support of this is not in my papers. Nevertheless, from the draft statements of Mr Symons and Mr Knight, together with the board minute of 7 May 2009 where it is stated that the area east of Seahouses had all the right characteristics for an oil deposit, it seems to be a clear inference that there would have been a large body of seabed survey documentation and reports from the survey team evidencing the prospects of oil being found in block 79452 (the Olen Horst field). This documentation

needs to be collected together and collated by Mr Knight for the purpose of establishing what was known in mid-2009 about the opportunity offered by obtaining a Production Licence for this area.

10. In my opinion, there is a good prospect of establishing that obtaining the Production Licence was a maturing corporate opportunity (*Industrial Development Consultants Ltd v Cooley* [1972] 1 WLR 443) or 'worthwhile opportunity' (*Bhullar v Bhullar* [2003] 2 BCLC 241) which was open to the Company in May 2009. This will be judged on the strength of the evidence available to the Company in 2009 on how likely it was that oil would be found in the Olen Horst field, and its likely value. The court should not look at this with the benefit of hindsight. Mr Gallagher in his letter dated 8 February 2014 asserts that this is such a case, and that no-one else had faith there was any oil in this area. This will be decided on the basis of the survey evidence mentioned in the previous paragraph, and on expert evidence (which should be obtained) from an oil industry geologist on the significance of the survey evidence available at that time.

Use of Company Information or Property

11. In addition to taking a corporate opportunity, in my opinion Mr Gallagher also made use of the Company's confidential information in deciding to apply for the Production Licence. As a director of the Company, and from his involvement in the surveying of the seabed, Mr Gallagher had access to the survey information which had been compiled on behalf of the Company at substantial cost. I am told that survey costs incurred by North Sea Shelf Drilling Ltd, and charged to the Company, amounted to £27.24 million in the 8 months to July 2009. This information was plainly confidential information owned by the Company, and Mr Gallagher obviously made use of it when deciding to apply for the Production Licence. Use of company information also falls within the no-conflicts rule in the Companies Act 2006, s 175.

12. Further, it is apparent that Mr Gallagher used the Company's name in his letter to the Department of Energy and Climate Change of 17 August 2009 in support of his application for the Production Licence. This case is therefore similar to *Quarter Master (UK) Ltd v Pyke* [2005] 1 BCLC 245, where the directors were held to be in breach of their fiduciary duties because they had used the company's database and goodwill. Here, Mr Gallagher made use of the work done by the Company under the Exploration Licence, enclosing a copy of its programme of works with his letter to the Department of Energy and Climate Change in support of his application for the Production Licence. Making use of company property is also caught by the Companies Act 2006, s 175.

13. If the case is defended it will be necessary to disclose the documentary records of the Company's survey work (as mentioned in paragraph 10 above), and in my view it will be necessary for an expert geologist's report to be prepared interpreting that material. Such a report should consider the strength of the evidence available in July 2009 for there being a commercially viable oilfield within the Olen Horst field.

The Company's Financial Difficulties

14. In July 2009 the Company, on account of the difficulties then being encountered by the Theobald Group, lost the source of its finances. On 16 July 2009 the Board of the Company agreed to avoid further expenditure until further notice. Certain fees have to be paid when applying for Production Licences, and a number of very onerous and

expensive obligations (contained in Schedule 4 to the Licence) have to be taken on by licensees. It seems clear that in July–August 2009 the Company was not in a position to honour that level of expenditure. Although a court is very likely to find that there was no possibility of the Company being granted a Production Licence in those circumstances, that is no bar to the Company obtaining relief against a director who has allowed his personal interests to conflict with those of his Company: *Regal (Hastings) Ltd v Gulliver* [1967] 2 AC 134, and the Companies Act 2006, s 175(2).

Authorisation by the Directors

15. It is provided by the Companies Act 2006, s 175(4)(b), that the duty to avoid conflicts of interest is not infringed if the matter has been authorised by the directors. Mr Gallagher in his letter in response to the letter before claim relies on the board meeting of the Company on 6 August 2009 for this purpose. I have been given extracts from the board minutes, which say that on that date a board meeting took place attended by Mr Gallagher ('MG') and Mr Walsh ('TAW'). The board discussed the difficulties of the Theobald Group (which holds 3,000 of the 5,900 issued shares in the Company), and agreed that 'Mr Gallagher [could] apply for a production licence in his own name.'

16. In the case of a private company, unless there is anything in the articles to invalidate this, an authorisation under s 175(4)(b) may be given by the directors by the matter being proposed and authorised by the directors in a board meeting (s 175(5)(a)). There is no provision in the articles of the Company invalidating such an authorisation, and in fact regulations 99 and 100 specifically allow this to be done. Such an authorisation is only effective if any quorum requirement is met without counting the director in question (s 175(6)(a)), and without the interested director voting (s 175(6)(b)).

17. Regulation 87 of the Company's articles provides that the quorum necessary for the transaction of business at board meetings is two, unless otherwise fixed by the directors. Subject to what follows, according to the extract from the board minutes, the meeting on 6 August 2009 was attended by two directors, so was quorate for ordinary business. One of the two directors present was Mr Gallagher, and by s 175(6)(a) he is not to be counted towards the quorum for the purposes of the resolution to authorise his application for the Production Licence. Mr Gallagher will only avoid this result if the directors had previously fixed the quorum for board meetings at one (Mr Walsh then constituting the quorum at the 6 August 2009 board meeting), as permitted by reg. 87. It will be necessary to obtain all the board minutes from the incorporation of the Company to check whether this was done.

18. Mr Gallagher's argument faces another difficulty in that under s 175(6)(b) the authorisation on 6 August 2009 will only have been effective if it would have been agreed to if his vote had not been counted. If the quorum for board meetings was two, he will fail on this ground as well. If, however, the quorum had previously been fixed at one, the authorisation will have been validly granted on the sole vote of Mr Walsh (assuming he is the 'TAW' identified in the extracts of the minutes).

19. If the quorum for board meetings was two, there was no effective authorisation for Mr Gallagher applying for the Production Licence for the reasons set out in the previous three paragraphs. If the quorum was previously set at one, although the purported authorisation will comply with s 175(6), it will in my opinion be ineffective if it is established that Mr Symons (and/or other directors) were not notified of the 6 August

2009 board meeting. Mr Symons specifically says he was not invited to this meeting, despite being the Chairman of the board. Regulation 86 of the articles provides that it is not necessary to give notice of a board meeting to any director who is at the time outside the United Kingdom. Subject to that, it is necessary to give notice to all board members (*Smith v Darley* (1849) 2 HLC 789). If even one member of the board was not given notice of the meeting, the meeting is bad in the sense of being an invalid meeting (*Young v Ladies' Imperial Club Limited* [1920] 2 KB 523, 530). If there was no meeting on this ground, of course the purported authorisation given to Mr Gallagher to apply for the Production Licence will be of no effect.

20. Although this may seem no more than a technical point given modern communications and travel, reg 86 of the articles preserves the long-recognised exception that notice need not be given to directors who are overseas. It is therefore essential to establish that Mr Symons was within the United Kingdom on 6 August 2009, and evidence, such as his passport, will be needed on this issue.

21. Finally, although I may be reading more into the very short extract from the board minutes of 6 August 2009 than is fair, what it says is that Mr Gallagher is 'to apply' for a Production Licence in his own name. The board therefore purported to approve a future application. According to Mr Knight, Mr Gallagher's application was made on 27 July 2009. What Mr Gallagher needed was a retrospective ratification of his past application. Technically, it is arguable that what happened was not therefore authorised within the meaning of the Companies Act 2006, s 175(5), in any event.

Duty to Disclose Information to the Company

22. There is authority to the effect that part of the no conflicts rule in the Companies Act 2006, s 175, is a duty on a director to disclose important information to the Company (*DPC Estates Pty Ltd v Grey* [1974] 1 NSWLR 443; *Industrial Development Consultants Ltd v Cooley* [1972] 1 WLR 443). It seems from the Board minutes before me that Mr Symons was dependent on Mr Gallagher for details as to the North Sea operation being conducted by the Company. In his letter of 8 February 2014 Mr Gallagher says Mr Symons was sceptical about the prospects of the Olen Horst field in 2008. Was this because Mr Symons did not have all the information available to Mr Gallagher? Was Mr Symons fully informed by July 2009? The reality of the situation was that there were two shareholders of the Company, ultimately owned by Mr Gallagher and Mr Theobald, with Mr Symons being Mr Theobald's representative on the Board. Was the Theobald side of the Company informed fully of the situation and Mr Gallagher's intentions when he met Mr Theobald in August 2009? Mr Theobald should be asked to provide a statement as to his conversation with Mr Gallagher, and any written record of it, and Mr Symons should be asked for the above details.

Renunciation of the Production Licence by the Company

23. Whether or not the Board decision of 13 July 2009 to incur no further expense would be regarded by the Court as a decision to renounce applying for the Production Licence for the Olen Horst field is unclear. Perhaps Mr Symons could also be asked if there was anything said as to how long the embargo on expenditure was likely to last, and whether it was contemplated at that time whether North Sea operations would resume. This certainly needs to be investigated, because there is a risk that the Court

will find the Company renounced its interest in the Olen Horst field unless it would have been possible to put in a 'holding' application for the Production Licence.

24. Mr Gallagher asserts in his letter of 8 February 2014 that express permission for him to apply for the Production Licence in his own name and at his own risk was given by Mr Theobald in August 2009. Again, Mr Theobald should be asked about this.

Effect of Resignation

25. It is settled law that a director cannot escape the consequences of a breach of his fiduciary duties by resigning his office in advance of the finalisation of the transaction in question if there has already been conduct by the director amounting to a breach of his duty to the Company. The Companies Act 2006, s 170(2), provides that a person who ceases to be a director continues to be subject to the duty in s 175 as regards the exploitation of any property, information or opportunity of which he became aware at a time when he was a director. In the present case the information from the exploratory work in block 79452, and the opportunity this presented, came about in 2007 to July 2009, which is a period ending 2 months before Mr Gallagher resigned.

26. Moreover, it is plain from his letter to the Department of Energy and Climate Change dated 17 August 2009 that Mr Gallagher applied for the Production Licence in advance of his resignation on 3 September 2009, so his resignation will not be a defence. As mentioned previously, Mr Knight in his draft statement says Mr Gallagher's application for the Production Licence was made on 27 July 2009. This application form should be obtained either from Mr Knight if he has a copy, or from the Department for Energy and Climate Change.

Resulting profit

27. I am instructed that Mr Gallagher, after obtaining written permission from the Secretary of State for Energy and Climate Change, assigned the Production Licence to Earlsferry in February 2011. Under that assignment he is paid a royalty, believed to be 1% of the price of sales, on oil produced from the Olen Horst field. Subject to the technical points mentioned above, there should therefore be a complete case under the Companies Act 2006, s 175, against Mr Gallagher.

Remedies

28. If liable, Mr Gallagher will hold the profits made under the Production Licence as a constructive trustee in favour of the Company, and will be liable to account to the Company for those profits.

29. In *Boardman v Phipps* [1967] 2 AC 46 the House of Lords allowed trustees whose personal interests came into conflict with the interests of their beneficiaries a generous allowance to compensate them for the work they had undertaken in earning the profits they had to disgorge to the trust. In this case Mr Gallagher apparently expended considerable time and money in confirming the presence of oil after he obtained the Production Licence. According to *Guinness plc v Saunders* [1990] 2 AC 663 such an allowance cannot be made in favour of a director as to do so will interfere with the management of the company's affairs. Indeed, no allowance was made in *Quarter Master*

(UK) Ltd v Pyke [2005] 1 BCLC 245, applying the principle that a director is not permitted to benefit from his breach of fiduciary duty. Although this seems to be the legal position, it is in practice often ignored by the courts, because in this situation the Company would inevitably have had to incur similar expenses to those incurred by Mr Gallagher. Probably the Court would regard the profits he has to return as the balance of the royalties he has and will receive after deducting the costs he has incurred.

Conclusion

30. Subject to the reservations I express regarding the directors of the Company having authorised Mr Gallagher's personal application for the Production Licence, and the points on the Company renouncing its interest in applying for a Production Licence, this appears to be a clear case of breach of fiduciary duty. If the board never reduced its quorum to one, and provided Mr Symons was within the United Kingdom on 6 August 2009, there will have been no authorisation. In which case the claim will succeed, subject to what appears to be a weak argument that the Company totally renounced its interest in applying for a Production Licence.

31. Before proceedings are started it is necessary to at least consider the use of ADR (PD Pre-action Conduct). A number of inquiries should be made before issuing proceedings, as outlined above, namely:

(a) Seabed survey documentation in relation to the Olen Horst field (para 9);
(b) Expert geologist's report on that survey material (paras 10 and 13);
(c) All board minutes (para 17);
(d) Evidence of My Symons' whereabouts on 6 August 2009 (para 20);
(e) Information available to Mr Symons relating to the Olen Horst field (para 22);
(f) Details on the embargo on expenditure (para 23);
(g) Whether Mr Theobald gave permission to Mr Gallagher (para 24); and
(h) The application form for the Production Licence (para 26).

32. Subject to the results of the further inquiries I have suggested, it would seem appropriate to apply for summary judgment in this case if Mr Gallagher acknowledges service.

A. BARRISTER
4 Gray's Inn Place,
April 2014

14.5 Suggested statement of case

IN THE HIGH COURT OF JUSTICE — Claim No.
CHANCERY DIVISION
BETWEEN

BEADNELL BAY PETROLEUM LIMITED — Claimant

and

MR MICHAEL RYAN GALLAGHER — Defendant

PARTICULARS OF CLAIM

1. The Claimant is a limited company incorporated and registered under the Companies Act 1985 for the purpose, among other things, of exploring for and extracting petroleum. Until his resignation on 3rd September 2009 the Defendant was a director and the managing director of the Claimant.

2. On 8th February 2007 the Claimant was granted an Exploration Licence by the Secretary of State for Business, Enterprise and Regulatory Reform under which it was permitted to search for petroleum in the strata in the seabed and subsoil in the seaward areas of the North Sea as defined by Regulation 3(1) of the Petroleum (Production) (Seaward Areas) Regulations 1988. A true copy of the Exploration Licence is served with these Particulars of Claim.

3. Pursuant to the Exploration Licence the Claimant incurred expenses exceeding £27.24 million in the period from 8th February 2007 to 1st August 2009 in searching for petroleum in the seaward areas of the North Sea, and in particular in an area approximately 60 miles east of Seahouses, Northumberland presently included in block 79452 as shown on a reference map deposited at Thames House South, 1 Palace Street, London SW1, the principal office of the Department of Energy and Climate Change.

4. In or about 2009, details of the exploratory work carried out by and on behalf of the Claimant in block 79452 were recorded in writing in a programme of works ('the programme of works'). The programme of works was property belonging to the Claimant within the meaning of the Companies Act 2006, s 175(2).

5. As a result of the searches pleaded in paragraph 3 above and of analyses conducted by or on behalf of the Claimant of samples, information and data produced by such searches (the 'search data'), the Defendant was privy to information that block 79452 was the potential site of a valuable reserve of petroleum (the 'site information').

6. The search data and site information (together referred to as 'the information') was confidential information belonging to the Claimant which was disclosed to the Defendant in his capacity as a director of the Claimant. As such it was information within the meaning of the Companies Act 2006, s 175(2).

7. In June 2009 the Department of Energy and Climate Change invited applications for Production Licences for areas in the North Sea including block 79452.

8. The invitation to apply for a production licence in respect of block 79452 was, by reason of the exploratory work carried out by and on behalf of the Claimant as set out in paragraph 3 above, together with the information, an opportunity which the Claimant could take advantage of within the meaning of the Companies Act 2006, s 175(2).

9. On or about 27th July 2009 the Defendant applied in his own name to the Secretary of State for Energy and Climate Change for, and on 19th September 2009 was granted in his own name, a Production Licence in respect of block 79452 ('the Production Licence'). The Production Licence gave the Defendant an exclusive right to search and bore for, and extract, petroleum (other than methane) in the seabed and subsoil of block 79452 for a term of 6 years from 1st October 2009, such term being capable of extension for further periods not exceeding 30 years. The Claimant will refer to the

Production Licence at trial for its full terms, and a true copy of it is served with these Particulars of Claim.

10. In support of his application for the Production Licence the Defendant wrote to the Department of Energy and Climate Change on 17th August 2009 making use of the Claimant's name and enclosing a copy of the programme of works. A true copy of this letter is enclosed with these particulars of claim.

11. In October 2010 substantial petroleum reserves were discovered in block 79452, and commercial extraction of those reserves began in March 2012.

12. In or about February 2011 the Defendant assigned the benefit of the Production Licence to Earlsferry Oil and Gas Public Limited Company, and is being and/or will be paid profits based on the oil or petroleum products extracted from block 79452.

13. In applying for and entering into the Production Licence the Defendant acted in breach of his statutory duties as a director of the Claimant under the Companies Act 2006.

PARTICULARS OF BREACH OF STATUTORY DUTY

The Defendant acted in breach of his statutory duties in that he:

(1) Allowed himself to come into a situation where he had a direct interest that conflicted with the interests of the Claimant by applying for the Production Licence in his own name, being an opportunity that could have been taken advantage of by the Claimant, contrary to the Companies Act 2006, section 175(1), (2).

(2) Allowed himself to come into a situation where he had a direct interest that conflicted with the interests of the Claimant by entering into the Production Licence in his own name, being an opportunity that could have been taken advantage of by the Claimant, contrary to the Companies Act 2006, section 175(1), (2).

(3) Allowed himself to come into a situation where he had a direct interest that conflicted with the interests of the Claimant by making use of the information when deciding to apply for the Production Licence in his own name, being information that could have been taken advantage of by the Claimant, contrary to the Companies Act 2006, section 175(1), (2).

(4) Allowed himself to come into a situation where he had a direct interest that conflicted with the interests of the Claimant by making use of the information when deciding to enter into the Production Licence in his own name, being information that could have been taken advantage of by the Claimant, contrary to the Companies Act 2006, section 175(1), (2).

(5) Allowed himself to come into a situation where he had a direct interest that conflicted with the interests of the Claimant by making use of the Claimant's name and the programme of works in his letter to the Department of Energy and Climate Change dated 17th August 2009, being property that could have been taken advantage of by the Claimant, contrary to the Companies Act 2006, section 175(1), (2).

14. In these circumstances the Defendant is liable to account to the Claimant for all profits he has derived and will derive directly or indirectly from his obtaining of the Production Licence.

15. Further or alternatively, by reason of the matters set out above the Claimant is entitled to equitable compensation for its loss and damage.

PARTICULARS OF LOSS AND DAMAGE

The Claimant has by reason of the Defendant's actions been deprived of the opportunity to extract and sell the petroleum reserves in block 79452, and has thereby lost the profits on such sales.

(i) Estimated capital costs for production facilities at block 79452	£
(ii) Annualised cost of production facilities if costs spread over [ ] years	£
(iii) The annual production figure for petroleum from block 79452 is estimated at [ ] barrels	
(iv) Price of [Olen Horst] petroleum in [date]	£
(v) Estimated annual operating and recovery costs for block 79452	£
Gross annual price of sales	£
Less annualised capital costs	£
Less annual operating and recovery costs	£
Annual loss of profit	£
Loss of profits from 1 March 2012 to the date of issue of the Claim Form in these proceedings	£
And continuing at the daily rate of	£

16. Further, the Claimant claims interest against the Defendant to be assessed pursuant to the Senior Courts Act 1981, section 35A and/or the rules of equity on the sums claimed and/or found due on the taking of the account claimed at such rate and for such period as to the Court shall seem just.

17. The parties have complied with the requirements of Practice Direction Pre-action Conduct.

AND the Claimant seeks:

(1) Equitable compensation.

(2) An account of the profits made and to be made by the Defendant directly and indirectly from his obtaining of the Production Licence.

(3) Payment of the amount found due to the Claimant on taking the account.

(4) Such other accounts, directions and inquiries as may be necessary.

(5) Interest under the Senior Courts Act 1981, section 35A, alternatively under the equitable jurisdiction of the Court, to be assessed.

(6) Further or other relief.

A. BARRISTER

Statement of Truth

(I believe) (The Claimant believes) that the facts stated in these Particulars of Claim are true.
I am duly authorised by the claimant to sign this statement.

Full name
Name of claimant's solicitors' firm   Daniels and Awford
Signed   Position or office held
(Claimant) (Litigation friend) (Claimant's solicitor) (if signing on behalf of firm or company)

DATED the day of 2014

Address for service
Daniels and Awford, 73 Grainger Street, Newcastle upon Tyne, NE1 3SL.
To: The Defendant
And to: The Court Manager.

14.6 Discussion

14.6.1 Approach to opinion writing in Company Law

Opinion writing and drafting in the context of company law should follow the same approach as that recommended for the main opinion writing and drafting courses at the City Law School. The principles laid down and the suggestions made in the main Manuals for these skills should therefore be followed when doing the same tasks in a company law context.

The main difference is that, unless Counsel is instructed by a specialist company law firm or a firm with a company law department, the probability is that the solicitor sending the Instructions is less likely to be familiar with the finer points of law on the subject than when the Instructions relate to one of the more mainstream legal areas, such as contract, tort and land law. As a result it will almost certainly be necessary to give more detail or to provide more references to primary sources than would be necessary in one of the more well-known areas. The other reason why more law tends to be discussed in company law opinions is that there is a greater prospect that one or more of the real issues in the case will be primarily issues of law, rather than issues of fact, which is the usual position in contract and tort cases.

Before starting your opinion (or statement of case) on a final assessment you should make sure you are fully conversant with the assessment criteria for the exercise in hand, as your work will be marked using the criteria published for that assessment (and on those criteria alone). The wording adopted will have been tailored to the requirements of the exercise.

14.6.2 The opinion

It is hoped that the Opinion at **14.4** will be fairly self-explanatory. It should be practical, identify and discuss the real issues, be legally and factually sound, ask for necessary additional information (see paragraphs 9, 10, 13, 17, 20, 22, 23, 24 and 26), and give reasoned answers to the issues raised by the Instructions.

Under the CA 2006, the fiduciary duties owed by directors were codified into statutory duties based on the former fiduciary and common law duties (s 170(3)). These provisions are discussed in **Chapter 7**. Although CA 2006, s 170(3), says that the provisions in ss 171–177 are based on established common law rules and equitable duties, and s 170(4) says that regard shall be had to the corresponding common law rules and equitable principles in interpreting and applying the new provisions, there are changes.

14.6.2.1 Nature of the duties in CA 2006, ss 171–177

The general duties placed on directors by CA 2006, ss 171–177, are statutory duties, and need to be pleaded as such in any statement of case. There is a concern that this may result in the duties on directors becoming too rigid. An attempt to avoid this has been made by providing in CA 2006, s 170(4), that the statutory provisions shall be interpreted and applied in the same way as common law rules or equitable principles. While it was intended to make some changes through the codification of directors' duties, the main purpose was to provide a readily accessible statement of what those duties are, so that non-lawyer directors will be able to see what their responsibilities are.

14.6.2.2 Breach of duty in this case

The general duties on directors laid down in CA 2006, ss 171–177, include a duty to avoid conflicts of interest (s 175). This covers situations of direct and indirect conflicts, and also situations where there is a possibility of a conflict. While it may be possible to characterise what has happened as a breach of s 172 (promoting the success of the company for the benefit of its members); s 176 (accepting benefits from third parties); or s 177 (declaring interests in proposed transactions), these are artificial approaches. The opinion and draft in this case have concentrated on the key duty, that of conflicts of interest.

The specific defence in s 175(4)(b) (authorisation by the directors) looks to be open to the defendant given the board minute from the meeting on 6 August 2009. However, it will not apply if Mr Symons is right in his draft witness statement that he was not informed about the board meeting on 6 August 2009, or if the quorum for board meetings is at least two (as is the starting position in regulation 87 of the articles of this company).

14.6.2.3 Continuing effect of the duties after resignation

A director generally remains under the duties set out in CA 2006, ss 171–177, while the director remains in post (s 170(1)). However, by s 170(2) a director remains under the two following duties despite ceasing to be a director:

(a) to avoid conflicts of interest under s 175, as regards the exploitation of any property, information or opportunity which the director became aware of when he was a director; and

(b) not to accept benefits from third parties under s 176, as regards things done or omitted by him before ceasing to be a director.

In the present case, the breaches alleged against Mr Gallagher relate to his conflict of interest in taking the Production Licence in his own name and taking benefits in the form of royalties in respect of the oil extracted under the Production Licence. These come under s 170(2), provided there is the necessary connection with what happened before his resignation. As regards the duty to avoid conflict of interests, the opportunity to apply for the Production Licence arose before Mr Gallagher's resignation on 3 September 2009. Indeed, he applied for the Licence on 27 July 2009 according to Mr Knight.

14.6.2.4 Duty to declare interest

In his letter of 8 February 2014, Mr Gallagher says that it was agreed that he could apply for the Production Licence himself. The board minute of 6 August 2009 records that it was agreed that he could apply in his own name. The minute says that the persons present were Mr Gallagher ('MG') and Mr Walsh ('TAW'). Mr Symons, the Chairman of the Board, in his draft witness statement says he was not invited to what he calls the so-called board meeting on 6 August, and that he was never told that Mr Gallagher intended to apply for the Production Licence in his own name.

In order to comply with CA 2006, s 177, it was necessary for Mr Gallagher to declare his interest to the other directors. If Mr Symons was never informed, this was not done.

Unless s 177(6)(b) means there is no need to declare interests where the person benefiting is the director personally (because the other directors either were aware or must be taken as being reasonably aware) there was a breach of s 177(1).

14.6.2.5 Consent or authorisation by members

If, despite the company's evidence, there was board authorisation under CA 2006, s 175(4)(b), or compliance with s 177 (declaration of interest to the other directors), the relevant transactions are not liable to be set aside (s 180(1)).

14.6.2.6 Remedies

Remedies for breach of the general statutory duties on directors are the same as would apply if the corresponding common law rule or equitable principles applied (s 178(1)). These therefore remain unchanged by the codification of the duties owed by directors.

14.6.3 The particulars of claim

The starting point with the particulars of claim is Counsel's analysis of the case. Here, this has been set out in the Opinion, and it is essential that the statement of case is consistent with the Opinion. The claim is based on the director allowing his personal interests to conflict with the interests of the company, contrary to the Companies Act 2006, s 175. Before the Companies Act 2006 was enacted, such a claim would have been brought as a claim for breach of fiduciary duty. These duties have been codified as statutory duties, so the modern approach is to plead the case against the former director as a claim for breach of statutory duty.

One of the problems with drafting the Particulars of Claim in this case is the lack of a particularly helpful precedent in the usual precedent books (such as *Atkin's Court Forms* and Bullen, Leake and Jacob, *Precedents of Pleading*). However, there are a number of precedents which can be used from analogous areas (such as constructive trusts and breach of fiduciary duty of trustees), which can be used to obtain some ideas. The overall structure used in the draft at **14.5** was based on general principles as set out in the ***Drafting Manual***. Paragraph 1 pleads the fact that the Defendant was a director of the Claimant, and hence owed it the fiduciary duties now to be found in the Companies Act 2006. Paragraphs 2 to 12 plead background facts. They appear in this sequence mainly for chronological reasons. Paragraph 4 seeks to set up the programme of works as property belonging to the company (within the meaning of the Companies Act 2006, s 175(2)). Paragraphs 5 and 6 plead that the Defendant was privy to company information concerning the site of the oilfield, and define this information in the terms provided for in the Companies Act 2006, s 175(2). Paragraph 8 pleads the invitation to apply for the Production Licence as a corporate opportunity within the meaning of s 175(2). Paragraph 13 pleads the complaints as breaches of statutory duty, with particulars. Paragraphs 14 and 15 plead the injury to the Company and the liability to account, with interest being claimed in paragraph 16. The prayer sets out the remedies claimed.

Index

D